THE GOLDEN WRECK

The Tragedy of
the 'Royal Charter'

The wreck of the *Royal Charter*, the fastest passenger liner of her day, only a few miles from her home port of Liverpool, shocked the nation when the news hit the headlines in October, 1859. With only 40 men saved out of a complement of passengers and crew numbering more than 500, it was one of the greatest peacetime disasters in maritime history.

About the author

Alexander McKee is best known for his twenty-year operation to locate and raise Henry VIII's warship the *Mary Rose*, in recognition of which he was awarded the OBE. The son of a naval surgeon he has spent most of his life on or under the sea, and has been associated with a number of expeditions to find and excavate buried wrecks, including, most recently, the Oxford University Expedition to raise the Etruscan wreck off the island of Giglio. The author of more than twenty books on aspects of military, naval and aeronautical history, Alexander McKee has covered subjects as various as the Spanish Armada and the Battle of Britain. His most recent books include *Dresden 1945: The Devil's Tinderbox*, *How We Found the Mary Rose* and *Tarquin's Ship: The Etruscan Wreck in Campese Bay*.

THE GOLDEN WRECK

The Tragedy of the 'Royal Charter'

Alexander McKee

NEW ENGLISH LIBRARY
Hodder and Stoughton

Copyright © 1961, 1986 by Alexander McKee

First published in Great Britain in 1961
by Souvenir Press Ltd

Second edition 1986

New English Library paperback edition 1988

British Library Cataloguing in Publication Data

McKee, Alexander
    The golden wreck the tragedy of the
    'Royal Charter'—2nd ed.
    1. Royal Charter (*Ship*)   2. Shipwrecks
    —Wales—Anglesey
    I. Title
    914.29'21   G530.R65

    ISBN 0-450-41906-1

Printed and bound in Great Britain for Hodder and
Stoughton Paperbacks a division of Hodder and
Stoughton Ltd., Mill Road, Dunton Green, Sevenoaks,
Kent. TN13 2YA.
(Editorial Office: 47 Bedford Square,
London WC1B 3DP) by BAS Printers Limited,
Over Wallop, Stockbridge, Hampshire

CONTENTS

PROLOGUE

The weather had been unsettled for days. 'A complete wintry scene, the vale as well as the hill entirely covered with snow,' wrote the Rector of Selworthy, the Rev J. Stephenson, on 23 October, 1859. Two days later, on Tuesday, 25 October, he noted in his diary that at midday it was 'so dull and dark that I could scarcely see to read. Violent storm of hail and rain at 4 pm.' What was coming now was the hurricane of the century, and these were its outriders.

The first indication had come an hour earlier in the Channel, when at 3 pm there had been a sudden shift of wind off the Eddystone. It caught the Channel Fleet at exercise off Land's End, fortunately with plenty of searoom in which to manoeuvre, for so violent a change in wind strength and direction could spell disaster within minutes to sailing ships standing close inshore. Even so, the ships, as they slid down into the troughs of the waves, disappeared entirely from sight of each other, hidden by the mountainous, overhanging crests of foaming water. And as the wind still increased in violence, gusting to one hundred miles an hour, the crests of the rollers were cut clean off and the entire surface of the sea was swept by driven spray that at times reduced visibility to a few dozen yards.

All along the rocky coasts of Devon and Cornwall the air was filled with the hoarse, booming roar of the breakers as they struck the cliffs with an impact that made the ground shudder and sent salt spray hundreds of feet towards the low, streaming clouds above. At several places where the South Devon railway line followed the coast, it was protected by massive embankments of granite and concrete which were sometimes as much as sixteen feet above the level of the highest spring tides. But the winds driving the breakers were moving at a speed never less than 110 feet per second, so that the waves rose to mountainous proportions and it seemed as if the entire level of the sea had risen more than a dozen feet. The embankments were battered, then swept away, collapsing into the sea or being scattered in ruin over the railway lines. Between Newton and Exeter there were places where, wrote a witness, 'the wind and waves made sport of the massive parapet as if it were mere shingle and strewed the blocks of granite and concrete masonry over the line in the wildest confusion.'

For a considerable distance, between East Cliff Tunnel and Dawlish, 'the wall was dismantled, so to speak, for five and six feet of its height, and an enormous granite slab, weighing not less than a ton and a half, was shifted to the opposite side of the rails.' At Powderham, parts of a wrecked vessel were found lying on the railway line. There was virtually no hope for any ship in distress or for any ship driven ashore, for the life-boats were unable to launch.

The shift of wind in the eastern end of the Channel came later than it had in the West Country. It was reported at Reigate at 5.30 pm and by that time amazing scenes had been experienced where the coast was flat; at Worthing, in Sussex, the sea itself rose bodily over the promenade, so that the normal shoreline entirely disappeared, and monstrous waves came roaring up the streets, to break in surging spray around the town hall.

By 8 pm the storm had engulfed Anglesey and by 10 pm was rising to full hurricane force. Outside Holyhead harbour the giant iron paddle-steamer *Great Eastern*, ungainly forerunner of the ocean liners of the twentieth century, was soon in deadly danger; inside the harbour, the masts of sunken vessels raised sheets of spray from the waves, while other ships, aground in the shallows, were rapidly being beaten into wrecks. In Penrhyn harbour, at Bangor, on the coast of North Wales, 'the effect was truly appalling,' wrote a witness. 'The vessels were driven from one side of the harbour to the other in the greatest confusion; some were run into, and actually ridden over; others scuttled or dismasted, with their sides or their sterns ripped open, and their boats smashed.'

The storm was terrible enough on land, but it was worse still for those actually at sea that night. A pilot-boat cruising north of Anglesey saw distress signals from some great ship caught by the hurricane close inshore, but was unable even to approach it, let alone give help; and the blue glow of the flares was soon blotted out by the driving rain and the darkness. There were wrecks all along the coast that night, but this was to be the greatest; the wreck that was to shock a nation as no other had done.

At midday on Wednesday, 26 October, the full force of the hurricane struck the Mersey, turning that sheltered water into a sheet of spray; even there ships dragged their anchors, riding uncontrollably, so that they smashed into other ships with a thunder of colliding timber and the crack of falling spars. At Liverpool Observatory the wind force was measured as 28 lbs to the square foot, greater than anything ever previously recorded; and the sea level rose four feet. A brand-new factory in nearby Flint was virtually levelled to the ground. By the time the hurricane had reached Scotland, the worst was over in the Channel and men were starting to count the wrecks and list the damage.

Admiral Fitzroy, of the Meteorological Office, described the storm as a 'complete horizontal cyclone.' It can perhaps best be pictured as a clock-face. Dead centre, in the heart of the hurricane, was a small circle of still air; and around it, maddened winds were revolving in a circle in an anti-clockwise direction. The diameter of the hurricane was only about 300 miles, so that, as it passed across the British Isles in a north-easterly direction, there were sudden and violent shifts of wind direction, totally without warning; and those winds were gusting at speeds up to and sometimes in excess of, 100 miles per hour. That is, at virtually twice the speed of a normal gale, which is Force 8 on the Beaufort Scale. The indications of Force 11, given by the Beaufort Scale, are winds of 64–75 mph, with the note: 'Very rarely experienced; accompanied by widespread damage.' But this was not Force 8, it was not even Force 11; it was Force 12. And, significantly, no indications are given for that. In British waters it is, quite simply, unprecedented; its effects incalculable.

The effects of that disastrous storm exceeded anything in living memory: 133 ships were sunk, 90 were badly damaged; about 800 lives were lost. Twice the number of people perished at sea within the space of two days of 1859 as in the whole of the previous year, when the total had been 340. Most of the ships lost were small sailing vessels, but one of them was a large iron ship, the great auxiliary steam clipper *Royal Charter*, and in her alone about 450 men, women and children lost their lives—more, in one ship, in half-an-hour, than in every ship sunk during the whole of 1858. And yet she had been within a few hours' sailing of her home port of Liverpool, after a voyage right round the world, when the hurricane had come howling down upon her out of the raging night.

Therefore it is not surprising that, although hurricanes were not then given code names by meteorologists, this hurricane should have a name; and that it should have gone down in history as the *Royal Charter* Gale.

Chapter 1

GOLD AND IRON

The *Royal Charter* was a hybrid; no such ship is in service today. She was the product of a certain stage of technology—a fleeting one—and she was designed to meet an historical accident which proved to be even more fleeting. Since it was a particular incident in history which shaped her and made her what she was, in effect her story starts before she had even been laid down. The accident that caused her was the finding of gold, at the beginning of 1851, in the British colony of Australia. Colony is hardly the word, it was a desert—at the other side of the world. In space, it was half the circumference of the globe away. In time, it was distant five or six months. When reached, it offered little but back-breaking toil. What you wanted to raise there, you had to take with you.

The emigrant ships of the first half of the nineteenth century carried not only people who intended to colonise the new land, but the cattle, the pigs, the dogs, and the seeds—particularly wheat—with which to do it. Conditions were insanitary, particularly when ships were becalmed for days, or even weeks, at a time in a hot, damp climate. For steerage passengers, who occupied the lowest deck, often underneath the cattle deck—not always well-caulked—the passage to Australia was indescribable. Fifty to a hundred deaths, per ship, per passage, was not considered unusual.

In August, 1852, the Eagle Line's *Albatross* sailed into Liverpool with £50,000 of gold aboard from the Australian diggings. And the Gold Rush began. Between 1852 and 1857 more than 226,000 people landed in Australia. Foremost among them were the English—100,000 of them—nearly half the total. But there were also 60,000 Irish, 50,000 Scots, 8,000 Germans, 4,000 Welsh, 3,000 Americans, and 1,500 French. In eighteen months the population of Melbourne rose from 23,000 to 70,000.

Aboard the crowded emigrant ships, making their slow passage through the doldrums, disease took a heavy toll. in 1834 the deaths through typhoid fever of twenty-two people aboard an East Indiaman had been thought unusual. It was not unusual now.

Speed is often a saleable commodity; on the Australian run it was vital. Soon, the shipping lines were able to supply it, although at first the solution took two different forms, both imperfect. The requirements were for a fast overall passage and, in particular, the avoidance of delay—sometimes as much as three weeks—in the belts of light winds and calms where outbreaks of fever were most likely to occur.

Two types of ship were immediately available, although in limited numbers. Representative of one type was the Eagle Line's iron-built screw auxiliary, the *Great Britain*. She made her maiden voyage in 1852, carrying more than 600 people to Australia for sums ranging between 70 and 75 guineas. On arrival at Melbourne, however, she was unable even to discharge her cargo—the entire crew, once they set foot on shore, departed in haste for the gold diggings, not many miles away at Ballarat. It was three months before her captain could obtain enough men to take the ship to sea again.

This 336-foot long vessel was a maritime landmark—the first large steamship to dispense with paddle wheels. Other revolutionary features were an advanced hull design, a flat double bottom, clipper bow, and watertight bulk-heads.

But the marine steam engine of the 1850s was extremely inefficient and none too reliable. The engine, and still more, the hundreds of tons of coal it consumed, took up space which, in a sailing ship, could have been used

The *Great Britain* in dock at Bristol, April, 1971, soon after her recovery from the Falkland Islands the previous year. The hull was towed back on a submersible pontoon. *Photo : Alexander McKee*

for cargo. Furthermore, the wind was free; coal was costly. Had it provided the power given by a modern steam engine, all would have been well; but it did not. The *Great Britain* was, therefore, apart from her iron construction, more or less a normal sailing ship; the engine was an auxiliary, used only to avoid delay in the areas of light winds or calm. Even by 1860, there were only 2,000 British-owned steamships, as compared to 25,663 sailing ships.

Representative of the rival type of ship was the Liverpool-owned clipper *Marco Polo*, commanded by the famous Captain 'Bully' Forbes. On her maiden voyage to Australia she carried 930 emigrants, and took 68 days for the passage out. As she was of only 1,625 tons, conditions aboard must have been cramped; but no more than two of the passengers died. She was better equipped than her predecessors—amenities included a sick bay staffed by two doctors, and rows of washing tubs, whereas on most of these ships, there was nowhere for the passengers to wash their clothes during many months at sea. 'Bully' Forbes made sure that his crew did not join the Gold Rush, by the expedient of committing them to prison immediately on arrival in Australia; and, after discharging her cargo and loading £100,000 in gold, the *Marco Polo* sailed back triumphantly to Liverpool, bearing the bold inscription, 'The Fastest Ship in the World.' This wiped the eyes of her rivals, but as the ship had been built at New Brunswick in Canada, it was not an all-British triumph. The clipper was virtually a North American invention, designed to take advantage of the breaking of the monopoly of the China tea (and opium) trade held by the old East India Company. The British soon copied the design, with great success, but the demand was such that British Lines had to place substantial orders in America; and in 1854, 'Bully' Forbes found himself collecting his latest command, the *Lightning*, from Donald MacKay's East Boston yard.

The strong suit of these sailing ships was speed—one American clipper averaged 15 knots for a full week, covering 2,550 miles. Admittedly, the winds were extremely favourable, but the speed attained was some four or five knots greater than that of the average coaster of today. It was enormously greater than that of the normal sailing ship; even the fastest warship could make only 12 to 13 knots, and then only at the cost of straining her spars and gear—whereas the clipper slipped effortlessly through the water at speeds much greater than this.

Three factors gave the clipper her superb performance. The first was sheer size—the larger the ship, the faster it will be, in proportion to its power. The reason is that the drag caused by the hull of a large vessel is proportionately less when compared to the available power, a rule which applies to sea creatures as well as ships. The second factor lay in the actual proportions of the hull—long and narrow, rather than short and tubby,

The Black Ball line clipper *Marco Polo*, 1,625 tons, arriving in the Mersey after a voyage to Australia. Her master, Captain James Nicol ('Bully') Forbes, used to boast that his destination was 'Hell or Melbourne'. From a coloured lithograph by W. J. Hammond after T. Dove. *Photo: The National Maritime Museum, London*

like an ordinary merchant ship. This was an old secret—the clipper was descended from the canoe, the galley and the Viking 'longship', all planned for speed, not cargo capacity. The human element was sufficiently important to constitute a third factor. The crews consisted of picked men; the captains were hard-driving characters, usually from the forecastle, with the additional ability to choose the fastest routes—which, because of the winds, were not always the shortest.

The clipper, however, had the disadvantage of being a sailing ship. Because of the unpredictability of winds her time of arrival could only be estimated—and might be wrong by a week or more. One sailing ship on the Australia run, the *Kent*, was not merely delayed but completely becalmed for seventeen days.

The *Royal Charter*, in the form in which she was completed, represented a cross between the *Great Britain* and the *Marco Polo*. In effect, she was the 'new look' on the Australia run, a combination of the good points of these two very different ships. She was large, she was a clipper, and she possessed auxiliary steam power. She was also, like the *Great Britain*, made of iron, not wood.

13

Here, again, she enabled the British to wipe the eyes of the Yankees, their only serious competitors. The Americans had vast supplies of timber available in their huge forests, whereas the British supply was dwindling. But the British had made the industrial revolution; they had both iron and the knowledge of how to make ships out of it. And, as iron was stronger than wood, weight for weight, a ship built of iron was more efficient and economical than a ship built of wood. That put the British ahead in the technical race—in the main department at least. And when American ingenuity produced a minor device which worked—the British were quick to copy it. One such was included by the builders of the *Royal Charter*.

The *Royal Charter* was built at the Sandycroft ironworks on the River Dee, in Flintshire, and was launched in 1855. The firm which had ordered her, Charles Moore & Co., of Liverpool, sold her while she was still under construction to another Liverpool shipping business, Gibbs, Bright & Co. Gibbs, Bright were in effect the Eagle Line, owners of the *Albatross* and the *Great Britain*, and a number of other ships. They operated this Line through a subsidiary company, the Liverpool and Australian Steam Navigation Co., Ltd. They therefore ordered a number of alterations to be made to the uncompleted hull, so that the ship should more closely fit their requirements for the Australia run; and to ensure that these were properly carried out, they installed at Sandycroft a Bristol shipbuilder, William Patterson, who had already built the *Great Britain* for them. The original builder at Sandycroft, Mr Cram, shortly afterwards went bankrupt, and so Patterson took over complete charge. The bulk of the necessary ironwork was already at the yard, the frames were up, and some of the plates had been fitted.

The principal alteration made by Gibbs, Bright was the lengthening of the hull at bow and stern, but without touching the keel, to give the *Royal Charter* finally a length which was seven times her beam—a proportion calculated to produce great and effortless speed. Because of her iron construction, her long, narrow shape should be at least as strong as that of a normally proportioned ship made of wood.

She was a large ship, of 2,719 registered tons, approximately 320 feet long; the length of her keel was $308\frac{1}{2}$ feet, and her length overall 336 feet. She had three tall, clipper masts and a single funnel; the auxiliary steam engine developed 200 horse power and she had bunker space for some 700 tons of coal—not nearly enough to take her to Australia, but ample for use when the winds were calm or contrary. Sails were her main motive power—basically, she was an iron clipper; and, when fitted out, a very luxurious one. But mishaps dogged her from the start.

Because the Dee was narrow and shallow at Sandycroft, she was to be launched sideways into the river. The great crowd which assembled to

Midship lines of the *Great Britain* seen in her Bristol dock, 1971, and (*right*), her clipper-type bow. *Photos: Alexander McKee*

watch the event were disappointed; when the moment for launching came, she did not move. It was only after a channel had been dug out for her, with much labour, that she was eventually floated. Shortly after, while being taken down the river, she grounded on a sandbank off Flint, and suffered serious damage. With her main keel bent, the *Royal Charter* was docked at Liverpool for lengthy repairs.

On her maiden voyage, a serious miscalculation caused a near fiasco. Her narrow hull and tall masts, it was believed, might tend to make her unstable; therefore hundreds of tons of stone ballast were laid in the hold. On top of this went the cargo. And instead of the expected small amount of cargo, there turned out to be a super-abundance. The result was that the ship, instead of drawing just under 20 feet of water, drew $22\frac{1}{2}$ feet. Her main deck was only six feet above the waterline.

In this state, the *Royal Charter* left Liverpool for Australia on 18 January,

15

Stern of the *Great Britain*, similar to that of the *Royal Charter*. *Photo: Alexander McKee*

Rudder of the *Great Britain*, seen in Bristol dock, 1971. In her final years, her engines were taken out and the ship reverted to sail only. On the left, the end of the propellor shaft is visible. *Photo: Alexander McKee*

1856. It was soon apparent that the greater part of the ballast was unnecessary; there was nothing unstable about the *Royal Charter*. The extra weight merely robbed her of her best qualities as a 'sea boat' and made steering difficult when sail only was being used. There was a device to lift the screw out of the water when it was not in use, as it would then cause drag and slow the ship's speed. But with the stern so low in the water the two-bladed screw, even in the lifted position, was dipping into the waves, causing water resistance and interfering with the steering. A more fundamental difficulty also became obvious. The top speed of the ship, using the screw only, was some seven or eight knots, whereas her top speed in a hard gale of wind was some ten knots faster than this. As soon as the ship began to reach about eight knots, she in effect over-ran the screw; instead of the screw turning and sending the ship forward, the high speed of her wake tended to make the screw revolve. Sailpower and steam were then in direct opposition, fighting each other, and a tremendous shuddering of the propeller shaft broke out. It was so bad, the first time it happened, that the engineer had to report to Captain Francis Boyce, the master, that if sail was not taken in and speed reduced, he could not answer for the safety of the machinery.

On 24 January, less than a week out, the *Royal Charter* was speeding through a moderate gale off Finisterre, with long lines of 20 feet high waves sweeping across the horizon and occasionally a 26-foot monster rolling majestically onwards. The ship was on the port tack when the Captain decided to try the operation known as wearing—turning the ship's stern to the wind. It was at once apparent that the deep-laden state of the *Royal Charter* was potentially dangerous. Instead of turning round onto her new course, she merely began the motion, then her head fell off again and she wallowed helplessly, paying little attention to the helm. This went on for an hour and consumed a distance of six miles. Had an inhospitable coast been ahead, she must have been wrecked. The effect of the rudder was being blanketed by the tip of the screw which normally, in the raised position, was a foot and a half above the water, but was now partially submerged all the time and wholly submerged part of the time. As the ballast was underneath the cargo, there was no remedy—except turn back to England. This the Captain was naturally reluctant to do, as the news that the *Royal Charter* had been forced to abandon her maiden voyage could seriously affect the commercial future of the ship. One further factor enabled him to make that hard decision.

Clippers were designed to lie low in the water, and had virtually flush decks, in order to reduce to a minimum all wind resistance—for the side of a ship, a large funnel even, acts as an unwanted sail. But six feet clearance was not enough, when combined with the unbuoyant, sluggish motion of the heavily over-weighted vessel; she shipped a great deal of water during the gale and much of that water found its way down below into the second and third class passenger accommodation. With every pitch and roll of the ship, dirty water slopped over the decks, washing in and out of the cabins; the upper berths were saturated with water as it leaked down through the deckhead above.

Boards, lids of boxes, even cabin doors, were laid on the deck, but even so, most of the clothing of the third class passengers was soaked through up to their knees; for the women, with their layers of underclothing, this was particularly unpleasant. And there was nothing to be done about it; no means of getting rid of the water, so long as it came in at such a rate, and no means of drying their sodden garments—or any point in doing so, even if it had been possible. All that could be done was to try to save their luggage, by stacking it in what few dry spots there were; and even in this they were not very successful.

When these facts were reported to Captain Boyce, he made up his mind to put back to England—not to Liverpool, but to Plymouth, distant little more than a day's sail. Not all the passengers were pleased—some were disappointed and annoyed, feeling that they had endured a good deal of discomfort for nothing, and irritated by the delay. On 26 January, her screw threshing deeply in the water, the *Royal Charter* steamed into Plymouth Sound, and the unloading of some 400 tons of ballast began. She was ready to sail again on 16 February, on a voyage which was to be as triumphant as her first attempt had been dismal.

CLIFF COLLEGE
SUMMER SCHOOL

75 PLACES AVAILABLE Why not come and join us in June 2013?

www.cliffcollege.ac.uk

'ENCOUNTERS WITH THE WORD'

'THINKING IT THROUGH'

'WORSHIP MATTERS'

'HEBREW IN A WEEK'

'REAL CHRISTIANITY'

DATES:
Monday 17th – Friday 21st June 2013

VENUE:
Cliff College, Calver,
Hope Valley, S32 3XG

COST:
£195.00 (including all teaching materials, meals and refreshments)

£295.00 (including all teaching materials, meals and refreshments, and accommodation in single study bedrooms)

£335.00 (including all teaching materials, meals and refreshments, and accommodation in single study en-suite bedrooms)

A subsidy on the course fee is available for students already signed up on Cliff College validated courses.

RESPONSES FROM SUMMER SCHOOL PARTICIPANTS

'An amazing week'

'Very welcoming'

'A special atmosphere'

'Lectures were spot on'

'A truly amazing experience – God's timing is great'

'I feel I have truly begun the journey I should have started years ago as a Christian'

'Meeting with other Christians from all walks of life has been inspiring'

'I have been really blessed'

'Inspired me to carry on preaching'

'It makes me realise how much I still need to learn!'

Q: ARE YOU WANTING TO BETTER READ, STUDY AND UNDERSTAND THE BIBLE STORY?

Q: ARE YOU WANTING TO BE REFRESHED IN YOUR MINISTRY?

Q: ARE YOU WANTING TO EXPLORE THE LANGUAGE OF THE BIBLE TO AID YOUR PERSONAL STUDY AND TEACHING?

Q: ARE YOU WANTING TO UNDERSTAND GOD BETTER?

IF YOU ANSWER *'YES'* TO ANY OF THESE QUESTIONS, THEN **THIS COURSE IS FOR YOU!**

Co-ordinated and led by Cliff College tutorial staff and guest lecturers, the 2013 Summer School programme is currently planning five streams of teaching to choose from:

'Encounters with The Word'; Bible Summer School – an overview of the story of scripture helping participants to handle biblical text in a deeper and more creative way. Ideal for those wanting a better understanding of the Bible, for fellowship group leaders and trainee preachers too.

'Thinking it through'; Theology Summer School – an opportunity to discover more about important Christian doctrines, such as the nature of God, the importance of the cross and an understanding of the Trinity. Ideal for all who want to dig a little deeper into the key themes of the Christian faith.

'Worship Matters'; Worship Summer School – an opportunity to explore understandings of worship, the importance of worship in the life of the Christian community, and different ways of creating and offering worship. Ideal for worship leaders, and those with a desire to explore new ways of worship.

'Hebrew in a Week'; Biblical Language Summer School – a framework to begin exploring the language of the Old Testament. Ideal for those wanting a starter course in this key area, for fellowship group leaders and preachers too.

'Real Christianity'; Wesleyan Summer School – an exploration into the story, theology, spirituality and impact of John and Charles Wesley, with practical implications for the life of discipleship in the 21st century. Ideal for those wanting to better understand the Wesleyan tradition and its continuing relevance for today.

All participants will share together in social times, meals, devotions, evening worship, and a shared event during the week. The different streams will be delivered through specific seminars, discussion groups, interactive workshops and lectures across the site.

Contact Reception for more details and a booking form:
admin@cliffcollege.ac.uk / 01246 584200

CLIFF
COLLEGE
www.cliffcollege.ac.uk

Cliff College is a registered charity in England and Wales: Registered Charity number 529386

Chapter 2

RECORD RUN

Some of the passengers were not paying their fares. One of these was Captain Thomas Taylor, an employee of the Line, who was going out to Australia to bring home an old East India ship, the *William Monies*. Another was a white-haired old gentleman, the Reverend W. Scoresby. Doctor Scoresby was a clergyman, scientist, and mariner. He was aboard, as a guest of Gibbs, Bright, in all three capacities, but primarily as a scientist. He was an expert on magnetism, and as wood was only slowly giving place to iron, little was known of the practical effect of iron hulls on the magnetic compass. Doctor Scoresby had a theory that the deviation caused by the mass of iron would not remain constant, as might be expected, but would vary when the ship moved from a northern to a southern magnetic latitude. The maiden voyage of this new iron ship would give him an opportunity to test his theory and to decide the best method of correcting the deviations.

It is thanks to Doctor Scoresby that we know as much as we do about life aboard the *Royal Charter*, for he afterwards wrote a book, *Journal of a Voyage to Australia and Round the World for Magnetical Research*, which was published in 1859: the year of the *Royal Charter* Gale. The era of the iron-built auxiliary clipper lasted so short a time that there is little literature on the subject. The uneasy transition from wood and sail to iron and steam captured no one's romantic imagination. There are actual examples preserved of the wooden line-of-battle ship and the Napoleonic frigate, and of the sailing clipper, too, but until the recovery and restoration of the *Great Britain* in the 1970s, there was no national shrine to the short-lived hybrid which bridged the gap between old and new.

Indeed, there was much opposition to iron and steam. Public reaction to innovations is always distorted by two opposite points of view, the conservative and the progressive. The former are irritated by anything new and advance irrelevant or inaccurate reasons against it, while the latter tend to over-claim, thus confusing Today with Tomorrow. There were, on the one hand, people who believed that iron construction could never match wood for strength and, on the other, people who thought that the day of the *Queen Mary* had arrived. It was in this atmosphere of critical

The auxiliary steam clipper *Royal Charter*, 2,719 tons. From a coloured lithograph by J. R. Isaacs after S. Walters. *Photo: The National Maritime Museum, London*

argument and speculation that, on 16 February, 1856, the *Royal Charter* sailed out of Plymouth to renew her maiden voyage.

Lightened by some 400 tons of ballast, she looked gracefully buoyant and 'bravely' lifted up her head to the Channel swell, noted Doctor Scoresby. She now drew 19 feet forward and 21 feet aft; the alteration in trim made a remarkable difference to her sailing qualities. She had now the true 'racehorse' action of the clipper, swooping effortlessly over the waves, with hardly any sound or disturbance of the water, at speeds which, in an ordinary ship, would have created a noisy turbulence.

This time, she went through the Bay of Biscay without trouble; with much less trouble than a ship lacking auxiliary steam power, which might be penned there by unfavourable winds for days on end, a factor which originally gave the Bay much of its reputation. When the wind was light or contrary, the screw was lowered and steam got up; when a fresh breeze blew from the right quarter, the engines were shut down and the screw raised. In a short while, the trick of stopping the engines at the right moment, before speed had increased sufficiently to strain the shaft, was thoroughly known to the Captain and officers. She rarely made less than seven knots, and, on 21 February, achieved a run of 200 miles in 24 hours.

20

It was a bright day, and the sufferers from seasickness had recovered; the first class passenger saloon was full at dinner that afternoon. During the day the passengers amused themselves by walking the deck, although the ladies mostly sat in fold-up chairs, reading or sewing. From below, mainly located in the third class accommodation, came strange noises; for some of the steerage passengers had brought musical instruments with them, and were in process of forming a band. Others were playing cards.

At daybreak on 23 February, after a stormy night, it was blowing a strong gale. The *Royal Charter* went racing on before the wind, heeling only to an angle of ten degrees, despite the large amount of canvas set overhead. The lowest sails on the three masts billowed out—those known as the fore-sail (on the fore mast), the main-sail (on the main mast), and the cross-jack (on the mizzen mast). The very tall sails above these—known as the fore, main and mizzen double topsails—were set also. The topsails on all three masts were divided into two parts, an upper and a lower, which was why they were known as double topsails; they represented a proportionately large part of the ship's sail power, and it was important that they should be kept in action as long as it was safe to do so.

With a normal topsail it was very often not safe, due to the time and labour factor involved in taking in these sails; men had to climb the tall masts and do the work by hand, hard enough in calm weather, and extremely difficult in a gale. But by dividing the topsails into two parts, and making it possible to drop the upper sail down to a position behind the lower, where it was effectively blanketed, the power of the sail could be halved in the time it took to give an order on deck and for a few seamen to let go the halyards; the upper topsails then came down of their own accord and lay snug in the lee of the lower topsails. This ingenious idea had only recently been invented by Captain Howes, an American, and the designers of the *Royal Charter* had promptly copied it. It was certainly working now.

The *Royal Charter* was running before the gale at a speed of 14 knots, carrying most of her square canvas, including the sails immediately above the topsails on the foremast and main mast— the fore and main topgallant sails. She maintained this speed for four hours and for a further eight hours achieved not less than 12 knots. She overtook two labouring ships, which were carrying only wisps of canvas, as if they had been at anchor—one indeed, could hardly have been doing more than three knots—and in the 24 hours from midnight to midnight sped 280 miles on towards Australia.

Two days later the weather and climate were very different from that of the wintry England which they had left ten days before—clear, warm sunshine, with flying fish breaking the surface of the blue sea; and, at night, new constellations in the sky. By day, it was so hot that an awning had to be rigged on the saloon deck. And, for the first time since leaving Liverpool, there was a failure at the dinner table—no roast beef!

Without counting the children, there were 54 first class passengers to be served in the saloon, plus four officers. The saloon itself was 100 feet long, divided in the centre by the mizzen mast; two tables ran down half the length of it, separated by the mast, and on these the food was served up on silver plate. Breakfast fare included tea and coffee, with milk from two cows kept aboard; bread or rolls, freshly baked aboard; and a choice of beefsteaks, ham, sardines, rice porridge, and stewed mutton. Dinner, which in the early part of the passage was served at four in the afternoon, usually offered a varied selection—joints of roast beef, roast or boiled mutton, roast or boiled chicken, mutton cutlets, mutton curry, ham, tongues, roast pork and apple sauce, and mutton pies, together with potatoes, carrots, rice, and cabbage. Afterwards, there were brandied plum puddings, rice puddings, fruit tarts, and sago pudding. For tea there were tea and coffee, with toast, plain bread and biscuits, and ample supplies of marmalade and jam.

This fare was served during most of the voyage, although some items, such as the beef, did not last more than a few weeks, because there was no refrigeration and the live animals could not be kept on board; and it was served, perfectly and punctually, in gale or calm. It was a very far cry indeed from the experiences of the early emigrants.

The second and third class passengers had their separate dining rooms—the third class mess-room being a large compartment, furnished with benches, far forward in the ship. Here, the amateur musicians practised and the card-players, many of them French, gambled for small stakes. But, as the weather grew ever more warm, the most popular apartment in the *Royal Charter* was the so-called 'ladies' boudoir'. This occupied the position which, in a warship, would have been taken by the Captain's cabin. It ran right across the ship, from side to side, and was ventilated by seven cabin windows overlooking the sea at the stern. In cold or heavy weather it was deserted, the deadlights being closed, but now it was cool and delightful. In the evenings there was, for the first class passengers, dancing on the deck above the saloon, with a dozen or more couples taking part, the music supplied by a succession of volunteer instrumentalists.

The *Royal Charter* saw few ships, and when she saw them, she passed them. Her auxiliary steam power enabled her to take a shorter route, not normally used by sailing ships at this time of the year, because of its light winds and calms. But in the engine room there was real suffering; in the coolest part of it the temperature was 93 degrees, and near the furnaces, where the firemen and stokers had to work, the thermometer reached 130 degrees and stayed there most of the day and night. A number of men

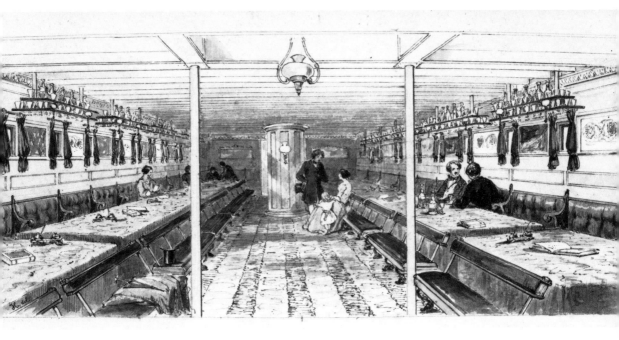

The grand saloon of the *Great Britain*. The interior of the *Royal Charter* would have been similar. *Photo: The National Maritime Museum, London*

fainted, and the Captain had to take special measures for their health, allowing them fresh provisions, together with beer, porter, or weak brandy and water, when they came off duty. The *Royal Charter* passed on, across the doldrums, with their sullen, oppressive heat, at a speed never less than seven knots, where often other ships had been detained seven, ten, or even nineteen days.

On 5 March she crossed the 'line', and on 17 March the first albatross appeared, enormous and majestic, following the *Royal Charter* without effort, soaring with motionless wings on the rising warm air currents the ship created. It was also Saint Patrick's Day and, as some of the saloon passengers were Irish, a champagne supper and ball was arranged, formal invitations being issued. A space of 70 or 80 feet, screened off by awnings, canvas and flags, was allowed for dancing, and as the ship pressed on through the Southern Atlantic at ten knots, with half a gale blowing and an occasional gust of wind rattling on the screens, toasts were drunk, speeches were made, and the dancing began. The band, by now, were extremely proficient.

Next day, the air on deck was noticeably chill, as the ship sped southwards towards Antarctica in order to round Africa (there being no Suez Canal then). She was making twelve knots, but only light spray occasionally came aboard at the bow. On the morning of 19 March, at about 6.30, many of the sleeping passengers were woken by the sound of spasmodic rifle fire coming from the stern, mixed with the noise of shotguns and other weapons.

The cloud of circling, enormous birds had proved too tempting to the 'sportsmen' aboard, and dozens of them were rivalling each other in their attempts to be the first to shoot an albatross. After half a hundred shots had been fired, one at last took effect, and an albatross went down onto the water, where it lay stricken and helpless, struggling in the waves. In a few minutes it had dropped astern, out of sight; but still the firing went on. These were 'savage birds', they had been known to attack human beings, it was proper to shoot them, averred the riflemen. Soon, the anglers joined in the sport. One of them threw overboard a baited hook on a long line, and while the ship was stopped temporarily in order to bring the screw into action, an albatross swooped down upon the bait and was trimuphantly hauled in and drawn up on deck by the angler. It was at that moment that the angler realised that the bird's wing-span was ten feet and that it possessed a powerful bill, eight inches long, which curved into a sharp point.

It was at this moment also that the bird realised that the only way of escape was to become airborne and that the deck in front of it offered the only take-off run. It came forward with a rush at the group of whooping spectators, who fell back in panic before it, shoving each other out of the way in their haste. It tried repeatedly to take off, at each failure the crowd closing in on it, and then falling back hurriedly as it rushed at them. Eventually, the albatross was killed. Next day, however, rain prevented this form of amusement from being continued.

On 26 March, the *Royal Charter* was fleeing across the Indian Ocean before a 'white squall'. It was full daylight, with a bright sun occasionally breaking through the clouds and bursts of driven rain. The waves rose rapidly in height, but moved forward only comparatively slowly, so that their tops were driven off them by the wind; the prevailing blue of the sea was streaked and speckled by the blown spray, a tempestuous maelstrom of torn blue and white; and behind the ship, the broken wake slid away astern, a seething streak of rich emerald green. With the coming of sunset, the scene took on an unearthly beauty, the waves rising to more than twenty feet in height, and the *Royal Charter* cutting through the water noiselessly at a speed of sixteen knots under an absolute cloud of white sail. All the square sails, including the royals, the highest of all, were set and taut before the wind; and the studding sails, sideways projections of

1	FORESAIL	20	MAIN TOPGALLANT STAYSAIL
2	FORE LOWER TOPSAIL	21	MAIN ROYAL STAYSAIL
3	FORE UPPER TOPSAIL	22	MAIN TOPMAST STUDDING SAIL
4	FORE TOPGALLANT SAIL	23	MAIN TOPGALLANT STUDDING SAIL
5	FORE ROYAL	24	MAIN ROYAL STUDDING SAIL
6	FORE SKYSAIL	25	CROSSJACK
7	FORE TOPMAST STAYSAIL	26	MIZZEN LOWER TOPSAIL
8	LOWER STUDDING SAIL	27	MIZZEN UPPER TOPSAIL
9	FORE TOPMAST STUDDING SAIL	28	MIZZEN TOPGALLANT SAIL
10	FORE TOPGALLANT STUDDING SAIL	29	MIZZEN ROYAL
11	FORE ROYAL STUDDING SAIL	30	MIZZEN SKYSAIL
12	MAINSAIL	31	SPANKER
13	MAIN LOWER TOPSAIL	32	MIZZEN STAYSAIL
14	MAIN UPPER TOPSAIL	33	MIZZEN TOPMAST STAYSAIL
15	MAIN TOPGALLANT SAIL	34	MIZZEN TOPGALLANT STAYSAIL
16	MAIN ROYAL	35	MIZZEN ROYAL STAYSAIL
17	MAIN SKYSAIL	36	JIB
18	MAIN TOPMAST LOWER STAYSAIL	37	FLYING JIB
19	MAIN TOPMAST UPPER STAYSAIL	38	JIB TOPSAIL

Sail plan of a typical clipper. *From a drawing by Maurice Young.*

the square sails, were spread like wings on either side. The wind shrilled in the rigging, and the waves rose higher, thrown up irregularly into peaks and crests, some of them measuring 35 feet from trough to crest, and collapsing under their own weight into a mass of white, roaring breakers. Occasionally, the ship's wake was enough to cause an up-heaving wave, already towering high, to dissolve into thundering foam, which struck the vessel's side and sent sheets of water sweeping across the deck, spouting upwards from projections on it.

Many of the passengers were on deck to watch the spectacle, and there would be a shout of merriment on such occasions, as some little group or other would be drenched or forced to dash for cover. Lightened of her ballast, the *Royal Charter* rode these seas, under press of canvas, without danger and without the swamping experienced in that first storm off Finisterre. For the 24 hours she logged a distance of no less than 352 miles, and for 30 hours she maintained an average speed of just under fifteen knots.

On the night of 31 March, with a heavy gale blowing, accompanied by squally blasts of wind and showers of rain and hail, the lookout reported an iceberg on the port bow. Passengers crowded up from below, their feelings a mixture of curiosity and apprehension. They peered out over the darkened sea, searching for some dramatic sight, and noticing only a slight but distinctive luminosity which was, in fact, the iceberg. The chief officer then called out that there was another iceberg in sight, almost dead ahead. The helm was put over and then, close on the port side, the passengers were able to see, half obscured by a black rain squall, a dim glowing shape some 300 yards long and perhaps 100 feet high. Some of the sails were taken in, and the speed reduced for a few hours, until Captain Boyce had judged that they were clear of the danger.

It was now the hurricane season in the Indian Ocean, and Sunday, 6 April, was the day on which the *Royal Charter* faced her severest test. Ships are built to withstand storms, but a hurricane is something else again. The principal danger to a sailing ship, which must use the tormented winds and try to profit from them, is that her bow will swing round under the impact of a wave, and that she will 'broach to', rolling sideways, helpless before the onslaught of the tempest. On this day the waves grew to an enormous height, forty feet or more, and they were not sweeping up from behind in regular lines; instead, two seas were meeting, and combating each other, swinging the bows this way and that in a turmoil of tormented water. Four quartermasters stood at the wheel, to force it round; a deck officer stood beside them. Just forward of the wheel, which was in front of the mizzen mast, stood Captain Boyce, looking out intently ahead and astern and to the side, to judge the next sea, and giving quick orders. 'Star-

board! Starboard!—steady so—port a little—meet her again—mind your
starboard helm.' And so the battle went on.

Above, reared the mizzen mast, denuded of all sail, the cordage swelling
out forward under the force of the wind. The ship went heeling over to
port, as a mountainous wave reared up under the stern and raised it high;
and on its heels another wave, rising up under the starboard quarter and
sending the ship still further over to port, the deck steeply inclined and
water rushing over it. If the ship broached to now, or if the tiller ropes
broke, which would amount to the same thing, there was no hope.

The screaming wind forced up the waves into great peaks which curved
forward and broke, as though they had struck a rock; they piled up one
wave on another, so that a following wave would overtake the breaker
in front, until a long stretch of ocean behind a mounting wave would be
one seething mass of white, jumbled water. The hurtling, high-velocity
winds, dissatisfied by the laboured, rolling progress of these surging mountains of water, would explode their tops, not merely blowing away the
foaming, snow-white crests, but slicing off masses of solid, rearing water

27

and drifting it away across the surface of the sea in sheets which, although it was full daylight, shut off the sun and restricted visibility to a few hundred yards.

This time, the water sweeping the decks did indeed penetrate below and seep into the cabins. The saloon tables, freshly laid for breakfast, were drenched, the table cloths, sugar and milk saturated with salt water. But they were relaid, and breakfast served at the usual time. There was an occasional inundation from the skylights, as water a foot deep swept over the deck above, and a torrent would pour down the forward gangway and through the doors; but the stewards bailed out the saloon and rewashed the suspended glasses. At 3.30, half-an-hour after the now usual time, the dinner bell was heard, and the surprised passengers found before them a properly laid dinner—with roast and boiled mutton, pork, cutlets, stews, curries and vegetables; and, in due course, plum pudding surrounded by brandy flame. There was no soup, and there had been an accident to the chickens, but apart from this, everything was normal. Two hours later the storm was beginning to lose something of its severity, and by midnight the *Royal Charter* was 306 miles nearer Australia than she had been 24 hours before. The only damage suffered was to one of the quarter-boats.

By 15 April, excitement on board was intense. Melbourne was only 240 miles away, but the breeze was light, and it looked as if the *Royal Charter* might be cheated at the last of the record for the Australia run. And so it proved. The *Royal Charter* anchored in the roadstead of Melbourne in just under 60 days from leaving Plymouth. She had not quite matched the performance of a steamship, but she had beaten every other ship, most of them by a very handsome margin. In the five months previous to her arrival, the shortest passage to Melbourne had taken 91 days. Her owners were now able to advertise 'The magnificent steam clipper *Royal Charter*— Australia in under 60 days.'

Chapter 3

BY TREASURE SHIP TO LIVERPOOL

In the last week of August, 1859, the *Royal Charter* lay in the roadstead at Melbourne. Her decks and cabins were a scene of bustle and confusion as passengers and their luggage came aboard, and were settled in. Alongside her port quarter lay a small steamer, from which some square wooden boxes were being handed up on to the clipper's deck. Each wooden box was marked with its weight and the name of the shipper as well as the bank to which it was being consigned; and each box was being checked personally by the Captain and an Australian customs officer, before being stacked below in the strongroom, deep inside the hull at the stern. For the boxes contained gold, valued at £4 an ounce. The gold had been weighed at the bank ashore, in the presence of representatives of the shippers and the ship's agent acting for the owners of the *Royal Charter*, and then the boxes had been secured and sealed. A police escort had convoyed them to the Melbourne quay where the small steamer was lying (on board which no one was allowed except the crew and the interested parties), and this steamer had carried them down the river Yarra to the waiting *Royal Charter*. On 26 August, all the gold had been loaded, and the Captain had given a receipt for the whole amount—£322,440. But the real total was much larger than that, for, apart from this officially consigned gold, many of her 390 passengers were carrying their own small personal fortunes on them.

The *Royal Charter* was a famous ship now. On her first trip she had beaten her fastest competitor by 13 days, the slowest by no less than 69 days. She never lacked for passengers. Her owners could promise, what many others could not, arrival in Australia within two months of leaving Liverpool; and the promise was kept, give or take a day or so. The return passage, which was normally by Cape Horn instead of round the Cape of Good Hope, took slightly longer. She was, in effect, what we would now call a liner—a fast passenger ship running on schedule like a train; and like the modern ocean liner, she also carried a small cargo—on this passage, copper, hides and wool, in addition to the gold. First class passenger fares varied between 60 and 75 guineas, second class between 25 and 30 guineas, while the third class fare was either 16, 18 or 20 guineas. Chil-

dren between the ages of one and twelve years went for half price, babies for nothing; the fare for a dog was £5.

The owners boasted of her seven 'Fire-proof and Watertight Compartments,' and had taken steps to remedy the minor structural defects which had shown up on her first round-the-world voyage in 1856. The main alteration was the fitting of massive stringers along her sides, between decks, in order to give greater longitudinal strength. There had also been some minor weakness at the bow, which had let in water, and a breaking of some iron gear on the upper topsail yard which had caused the yard—which weighed five tons—to fall towards the deck. Luckily, it was arrested in its passage by the yard below it, so that the damage was not so serious as it might have been. The art of working in iron was still by no means perfect and there was a practical limit to size, which could only be overcome by the introduction of steel.

Nevertheless, with her ladies' boudoir, baths, comfortable fittings, luxurious meals, and water-tight compartments, she represented an early step in a process now almost complete—the insulation of ship passengers from the sea. For such a ship to sink, then or now, is unthinkable—until it happens.

As the *Royal Charter* lay at anchor in Melbourne roadstead, under the southern sun, she was a miniature *Titanic*, an old-fashioned *Andrea Doria*.

Her previous master, Captain Francis Boyce, had in 1852 established a record of 76 days for the passage Melbourne to London in the Australian packet ship *Eagle*. According to tradition in his family, passed on by his daughter, Katie Boyce, he retired 'because owing to the intense competition, especially with the *Great Eastern* coming along, he thought the owners were pushing their ships too hard, thereby forcing their captains to take greater risks than was always wise'.

Her Captain now was Thomas Taylor, who had gone out in her on her maiden voyage to Australia as a passenger, under Captain Boyce, and who had helped Doctor Scoresby with his magnetical experiments by 'swinging' the ship after she had arrived for the first time in Melbourne. He was, as clipper captains had to be, what a later generation was to call a 'press-on' type. 'A rough diamond,' recollected William Gilmour of Aylesbury, who was surgeon superintendent of the *Royal Charter* during four of her Australian voyages, but had taken up private practice ashore before she made her last voyage. 'Almost everyone is a rough diamond, who has risen from the ranks of the forecastle. Thomas Taylor never had been a gold-laced, kid-gloved middy, with more money than brains, but had got up to what he was by his own perseverance and proficiency. A

Sailing bill of the *Royal Charter*, 1856. *Photo: Merseyside County Museums*

31

better commander and seaman never had charge of a ship. He was a strict disciplinarian with his officers and crew—almost too much so. He was very fond of carrying all the sail he could possibly have spread out, and he took every advantage of the wind.' Taylor's contemporaries allowed that he was a 'very smart man'. He was a proud man, too, Captain of the crack ship on the Australia run. He had a wife and daughters at home in Liverpool and, within two months, he would see them again; they usually met the *Royal Charter* at the quayside when she docked.

The city in whose roadstead his ship now lay was very different from the shanty town of some twenty years before, when the population of Melbourne had been less than 500. It now exceeded 80,000. Doctor Scoresby had been most impressed by the fineness of the buildings, the width of the roadways, and the bustling air of prosperity, when he had visited Melbourne three years earlier, in 1856. The process was very similar to that which he had seen in the United States, where colonial expansion was also in full swing. There were simple buildings of wood or corrugated iron, more permanent houses of brick or stucco, and many substantial structures some three or four storeys high, built of stone. Melbourne, he wrote, was 'much finer in the width of the streets and the costliness of many of the newer buildings, than almost any strange place in a distant country I remember to have visited.' The main streets were 100 feet wide, with pavements five or six yards across; the traffic consisted of English-type gigs, phaetons, and broughams mixed with Australian wagons drawn by bullocks and buffaloes. It seemed strange to him that, in a city built in so short a time in a reclaimed desert at the opposite side of the globe to England, the dress, manners and classes of the home country were almost exactly reproduced, 'except some peculiarities with the working classes.' In great enthusiasm, he concluded, 'It is like a city raised by the power of an Aladdin's lamp.'

That power was gold. Every ship brought in men and women hungry for it, and every vessel that left carried back successful miners to spread the tale at home, and so encourage more to come out, In the end, Australia gained more people than she lost. The passenger list of the *Royal Charter* gave a fair sample of them. Nearly 400 people, with their different hopes and ambitions: the successes and the failures, the rich and the poor, the fortunate and the unfortunate, the long-married and the newly in love.

James Dean, a north country man from Wigan, was one of those who intended, if he could, to come back to Australia. He had left his wife in England three years before, after only twelve months of married life, because the wages of a skilled labourer were far higher in Australia than at home. In his trade of smith, he had expected to make good money. And so he had. But a visit to the gold diggings had shown him a quicker

A Portsmouth emigrant packing for the passage to Australia in 1853. *Photo: Alexander McKee collection*

way, and he was now taking passage in the *Royal Charter*. He had on him a considerable sum of money, mainly in the form of a cheque on an English bank, which he wore in a waterproof belt round his waist. Dean was a prudent man. In cash he had only enough to cover his expenses on the journey. Once home, he hoped to win round his wife to the idea of settling permanently in the colony.

There were easier ways of obtaining gold than digging for it, and Mrs S. A. Foster, wife of John Foster, owner of the Shakespeare Hotel, Manchester, represented the business side of the boom caused by the gold rush. John Foster had seen his opportunity at the very beginning. Leaving the Shakespeare Hotel in the capable hands of his wife, he had spent four years in the colony, and in that time had established two new hotels. Once the business was on its feet, he had handed over the management to two of his nephews, and returned home. Early in 1859, however, some matters arose which could not be handled satisfactorily by correspondence, and Mrs Foster sailed in the *Royal Charter* on 26 May; having transacted her business within a month, she was now returning in the same ship. When she got back to Liverpool she would have sailed right round the world—a distance of some 30,000 miles—in the *Royal Charter*. She was not to know that she would never complete the last fifty miles of that tremendous journey.

Mrs Foster had with her some of the profits of the Australian business—nearly £5,000 in money and valuables. And, although she had travelled out alone—a most unusual proceeding, thought to demand great courage of a woman—Mrs Foster had a companion on the return trip. This was Mrs Woodruffe, a very handsome girl from Stockport, who had married

33

one of Mr Foster's nephews. Mrs Woodruffe was soon to attract a number of admirers on board—including Captain Withers, whose ship, the *Victoria*, had been lost off the Fiji Islands. There was another ship master due to join later—Captain Adams, of the *Red Jacket*, sunk by collision off Buenos Aires.

These four were to form a friendly group with a number of other passengers, mostly family men. There was Henry Carew Taylor, a New South Wales magistrate, who was travelling first class with his little daughter and her nurse. There was a Scotsman from Linlithgow, James Russell, with his wife and two little girls, one aged ten, the other two-and-a-half; the family had been in Australia seven years. And there was James Watson of Rochdale, son of Thomas Watson, of the firm of Watson and Healey, silk manufacturers. Young Watson had helped form a company to exploit the diggings and had been very successful—one nugget alone had been worth £5,000. He was bringing home samples, which he showed to Russell. Now in a position to marry, he had just proposed by post to a young lady in Preston, and was hurrying home for his answer.

Another prosperous man aboard was a New Zealand farmer, Samuel Edward Gapper. He had come out from England in 1841, farmed successfully for fourteen years, and was now returning to England with the sum of £500 set aside for the purchase of agricultural machinery. Before the *Royal Charter* left Melbourne he was introduced to 23-year-old Mrs R. Rose by her brother, Mr Pratt. The young and pretty Mrs Rose was returning alone to London to join her father, and had no companion on the voyage. Having already been introduced, she was willing enough to be friendly with Mr Gapper, and to be seen about with him, as this would keep away less desirable admirers. As Gapper afterwards said, 'Attempts were being made to impose on her; I offered my services, and she accepted them.' For him, it was to be a very happy journey; and because of that, his loneliness and misery at the end the more terrible.

There were several families who were related, including two married sisters, Mrs Davis and Mrs Fenwick. Mr Fenwick was remaining behind in Melbourne, while his wife and their four young children travelled to England. Mrs Davis was making the journey with her two grown-up daughters, one of whom, Sophia Davis, was soon to become friendly with 17-year-old Jane Fowler, elder daughter of Mr and Mrs Edwin Fowler. The Fowlers had two daughters, the younger of whom, Ida, was only five-and-a-half; travelling with them, as nurse to the child, was a girl of about twenty, Emma Calf, who was devoted to her charge.

All these passengers were travelling first or second class; the humbler gold miners had booked steerage accommodation. They were poor, but only comparatively so. Two of them, from the West Country, had met at the diggings, chummed up and were now returning together. Thomas Bowden, of Torquay in Devon, was returning with £200 to 'his old woman,' as he put it. Unlike the prudent Mr Dean, he was carrying the money in cash. His chum was Samuel Grenfell, of St Ives in Cornwall. Many of these men carried their newfound riches in money-belts or wallets; as safe as it could possibly be—unless the ship sank, in which case the weight of the gold was likely to take them to the bottom. They were not even dreaming of that possibility, and were in boisterous mood, elated by their success at Ballarat and the prospect of a triumphant return to their wives, families and friends. One young man, T. Bakewell, had not even told his parents in Manchester that he was returning, as he hoped to give them a pleasant surprise; he became friends on board with John Bradbury, an excellent swimmer, whose destination was also Manchester.

In contrast, there was James Potts, another miner. A tall, stout man, with whiskers and moustache, he had been extremely unlucky. He came from Crewe, and had gone to Indigo diggings, where he had broken his thigh. He had been in two hospitals, while his bones were mending, but was almost penniless. A friend had obtained for him a free passage in the *Royal Charter*, but as he could not work and had a wife in England to support, the future was bleak. However, he soon made friends in the ship and a subscription was got up for him, so that he could obtain the services of a London surgeon after arriving home. They were a rough but good-hearted lot in the steerage, dressed, mostly, in loud checked shirts, under black waistcoats, with moleskin trousers and boots. There was a distinctly 'Wild West' aspect to them—hardly to be wondered at, because the American West was being opened at the same time by the same sort of people. The parallel was complete in the person of an old lady of eighty, another third class passenger, whose gold-miner husband had been shot down in a gunfight at Ballarat the previous year.

Among the miners was Thomas Brough, possibly travelling as John Brough. He had been deported to Australia for a period of seven years, had served his sentence and then settled there. In 1852 he went to the gold diggings and made a fortune. To his relatives he wrote letters announcing his return to the country which had rejected him, telling one relative that no one in his family would ever work again, informing another that no Brough would ever want again.

One passenger came up the gangway under guard, and was escorted below. He was something of a mystery. It was said that his name was Samuel Henry, that he was a jeweller and highly connected in London; but that he was now insane. He was kept locked in his cabin.

Another passenger also came aboard unwillingly and under duress, although of a different sort. This was the Reverend Charles Vere Hodge, vicar of Claresborough. Shortly after taking up the living of Claresborough in 1844, his wife had left him on the excuse of visiting a distant relative in New Zealand; and, despite his protests, to New Zealand she had gone—alone. The poor man was left to look after all their ten children—seven boys and three girls. She returned to England after a few years, found life with the vicar again intolerable, and decided to set off once more for the other side of the globe. This time her husband decided to accompany her, with the whole family, so that she could not escape. After a no doubt embarrassing interview with his bishop, he obtained leave of absence from the diocese for two years. When the two years had passed, his wife informed him that she had no intention of leaving New Zealand; so the Reverend Hodge remained there until the Bishop, losing patience at last, issued a monition for his return. That was why the poor, henpecked man, a figure of fun to those who knew of the pitiful character of his domestic life, was aboard the ship. But, for the Reverend Charles Vere Hodge, the *Royal Charter* was to provide a brief gleam of glory.

As the last boxes of gold were stowed down below and the *Royal Charter* prepared to cast off, a last-minute passenger came aboard. He gave the name of Garden, but his real name was William Gardiner. He had with him £4,000—not his own. A commission agent in Melbourne, he was absconding with other people's money. There was another mystery passenger, a young man who gave his name as S. Perry. Some of the other passengers found out that this was false, but his real name is still unknown.

One family with nine children turned up just to see the *Royal Charter* sail. They had settled their affairs and paid their passage, when the wife's pocket had been cut by a thief. With her money went the sailing documents. Nevertheless, although they now had to find a place on another ship leaving Melbourne later, this family went to the dock to witness the splendid clipper depart for England, and to wish that they were on it.

On 26 August, 1859, the anchor was hove up and the ship cleared of people from the shore. The *Royal Charter* went astern and, when clear of other shipping, turned round in the roadstead of Port Philip, and headed for the open sea.

One of the crew, 15-year-old Charles Thomas, had written to his mother, Mary Thomas, a fortnight before, announcing the imminent sailing of the *Royal Charter*: 'Mother, pray for a fair breeze, and I shall whistle for the wind.' And indeed, a wind was coming. One of the seamen working aloft was Isaac Lewis, who came from the obscure little village of Moelfre, nestling on the rugged and desolate northern coast of Anglesey, half the world away. By a coincidence too sardonic to be dared by any fiction writer, Isaac Lewis was to see his home again, just once more before he died.

Chapter 4

THE ONSET OF THE HURRICANE

The *Royal Charter* sped on across the vast expanses of the Pacific towards the tip of South America. As she neared Cape Horn, the balmy days were left behind and sometimes there was ice on deck. At dead of night, when rounding the Horn, the lookouts saw what appeared to be low clouds lying over the water. They were, in fact, immense icebergs, some of them merely flat sheets of ice, others with lofty turrets and spires. But it was not long before, scudding in front of the sudden gales which often blow up off South America, the ship was nearing the equator. Most of the birds that had been following the clipper now left her, as she drove north into warm, blue waters. Awnings were spread, and the passengers changed into lighter clothing. Many of them had bought parrots, and these, in their cages, were brought on deck now. There were literally hundreds of them, in spite of the attrition of the voyage and of the fighting that ensued when a number of parrots were kept in the same cage. Some escaped, when the cages were brought on deck and opened, and took up perches in the rigging. Valiant efforts were made by their owners to recapture them, for the profit on a pair of parrots was very high.

Amateur dramatics were performed, and there was dancing on deck again for the saloon passengers. There was some resentment among the steerage passengers that this was reserved for those who had paid first class fares. Samuel Gapper and the pretty Mrs Rose were now inseparable, although, to avoid scandal, he also partnered other young girls at the dances. He was to recall that the two Misses Davis, in particular, 'were very fond of dancing'. The passengers also organised concerts among themselves. There were a number of French and Germans aboard, very musical people. One, Carl Bartel, whose home was in East Prussia, was a professional musician of high standing who had just completed a concert tour in Australia.

The passengers had not only got to know each other, and formed firm friendships among themselves, but had come to accept certain members of the crew as almost part of their daily lives. In particular, Miss Wareing, the stewardess, was deservedly popular throughout the ship; she was supposed to attend only to the saloon passengers, but spent much of her spare

37

time nursing anyone who fell sick. On a previous voyage, she had nursed back to health one of the sailors who had fallen from the mainyard to the deck and was severely injured. A real 'character', known to everyone who had ever sailed in the *Royal Charter*, was 'Piping Judd', the sweeper. He had a tin whistle which he played whenever there was hard work to be done, such as hoisting up coal. He was invariably a performer at the ship's concerts, when he would give renderings from well-known operas, without actually being able to read a note of music.

It was noticeable that thirty-year-old William Bean, the quiet and reserved Third Officer, was often in the company of a lively girl who was travelling as a steerage passenger. Such shipboard romances are often lightly regarded, but this one, like that of Mr Gapper and Mrs Rose, was to be broken only by death. As the clipper ploughed north, ever nearer to her destination, which could be the parting point for the involved couples, no doubt they were making plans for the future. What plans Mr Garden, alias William Gardiner, was making we cannot know; but he was probably worrying about how to get his ill-gotten £4,000 through Customs. A man by the name of Garden did get off at Queenstown; according to newspaper reports, he left his 25-year-old wife on board to continue on to Liverpool. If it was really William Gardiner, then a convenient fate was about to wipe out his tracks, for the passenger list of the *Royal Charter* was lost in the wreck—no one was ever able to say exactly how many people died, but only who survived. If it was not the insolvent commission agent who landed at Queenstown, then he met a worse fate than bankruptcy.

*   *   *

At daybreak on Monday, 24 October, land was sighted—the Old Head of Kinsale, on the southern coast of Ireland. They were nearly home. Since leaving Melbourne two months before, the *Royal Charter* had not called at any port; she travelled non-stop across the world. But there were some passengers to put ashore at Queenstown and, to avoid delay, the ship would lay off outside for a short time while they were transferred to a pilot-boat. When this news got around, a number of people wrote letters, to be posted in Queenstown, giving relatives and friends warning of their imminent arrival.

One of these was young Frederick Foster, an orphan, and the only midshipman in the *Royal Charter*. William Gilmour, former surgeon of the ship, had no very high opinion of him, complaining that he was 'fonder of his bunk than the deck', that he frequently feigned illness, had to be roused with a bucket of water, and spent many hours at the masthead as a punishment. 'He never would have made a sailor, but now all his troubles are over,' wrote the doctor, rather unctuously, circumstances considered. The letter that the young midshipman penned off Cork was the last he ever wrote.

'We are now coming up Channel with a slashing breeze. We ran out in fifty-nine days, and should have come home in forty-seven, had we not had strong head winds all the way from the line. You may expect me and one or two friends at your house Tuesday or Wednesday night, so be prepared. How is Alice? Remember me kindly to her and all. Excuse bad writing.'

Another letter which has survived, although the writer did not, was then being written by Joseph Robinson, a passenger, to his sister. 'Isabella, you must make a good apple cake, and we must have tea by ourselves. Don't tell anyone I am coming, not even a relation, till I have seen you all. And Isabella, you must come down to meet the night train, and stand in front of the ladies' waiting room. In order that you may know me, for I am much changed in my appearance since I left, I will call the word "Brown".'

Another passenger impatient to see friends again was Mrs Edwin Fowler, mother of Jane and Ida. She wrote to a family living in Ireland, asking them to meet her at Liverpool. The family concerned had made all preparations to leave for Liverpool, but had not actually left, when news of the disaster reached them; instead, they went at once to the scene of the wreck, and later wrote a book about it, under their initials only, which they gave as A. and J.K. 'K' may possibly have stood for Kennedy, for there were passengers of that name also travelling by the *Royal Charter*.

When the *Royal Charter* hove to off Queenstown at about 1.30 pm on Monday 24 October, she had some 500 people aboard—a crew of 112 and a passenger list of about 390. The pilot-boat *Petrel* ran alongside, and took off 14 passengers whose destination was Ireland. It was 58 days since they had left Melbourne.

At the last moment, while he was actually shaking hands with some of his friends who were leaving in the pilot-boat, a Mr M'Evoy, brother of the MP for Meath, suddenly decided to join them, and had his luggage transferred to the *Petrel*. Emotional impulse, or premonition, or whatever it was, the decision almost certainly saved his life.

About three hours after stopping off Queenstown, the *Royal Charter* was under way again, her voyage almost completed. Her passengers were in a cheerful mood, looking forward intensely to the tales they would have to tell of their adventures in Australia, and of a new, exciting continent. Their friends, they flattered themselves, would hardly recognise them now. Besides this, there was the pleasurable, on-top-of-the-world feeling produced by gold-lined pockets, topped by the satisfaction of having almost completed an exceptionally fast trip half across the world. So pleased were the saloon passengers with the ship and the good time she had made that they were getting up a testimonial to present to the Captain; only two out of more than three-score failed to sign it. Captain Taylor, 'rough diamond' as he was, was flattered and delighted by the testimonial, which he received that evening. In return, he promised that he would have them in Liverpool within 24 hours—59 days out from Australia. By Tuesday night, he pleasantly assured them, he expected to be 'on the lee side of Mrs Taylor'. That promise was later to be remembered, and held against him.

He had under his command a veritable treasure ship. Few so-called 'treasure ships', not excluding the Tobermory galleon, are literally such; but the *Royal Charter* really was; as she sped away up the Irish Sea, she was a wrecker's dreamboat.

To one man, however, her speedy departure gave great indignation. He had risked a quick run ashore, in order to transact some trifling business, while the *Royal Charter* lay for three hours off Queenstown. Aboard her was his wife, with £700 in her possession. He was too late in getting back and now, helplessly, he had to watch the tall, graceful clipper disappearing over the horizon. Fuming, he set out to find the quickest alternative means of getting to Liverpool in time, if not to meet her, at least to arrive soon after she had docked. But the *Royal Charter* was never to dock again.

*   *   *

In the dusk, the beams of the Irish lighthouses shone out over a sea that was calm and quiet. At 7.30 that evening the *Royal Charter* was abreast of Ballycotton; an hour later she was passing Youghal. Her last sight of Ireland was the Tuskar Light, which was in view half-an-hour before midnight. One of the quartermasters at the wheel was Owen Williams, of Caernarvon. Most of the crew were from Liverpool, but a number, like Williams, were Welshmen. The weather that night was very fine, he recalled, with only a ripple on the water. But the clipper's decks were almost deserted, for the light breeze held the chill of the cold northern waters.

The dawn of Tuesday, 25 October, was grey and bleak, with no sight of land anywhere; but the coastline of Caernarvonshire lay only just over the horizon beyond the bow. Williams came on deck at 8 o'clock, taking over the wheel two hours later. The wind was still at south-east, as it had been the previous day—light but favourable. A thin line that shortly appeared on the horizon was Bardsey Island, lying off the Caernarvon coast. Williams was almost home.

Very far from his homeland was George Suaicar, the boatswain's mate. He was Maltese, but his home now, and his wife, were in Liverpool. He was soon needed on deck, because the wind began to freshen and to veer somewhat to the north, so that it became foul for the clipper. First the square sails were taken in, and then, as the wind increased still further, all the fore and aft sails also; but the *Royal Charter* continued to forge ahead, to the steady beat of her 200 hp engine.

Close to Bardsey Island, the steam tug *United Kingdom* ran alongside the homeward bound clipper, and bundles of newspapers were handed on board. Shortly afterwards, 11 men from the tug boarded the *Royal Charter* and went below. They were riggers who had been taking the ship *Typhoon* round to Cardiff in South Wales. In search of a return passage to Liverpool they had joined the tug, which was bound there as soon as she got a tow. However, they saw a chance of getting home earlier in the *Royal Charter*, if her Captain would agree to let them work their passage. It was a fateful decision for more than half of them.

At about 1.30 pm the *Royal Charter* was in sight of Holyhead, a small island off the Island of Anglesey on the coast of North Wales. There was a considerable haze over the land, shrouding the Welsh mountains, although the sea was still calm. One of the ship captains aboard as a passenger averred that it would be a 'dirty night'—or so witnesses recalled afterwards. The haze was peculiar, and there was an unnatural look about the sky, but no one had the least idea of what was really in store for them. The clipper carried three barometers but, as the barometers ashore had given the land observatories no warning, it was unlikely that those of the *Royal Charter* had so much as hinted at what was coming. There was no broadcast weather report to tell of the tempest that had already struck Devon and Cornwall and was now imminent in the Irish Sea. The *Royal Charter* plugged slowly northwards, her small engine beating away, the sea parting evenly at her bow, the long wake stretching astern, and the rising wind beginning to drum in the rigging. Her progress seemed very slow to those aboard, perhaps because they could hardly endure any delay so near to home.

Very many of them had sent messages from Queenstown, and expected to be met at Liverpool. Captain Taylor's own two daughters would be at the quayside tomorrow, to welcome their father home. John Foster would be there, too, meeting his wife and Mrs Woodruffe; he was already planning a party for that night at the Shakespeare Hotel. A miner had telegraphed his wife at Blyth to meet him at Newcastle on Thursday; but he, too, failed to keep his rendezvous.

The watches on board changed over at 4 pm. David Strongman was one of the quartermasters who took over at the wheel; Joseph Rodgers

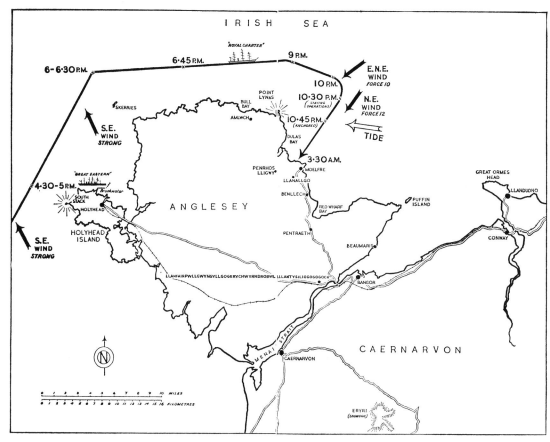

Map I. The course of the *Royal Charter* through the Irish Sea until she was caught by the hurricane at 10 p.m. on 25 October, 1859.

was one of the seamen who came on deck. Like Suaicar, Rodgers was Maltese. But where Suaicar was boisterous and talkative, Rodgers was quiet and confident. The modest impression he gave was quite at variance with the skilful daring which he often showed aloft when tackling work which not everyone would venture. His real name was Joie Rodriguez, and he was born in Malta in 1830; after some years at sea, he settled in Liverpool where, inevitably, his name became changed to something easier for the English tongue to manage. He had joined the *Royal Charter* two years before and had completed five voyages in her. In one respect he differed markedly from the ordinary British seaman who, although showing natural ability on the sea, was not at all happy in it. Like most Maltese, because of the warm, buoyant water of the Mediterranean, he was an excellent swimmer and proud of his skill. So, too, was Suaicar, but he lacked some intangible spark which was more than a mere physical skill.

The highest sails on the three tall clipper masts—the royals—had already been sent below, together with the topgallant studding sail. Rodgers and other seamen of the watch on deck now began to take in some of the fore-and-aft sails—the staysails—from the main and mizzen masts, and to stow them below. Her masts mostly bare of canvas, and the twin-bladed screw thrashing the water, the *Royal Charter* moved slowly up the coast of Anglesey, about five miles out to sea. It was not until 4.30 that afternoon that she came abreast of Holyhead harbour, its uncompleted breakwater a mass of scaffolding and cranes. In front of the breakwater reared a monstrous shape, topped by what looked like a row of factory chimneys and masts. Set in her vast slab sides was a pair of ungainly paddle wheels. Excited passengers, among them the Scotsman, James Russell, began to point it out to each other. Below, in the saloon, most of the first class passengers were having tea. A steward came clattering down the gangway, and said excitedly to Henry Carew Taylor, whose child was being fed by the nurse, 'Mr Taylor, would you like to go on deck and see the *Great Eastern*?'

In the light of a murky sunset, Taylor stood at the rail and looked out across miles of heaving water at a ship so massive that it could not be got inside the harbour of Holyhead and had to lie outside the breakwater in what was virtually open sea. This unshapely iron leviathan was the steamship *Great Eastern*, designed by the famous engineer I. K. Brunel, launched the previous year, and now undergoing her trials. Nearly 700

I. K. Brunel's monster ship *Great Eastern*, 19,000 tons, passing a frigate and a paddle steamer. From a coloured lithograph by T. Picken after S. Walters. *Photo: The National Maritime Museum, London*

feet from bow to stern, she was more than twice the length of the *Royal Charter*, and of far greater tonnage—not far short of 20,000 tons. She was powered by engines which drove either a screw or a pair of paddle wheels, was intended to carry either 10,000 troops or 3,600 passengers—and was the most publicised ship of the century. She was virtually flush-decked, but her steep iron sides were topped by no less than half-a-dozen masts and five tall, spindly funnels. On deck were 20 lifeboats and space for two one-hundred-foot long steamers for landing the passengers. Her maiden voyage across the Atlantic was to be made in June 1860; and her subsequent history was to be an awful warning to make haste slowly—or, rather, not to build a *Queen Mary* before the requisite technical knowledge is available and the economic demand exists. But, at this moment, the *Great Eastern* was a gigantic magnet which drew wildly excited and enthusiastic crowds in every port at which she called. Even the stately *Times* thought her sufficiently important to instal aboard their own Special Correspondent. In a sense, that was fortunate.

When plain seamen, caught at sea in the *Royal Charter* Gale, tried to describe afterwards that explosion of demented winds, then, quite literally, words failed them. They could say only that it was the worst gale in living memory, and that they felt very lucky to be alive. But to describe it, to say what it looked like, and above all what it felt like, to be at sea in that tremendous hurricane, was beyond them. It was not beyond the Special Correspondent of 'The Thunderer'. Indeed, he stayed up most of that night, expressly in order to observe the occurrence and to record it with accuracy. Doubtless Doctor Scoresby, with his technical knowledge of wave motions—a still imperfectly understood subject—would have been more informative; but the man from 'The Thunderer' grasped fully the drama of what was about to happen.

He noted now:

The wind gradually freshened during the afternoon, though not very much, till over the mountain came a thin black haze, which rose into the air with ominous rapidity and overspread the sky. The sea and wind kept rising as the glass fell, and before eight it blew a heavy gale from the eastward, with fierce squalls and storms of rain. As night wore on, the wind increased and came in fearful gusts, tearing away among the spars and rigging with a hoarse sustained roar that was awful to listen to, especially when one bore in mind that the glass was still falling, and that what we saw was only the commencement of the gale.

The *Royal Charter* could have run in to Holyhead for shelter; had she done so, it would have delayed her arrival in Liverpool by less than a

44

day. But she was a crack ship of the Australia run, always making the passage in 'Under Sixty Days'; and, besides, Captain Taylor, flattered by the admiration of the first class passengers, had promised them that they would be in Liverpool within 24 hours of leaving Queenstown. He could never now make good that boast for, instead of being in the Mersey that Tuesday evening, the *Royal Charter* was battling with foul winds seventy miles away. But at least he could try to get them there early on Wednesday morning, still within the magic figure of 60 days.

Besides, there was no warning of danger. The *Royal Charter* was an excellent sea boat, had weathered many gales, and a hurricane, too. True, she was close to land, but when she rounded Anglesey the coast would lie to the south, while the wind, although rising, was blowing from the east. If trouble developed then, from almost any point off Anglesey, or even in Liverpool Bay, she could run westward before the wind, the whole of the Irish Sea before her. So the clipper drove on, under the beat of her engine, lights blazing along her sides, indicative of the warmth within, while the cold wind roared through her rigging and the giant waves came riding out of the murk to the eastward. Her motion was not uneasy, for she rode the waves buoyantly; her passengers were not alarmed, although some, no doubt, were seasick. They all had perfect confidence in the ship and her Captain. Captain Taylor, for his part, intended to pick up the pilot-boat which patrolled north of Anglesey, off Point Lynas, where the lighthouse was. He, too, had no premonition, and did not come on deck until some hours later.

The *Royal Charter* plugged northwards, making barely six knots; slowly she rounded the Skerries—a group of small islands off the north-west corner of Anglesey—and at about six o'clock that evening was turning in a wide circle eastwards into Liverpool Bay. Anglesey now lay to the south, some three miles or more away on her starboard side. As the wind got up, out of the dull and gloomy sky, white horses began to appear on the wave crests, and spray occasionally drifted back over her bows. The note of the wind in the rigging changed ominously in pitch, higher, more menacing; darkness was beginning to shroud the horizon.

Although the *Times* man in the *Great Eastern* had spoken of a falling glass, he may merely have assumed it. At Liverpool Observatory, most certainly, the barometer readings hardly varied all that day or the next, even when the hurricane was overhead. 'A singular circumstance,' said Mr Hartnup, of the Observatory, when called upon to give evidence. There was, in fact, no advance warning of the tempest—except that ominous thin black haze over the land, heralding the howling outriders of the swiftly northward-moving hurricane. The south-west had already been swept and devastated, ships driven ashore, stone embankments bat-

From Point Lynas, the outriders of a 'severe gale', Force 9, seen sweeping over Anglesey in September, 1985. *Photo: Alexander McKee*

tered to pieces, trees blown down or sent whirling, uprooted, across a hail-swept, devastated landscape. Hundreds of men and women had died. It was, as Admiral Fitzroy of the Meteorological Office said, a complete horizontal cyclone.

And now, the north-west quadrant of the hurricane was about to stream across Anglesey and out over Liverpool Bay, lashing the sea into mountains with gusts of 100 mph and upwards. At the top of the quadrant, the winds screamed like wild cats from the east; but, as the hurricane was blowing air in a circle round a still centre, and the whole of it was moving steadily northwards, the easterly winds would soon be replaced by north-easterly winds, and then by northerly winds. The tempest would appear to turn through 90 degrees, from east to north, within the space of a few hours. When that happened, the *Royal Charter* would most desperately need sea-room, not to the west, but to the south; and now, as she rounded Anglesey and stood into Liverpool Bay, she no longer had it. There was nowhere to run to—the grey, granite rocks of a desolate coast hemmed her in. At about 6.30, there was the bang of a gun, and rockets soared into the air, as she signalled for a pilot.

Miles away to the east, a member of the crew of Pilot Boat No 11 saw those rockets, and reported to the master, Richard Parry. Half an hour later, at about 7 pm, Parry himself saw a blue light to the west, apparently

46

from a ship some seven or eight miles out to sea from Point Lynas. It was probably the *Royal Charter*. There was no help he could give; even if he had been able to close the vessel signalling for a pilot, he could not have boarded. It was now blowing very hard, blotting out the signals of the unknown vessel; even the flashing beam of Point Lynas Light was only dimly visible. By 8 pm a gale of terrible violence had engulfed the tiny pilot-boat, which was blown before it with all sails reefed. In the murk and driven spray, Parry lost sight altogether of the lighthouse; until nearly noon the following morning he had no glimpse either of another ship or of the shore. It was not a question now of whether he could give assistance to the *Royal Charter*, but of whether or not he himself could survive.

Although the *Royal Charter* was not the only vessel in the area that night, almost certainly the blue light burning aboard her was the one seen by Parry. David Strongman, one of the quartermasters then at the wheel, testified that he first saw Point Lynas Light at about 6.45 pm, broad on the starboard bow, and some six or seven miles distant. During this time the *Royal Charter* continued to fire signal guns and rockets, and to show blue lights, in an endeavour to obtain a pilot. A few minutes after sighting Point Lynas, Strongman was relieved at the wheel, and went below to get his supper.

There was some alarm among the passengers. 'When the gale became so strong, opposite the Skerries, the ladies and the passengers became exceedingly nervous,' recalled Thomas Gundry, who was travelling first class with his fiancée and her family. Gundry himself, however, had such confidence in the ship, and in her Captain and officers, that he decided to have an early night; he turned in at about 10 pm. Long before that, the crisis was on them. The *Royal Charter* was now pitching and rolling heavily, the bows smacking down into the waves and sending spray sweeping over the forecastle like small shot. The high, rearing waves could hardly be seen, as they came surging heavily out of the darkness upon the labouring ship, except for the broken foam upon them, gleaming like fresh snow in the black night. Line upon line of such ponderous hills of water bore down upon the vessel, sent on their thundering course now by a full gale; and still the wind was increasing.

At 8 pm it was time for Owen Williams and David Strongman to come on watch again. Williams took over at the wheel for a spell, and found the *Royal Charter* only slackly answering her helm. Laboriously the three great masts, almost bare of canvas, swept across the horizon as she rolled, then swept back, to pause, and then heel again. The hull trembled with the slow rhythm of her small engine, but the two-bladed screw, driven by only 200 hp, had little effect; the *Royal Charter* hardly moved through the water.

The wind plucked at what little canvas she had set, bending the rigging in an arc, drumming on the masts and spars. Because her course was very close to the wind, which was still from the east, the few sails set were mostly fore-and-aft sails, although there was one topgallant sail. At about 8.45 Captain Taylor came on deck to take charge. He ordered the maintopmast staysail to be set, to try if that would improve matters by getting a little more way on her. But within ten minutes it was clear that the expedient had failed; and Joseph Rodgers, with other seamen, found himself climbing the swaying mast in an attempt to reef the billowing, flapping sheet of drenched canvas.

Shortly after 9 pm, Captain Taylor turned to the helmsman and gave the order to starboard the wheel. Williams was one of the four men who were forcing the wheel slowly round, angling the rudder against the sea, so as to bring the clipper's bow away from the rocks of Anglesey into deeper water. The four men strained at the wheel, momentarily, but could not get it over any further. The helmsman's voice rang out, and rang out, too, the doom of the great clipper. 'Helm is hard-a-starboard, sir.'

The *Royal Charter* was no longer answering her rudder.

This could only be because she was no longer moving ahead through the water—the power of the howling wind and sea had overcome the efforts of the labouring, thumping auxiliary engine, with its mere 200 hp. The big, twin-bladed screw was thrashing the water astern to no effect. The *Royal Charter* was out of control, swept away before the storm like any log of driftwood, the five hundred souls aboard her at the mercy of any shift of the wind. It was time, high time, for emergency measures.

The backs of breaking waves in a spring tide Force 10 gale off Hayling Island in November, 1963. The entry to and exit from the water was a steep shingle beach, avoiding wooden and concrete breakwaters against which the swimmer would have been smashed to pieces. Even so, the swim was only possible because the wind, blowing at 60 mph, was westerly and therefore moving parallel to the beach and not directly at it, as with the *Royal Charter*. Even so, it gives some idea of the power of storm-driven water. *Photo: Alexander McKee*

Chapter 5

THE SONG OF THE 'WHITE SQUALL'

The *Royal Charter* was not the only ship in trouble that night. A few miles ahead of her was the brigantine *Maria*, of Barrow, being driven helplessly towards the Anglesey coast. Already her crew could hear the hoarse booming of the surf on the sands in Red Wharf Bay, eastwards of the headland of Moelfre. In total darkness, lit only by the occasional lightning flash, she was tossed towards the shore. Had she been caught a little earlier, she might have struck on the rocks around Moelfre, or on the submerged ledge off the cliffs at Benllech; a little later, and she might have been shattered on Puffin Island. But when she grounded in the pounding breakers, it was on the wide flat sands of Red Wharf; with the water pouring over her like a half-tide rock, the survivors of her small crew climbed the rigging to wait for dawn and rescue, if dawn should come before the vessel broke up.

No life-boat could launch in that sea, however; if rescue came, it would have to be by rocket line. Rowland Hughes, cox of the Moelfre life-boat, was out in Red Wharf Bay that night in the small fishing smack which he owned. The *Royal Charter* was only a few miles away to the westward of him, but in the driving murk of the gale he never saw her, nor did he see the lights and rockets, or hear the bang of her distress guns. When the gale got up and the wind began to veer round to the north, it was clear that he would soon have to run for shelter. 'It chapped round to the north-east between 10 and 11 o'clock that night, and then it began to blow a complete hurricane,' he recalled. Soon after midnight, he was back at Moelfre, and would not put to sea again.

The life-boat station was on the little shingle bay at Moelfre, in the curve of the headland which pointed out towards the north, with rocky Moelfre Island—Ynys Moelfre—just beyond. With the wind at north-east, it was blowing almost dead on the slipway. 'The sea upon that beach,' said Rowland Hughes, 'was such as I had never seen in my life before.'

A modern motor life-boat might, just possibly, have been able to cross in time the critical area of the breakers; but there is no certainty of it. For Rowland Hughes' boat it was impossible. She was a self-righting life-boat, pulled by six oars. The double crew, with other helpers, totalled

16 including Hughes, the cox, and Thomas Owen, the second cox. That night, Owen was on call with the second crew. To bring a boat to shore in a rough sea is one thing, for she rides the wave crests and is deposited on the beach; launching is quite another, for the wave crests thunder down on her from above and the violently broken water shoves her bows this way and that. She broaches to, the oars on the shoreward side are broken off, possibly injuring the men, and she is rolled sideways up the beach; if she capsizes in the process, there is insufficient water for her to right herself and her crew probably drown, upside down in the surf.

No fewer than 133 ships were totally wrecked around the British Isles that night, and a further 90 driven ashore and badly damaged; to very few of them were the life-boats able to get out. Ships in distress might make all the signals they chose; for, even if their signals were seen and understood, the hope of help from shore was negligible.

Most of the ships so destroyed were small, but nearly 400 lives were lost in them. Even the huge *Great Eastern*, iron-built and steam-powered, was now in trouble. One by one, her saloon skylights were blown in, and a deluge of driven rain and spray poured down onto the expensive carpets and furnishings, reducing them to a soggy mess. It was impossible to stand on deck, in the violent gusts, except by holding on. The great ship was steaming to her anchors, the screw going in order to ease the strain on the tortured iron cables. Inside the breakwater, the masts of a vessel which had sunk at anchor raised spouts of spray at every passing roller as it went racing for the shore; four ships lay aground in the shallows, pounding on the seabed, their sails torn out into tattered ribbons by the 100-mile-an-hour winds. Those vessels still afloat in the harbour seemed hardly better off, plunging their battered bows deep under with every wave. As he gazed

The old life-boat house at Moelfre, seen from the diving boat, September, 1985. During the 'Royal Charter Gale' of 1859, it was impossible to launch from here. *Photo : Alexander McKee*

shoreward at the uncompleted breakwater, the horrified correspondent of *The Times* saw it appear to come apart like a child's jig-saw puzzle. Scaffolding, cranes, machinery, all fell into the sea and vanished, as if dissolved by acid; there seemed nothing left, nothing at all. In fact, the damage was not so great as he had feared; the stone structure was still virtually intact, but all the elaborate apparatus assembled for the lengthening of it had been swallowed by the sea in a few minutes. In the darkness, the black baulks of timber came floating down on the *Great Eastern*, looking like jagged rocks, and making it impossible to use the paddles for fear of knocking the floats to pieces on the heavy wreckage. Only the screw could be used, to keep her steaming ahead to her anchors, and it was questionable whether that would be enough.

Over a wide area in Britain it was a night of horror; on Snowdon rocks were sent bounding down the slopes like pebbles, before the ruthless, screaming blast of the hurricane. And on the rocky coasts of Wales, the dull, threatening boom of the breakers was continuous, with sheets of sea spray rising a hundred feet and more into the black night. On the tiny, rocky island of South Stack, which carries the lighthouse at Holyhead, a man was huddled on his hands and knees. He was John Jones, assistant keeper of the light, who had been making his way across the bridge onto South Stack in order to join the principal light-keeper, Henry Bowen, already on duty. Now he would not have recognised his closest friend, for a stone, flung from the cliff above by the storm, had struck him on the head. His limbs twitched uncontrollably, as he tried to drag himself up the narrow path that led to the lighthouse. His cap had fallen off, and it could be seen that his head and face were drenched with blood; his eyes blazed wildly with the light of incomprehension, open and staring.

Every inch he crawled forward up that gale-lashed path was a mile to an ordinary man, for John Jones had been reduced by one concussive blow to a thing less than human, but which still knew somehow that it must reach the lighthouse or die. Frequently he stopped and, feebly waving his hand, cried out for help in a voice strangely thin and cracked, and which the wind instantly snatched away. His bloodied head fell forward into his hands, and he ceased to struggle.

It was there that Henry Bowen found him on Wednesday morning, calling out dolefully, waving his hand, and groaning, unable to move. His hair was matted with blood, but on the path where he lay there was no blood. Down by the bridge, however, there was a great pool of it, beside which lay the stricken man's cap. He had crawled far, but not far enough. A doctor, called to that desolate spot, diagnosed compound fracture of the skull. Within three weeks, John Jones died, merely one of more than 800 souls lost as a result of the *Royal Charter* Gale.

The keeper of Point Lynas Light meticulously logged wind strength and direction on Tuesday, 25 October, and the following day, Wednesday, the 26th. On Tuesday, from nine in the morning to nine at night, the wind was from the south-east at Point Lynas. The weather was clear in the morning, with a light wind; dull and gloomy in the afternoon, with a strong breeze. At 10 pm the wind abruptly changed direction, and blew from ENE at gale force, with much rain. That was the critical change for the *Royal Charter*, then in Liverpool Bay, somewhat to the east of Point Lynas and perhaps opposite Moelfre. At 11 pm, the gale had still further increased in velocity and was blowing from the north-east; it continued to blow, at hurricane force and from that direction, until 4 am on Wednesday, 26 October, when it veered further round to NNE. It was still as powerful as ever, with sheets of rain, and did not moderate until 1 pm on the Wednesday, when the wind went round completely to the north.

At 9 pm on Tuesday, having rounded Point Lynas, the *Royal Charter* was now compelled to sail very close to the wind, which was south-easterly. Soon the tide would be flowing out of Liverpool Bay, adding its strength to that of the increasing gale which was beginning to go round to the north. When the wind made that critical change, at 10 pm, from SE to ENE, it then began to scream through her rigging from almost dead ahead. Captain Taylor ordered starboard helm, so as to bring her up to the wind and also head the clipper away from the land out into deeper water. But at that moment she was virtually stationary. Her rudder had no bite; there was insufficient flow of water past it to give a grip strong enough to force her head round against wind and tide on to the opposite tack. One of the reasons, no doubt, was that, being at the end of her voyage, she was lightened of a good deal of coal—some 300 tons at least—which she had used up in steaming. Riding high in the water, her hull and upperworks became in effect sails which could not be furled. This, then, was the situation which developed between 9 and 10 pm.

It was a ridiculous situation, irksome to the pride of the bustling, expanding nineteenth century, with its growing belief in the inevitability of progress and of the mastery of man over nature; the humbling lesson of the *Titanic* was yet to come. The *Royal Charter*, a floating hotel, luxuriously appointed and lit, was remorselessly revealed in all her terrible fragility, tossed buoyant but helpless in a storm-torn sea, lost in a waste of foaming waves and roaring darkness, off a savage coast which would, in these conditions, shiver her iron hull like a cracked wine-glass, let in the mountainous cold ocean to snuff out like candles all the human life aboard her.

Owen Williams was one of the group of quartermasters at the wheel, faces tense with responsibility, as they tried to anticipate the effect of each

Point Lynas lighthouse, September, 1985. *Photo: Alexander McKee*

Looking out over the Irish Sea from Point Lynas in September, 1985. This is the route the *Royal Charter* took on her last voyage. *Photo: Alexander McKee*

rearing sea. Ahead of them stood Captain Taylor, facing slightly sideways, so that he could watch both fore and aft. He was obviously worried that the *Royal Charter* might be drifting astern. He told David Strongman to heave the lead and, from the starboard bridge, Strongman threw the weighted line out into the night. When it had run out, it showed that the clipper was in 18 fathoms of water. As she drew a trifle less than 20 feet aft, that meant that she had nearly 90 feet of water under her keel. She was some miles from shore and in no immediate danger. At this time the screw was churning the water, but there was only one sail set, the spanker, a fore-and-aft sail at the stern. The ship was headed ESE, roughly towards the Mersey. Ten minutes later, Strongman took the second sounding—which would tell the tale. He found extreme difficulty in heaving the lead. The ship appeared to be drifting so fast that the line was being overtaken by the hull and went under the ship, even though he threw the lead as far to leeward as he could. The sounding he eventually got was 16 fathoms. The *Royal Charter* was drifting rapidly towards the shore.

The time, he thought, was then shortly before 10 pm. The ship's log was lost and all times given by the survivors are therefore estimates; however, they accord well enough with the times given by the cox of Moelfre life-boat, at sea somewhere to the eastward of them, and with the log kept at Point Lynas lighthouse. It began to blow a 'complete hurricane' between 10 and 11 pm.

Between the taking of the two soundings, Captain Taylor had ordered the lower maintopsail—the lowest sail but one on the mainmast—to be loosened from the spar, in order to get some way on his vessel. Immediately after the second sounding had shown, just before 10 pm, that the *Royal Charter* was drifting on shore, he gave the order: 'Prepare to let go anchors!' A body of seamen ran forward to make the necessary preparations, which included making sure that ample lengths of cable were ready to be let out, whenever the order to anchor was made.

As he gave the preparatory order, and as the men went forward, the skies opened and a fresh deluge of rain, blown by the screaming wind, engulfed the ship. Gust after gust, each seemingly stronger than the last, struck her like blows from a hammer. In seconds, everyone on deck was soaked to the skin, and barely able to see, even through eyelids half-closed to avoid the solid blows of that downpour. The massive masts, spars, and rigging drummed and roared aloft with the howl of the rain-laden wind, the crests of the more mountainous seas were skimmed clear off and the spray swept the deck in sheets. No one could see the length of the ship; visibility was reduced to a few yards. At the same time, the wind began to go round to the north. Instead of blowing the clipper out to safety in

Ynys Moelfre, the tiny island at the tip of the headland. Had the *Royal Charter* struck on the seaward side of the island, no one could have survived. Taken at low water, September, 1985. *Photo: Alexander McKee*

the wide expanses of the Irish Sea, it was hemming her in towards the granite, spray-capped coast of Anglesey. And for a third time, David Strongman took a sounding. Fifteen-and-a-half fathoms now.

It was only a few minutes before 10 pm that Thomas Gundry, saloon passenger, had gone below to his cabin, confident that all was well and that the passengers might sleep soundly in the knowledge that they would be safe in Liverpool next morning. There was nothing in the motion of the great clipper to suggest danger; always a smooth-riding ship, she crested the waves like a bird. The engine still gave forth its comforting, throbbing beat; all appeared to be well. Many of the passengers were similarly convinced of their safety.

One who was not convinced was Henry Carew Taylor. He came on deck, alarmed at the change in the weather, while his little daughter, comforted by her nurse, stirred restlessly below: he was still on deck an hour later. Another passenger who doubted was Samuel Edward Gapper, the friend of young Mrs Rose; and he was very worried indeed. He had several times anxiously asked Captain Adams, who had lost his ship in collision off Buenos Aires and was travelling as a passenger, too, what the present position of the *Royal Charter* was. Adams, slightly exasperated, had at length produced a chart and shown him. On being asked again, at about 10 pm,

Adams had replied, shortly, that she was on her correct course. And then he hurried away for a conference with Captain Taylor, Gapper calling after him to ask Adams to be sure, when he came back, to tell him the latest news. Captain Withers, the shipmaster who had lost his vessel off the Fiji Islands and was also just a passenger aboard the *Royal Charter*, went with Adams. It seemed that Captain Taylor wanted their advice and, if so, the position must indeed be serious. What these three experienced seamen talked about, we do not know, for none survived; but at 10.30 pm, immediately after they had conferred, Captain Taylor made the first of three successive attempts to stay the ship.

It was the change in the wind direction, from SE to ENE, that must have influenced the decision. At the moment, the *Royal Charter* was drifting astern. To put her in stays—that is, to force her head right round, by the pull of certain sails combined with the helm, so that she would be able to run out into the Irish Sea, was worth trying. But this swift change of direction almost in the teeth of the wind and against the tide, was a ticklish proceeding. It would not be easy even with a small yacht, handled by two or three men sitting down. The *Royal Charter*, with her tall masts and large expanse of heavy canvas, was an altogether tougher proposition. Men must climb the rigging supporting her wildly reeling masts, and, battered by almost solid sheets of water blown at them by the wind, which was gusting to nearly 100 miles an hour, fumble with numbed fingers to undo the ropes which held the heavy sails to the yards.

It was Force 10 now and, wisely, Captain Taylor sent Suaicar, the boatswain's mate, down to the engine room to ask the Chief Engineer for all the steam he had. It was vital to get some forward speed on her. With engine shuddering at full revolutions, the watch was called to back the after yards and put out a spanker. Slowly the great clipper's head came round to the wind, but just when it seemed she was about to swing round past the wind, which would be the preliminary to her shooting forward once more with swelling sails, the solid force of the gale blew her off again. Like a racehorse that has baulked at a jump, she quivered a moment, sails wildly flapping, and then heeled wearily back. Again the watch on deck attempted the impossible, brailing the after yards and squaring the head yards. Again her bows came slowly round, and then fell off again. Defeated by the gale, the *Royal Charter* wallowed helplessly.

Captain Taylor ordered one final attempt to wear the ship, and the sodden, chilled men clinging to the yards set the maintopsail. Nothing happened. The helm still produced no effect. The *Royal Charter* drifted astern, wallowing and pitching, the men out on the yards swaying dizzily up and down in gigantic sweeps that kept time with the onslaught of the waters foaming past below.

Not only had their work been for nothing, but they would have to undo it and take in the maintopsail, otherwise it would merely help to force the ship backwards. Loosing the sail had been easy, compared with what was to come now. The bellying, sodden canvas, brutal with weight of water and the booming wind that filled it, jumped under their hands like a wild horse, threatening to pitch them off the yards. Once, Joseph Rodgers was half-shaken loose from his hold high above the deck and nearly pitched into the sea. The robing poles were broken away and the sail, as if it possessed a violent spirit of its own, nearly leaped from the yard. Then, in one of the lulls between the fearful gusts, it became entangled on the starboard side, and nothing that the watch could do served to capture it. A mob of seamen, led by Suaicar, tried to clew it up, and failed. William Bean, the Third Officer, lent a hand. Rodgers, and others working high above the deck, did their best. Eventually Rodgers came down and reported to W. B. Stephens, the First Officer, that it was impossible to

Looking out from the Pilots' observation room in Point Lynas lighthouse, with a 'severe gale' imminent, September, 1985. The *Royal Charter* passed this point, her Captain unaware of the change of wind strength and direction which he was to meet within a few hours. *Photo: Alexander McKee*

furl the sail. 'Go back and make it fast to the yard,' was the reply; and this they did.

By 11 pm the wind had backed round almost to the north; and unbelievably, impossibly, the gale was still increasing in violence, rising to full hurricane force. Force 12. Winds of more than 100 mph.

Somewhere in the track of the *Royal Charter* was Liverpool Pilot Boat No 4, a little sloop of 23 tons, commanded by John Sheppard. Her storm jib and stay foresail were gone, torn to shreds; her light was put out once, lit again, and again put out. 'At 11 pm, the gale was more violent than before; it was dreadful,' he afterwards testified. 'We could not hear each other speak at a distance of eight feet on deck.' Sheppard and his six-man crew were given up for lost that night; never, in his 39 years as a pilot, 29 of them as master pilot, had he experienced such weather or known an easterly gale back to the north.

There was only one chance now left to the *Royal Charter*, if she was not to be driven on to Anglesey and destroyed: to anchor, and to hope that the anchors would hold. At 11 pm her port anchor was let go, the thick iron chain roaring out through the hawse hole until 75 fathoms of it had been paid out. The weight of all those tons of cable, lying on the bottom, would help to hold the ship and ease the strain on the anchor, which must otherwise drag. Still further to reduce the strain, the clipper's engine continued to pound, her screw thrashing the water. As she pitched violently under the combined assault of wind and tide, the iron chain groaned in the hawse hole. Now, it stood rigid out of the water like an iron bar, and then, in the momentary lull before the next howling gust, slacked for a few seconds before it was again drawn taut.

And it was at 11 pm, that Henry Carew Taylor, tired of his long and anxious vigil on deck, decided that everything was now under control and went below. It was comfortably warm down there, and the motion of the ship was now more regular. As he was settling into his bunk, he heard someone say, 'She rides nobly.' He put his head down on the pillow and tried to ignore the sickening motion of the cabin, accentuated by the stale air; the repeated heave and descent as the bow rose and fell; the dull thumping of the engine and the quivering of the plates, which showed that the ship was alive and struggling strongly for life; muted now, the hoarse roaring of the hurricane that battered the deck above his head.

What he could not guess was that the *Royal Charter* was slowly drifting astern, the anchor dragging across the seabed, towed by the links of the chain; like a monstrous skeletal snake, the cable slithered over the bottom in the gloom of the undersea. Captain Taylor, watching keenly from the forecastle, detected the drift and ordered another 25 fathoms paid out, to increase the tonnage of metal on the bottom and so halt the ship. There were 100 fathoms out now, on the port anchor, and still her drift was not entirely checked. The space left between the *Royal Charter* and the shore could hardly be more than four miles, and might be less. Captain Taylor gave another order. The starboard anchor fell like a plummet into the waves sweeping the bow, and 70 fathoms of cable went roaring out after it. Momentarily, the *Royal Charter* checked, tugging and rolling to the cables as if she would bring up a mountain from the seabed.

An enormous wave came surging at her, its foaming crest blown to fragments by the wind, so that the air was filled with what seemed like snow, but was really partly rain, partly spray, and partly low cloud. Her bows dipped under, then rose again, the water cascading down the decks and along the scuppers and pouring out over her sides. The cables made strange sounds, groaning and stretching, the iron links distorted by the enormous and unbearable pull exerted on them.

Owen Williams was still at the wheel. When the starboard anchor thundered down, he noticed the ship's head come up east-half-north, then slowly fall off south-east again; but her motion became much steadier. The helm was still hard-a-starboard, and quite ineffectual; probably, she was still drifting, although only very slowly. David Strongman was sent below to get up the deep sea lead, in order to check this, and when he had done so, took Williams' place at the wheel. It was now 11.35 pm. Rockets were again sent up, briefly bathing the tormented water around them in a metallic glow, showing wave crests towering high above the ship, effectively blotting out any sight of other vessels which might have been near. Now and then the bang of a distress gun competed with the roar of the hurricane, and blue lights were shown. 'We set the bay on fire with distress signals,' said a survivor. But the night was too thick with spray; neither of the two pilot boats saw them, nor did Rowland Hughes, riding out the storm in his fishing smack. And none of them saw the *Maria*, of Barrow, or knew exactly at what time she was driven ashore.

The crew were very tired, from lack of sleep and from their exertions in putting out and taking in sail and labouring with the cables; and they were bone-weary with the battering of the hurricane. The passengers slept fitfully, and some did not sleep at all. Mr Gapper was still up, waiting for news, anxious not so much on his own account, but for Mrs Rose, and faced by conditions he could not interpret. When at last Captain Adams returned, Gapper button-holed him and Adams again had to produce his chart. There was the position of the *Royal Charter*, so far as it could be estimated, eastward of Point Lynas, and probably not much more than a mile or so from the shore. And there was the new wind direction, driving her towards it. Was there no possibility of escape? asked Gapper. Adams showed him how the *Royal Charter* was now embayed in the great semi-circular sweep of the Anglesey coast between Point Lynas and Puffin Island. 'It is impossible to get off,' said Adams quietly, 'and I shall not be surprised if we are on shore by morning.'

Gapper was in the middle of a torrent of desperate questioning when John Croome, the Fourth Officer, entered the cabin. Croome was a young man, only recently promoted from midshipman. 'Captain Adams,' he began, in a formal manner, 'Captain Taylor would like to speak to you immediately in the saloon.'

Probably not the least factor in the tragedy was the Captain's conscious-ness of the trust the passengers had in him and in his ship, and his extreme reluctance to allow, to their faces, that there was any danger at all. It made him unwilling to take any obviously desperate measures. He had already spoken reassuringly to some of the more anxious passengers, who had refused to go to bed and were waiting about in the saloon. He had her 'fast by the nose,' he said. There was no need to cut away the masts, they might be needed again. But to Captains Adams and Withers he now spoke confidentially and less confidently. Captain Withers agreed that the danger of the situation ought to be minimised, to avoid the risk of panic among the passengers, and subsequently did his best to radiate optimism. Captain Adams preferred frankness, at least with his friends. On his return to Gapper's cabin, and in answer to Gapper's enquiry if there was any danger, he replied bluntly, 'Yes, there is.'

Then he looked Gapper straight in the face. 'If it were possible to sing the Song of the "White Squall", it might now be sung with feeling.' Dumbfounded, the New Zealand farmer gaped at him. What on earth was a 'White Squall'? The old mariner impatiently made vigorous swim-ming motions with his arms.

'I have no doubt we shall have to do this before we get ashore.'

Chapter 6

DARKNESS BEFORE DAWN

It was Wednesday, 26 October. At 1.30 am, an hour and a half after midnight, the *Royal Charter* was still pitching to her anchors, still steaming ahead to relieve the strain on the cables. In the frequent lulls between the fiercest gusts, she tended to move forward in the water, under the thrashing of the screw, and to over-ride her anchors; but when the blasts of 100 mph or more came screaming at her, she drifted astern until the chains were taut and groaning at the hawse holes. But she still breasted the mountainous seas like a floating seabird. Captain Taylor was no longer on deck. He had gone down below a few minutes before, into the saloon, to order coffee for himself and for those passengers who were still up. He gave the order to the Chief Steward, Mr Emery, who went forward to wake the Second Steward, Thomas Cormick. Cormick, who had turned in at 10 pm, got up and went sleepily aft. While he prepared the coffee, Captain Taylor spoke reassuringly to the passengers, particularly the ladies among them. There was no immediate danger, he said; the ship was riding very easily, almost over-running her anchors. Henry Morse, the New South Wales magistrate, who was there and partook of the coffee when it was made, thought that his main reason in coming below was to calm the females, many of whom had children with them and were extremely anxious. But Captain Taylor never had time to drink his coffee.

At about 1.30 am, the port cable of the *Royal Charter* parted near the hawse hole, where the strain was greatest, stood up for a moment from the waves like a striking cobra, and then whiplashed down into the depths.

John Croome, the young Fourth Officer, came tumbling down the gangway into the saloon to report to Captain Taylor, who instantly went on deck. He ordered the stream anchor, or drogue, to be got up from below, and men ran aft to obey. He ordered more cable on the starboard anchor, which still held, until 90 fathoms had been paid out. Then he sent John Croome to fetch Captain Adams and Captain Withers once more. Leaving Mr Gapper, Adams hurried away, grim-faced. William James Ferris, who had prospered as a storekeeper at Ballarat, heard some of the passengers crying out for the masts to be cut away, and believed that it was through the advice of Captain Withers that this was finally done.

61

The tall heavy masts and yards, with their standing and running rigging, represented a considerable obstruction to the wind, and so did the funnel; they acted as permanent sails. But if the masts were cut away, there would be less resistance to the wind, less drag, and therefore less strain on the the one remaining anchor cable. The ideally safe position was to have a mastless hull, firmly anchored, and with the screw going. The reason, no doubt, why Captain Taylor wanted to talk to Adams and Withers, was that this state of theoretically ideal safety could not be achieved without running serious risks which might destroy the ship.

The main factor in easing the strain on the anchor cable was the power of the engine applied to the screw thrashing the water astern. If the masts were cut away without stopping the screw, the rigging, when it fell into the water, might entangle the screw and stop it turning. If the engine was stopped and the screw hoisted out of the water while the masts were cut away, this would prevent any fouling. But both courses meant stopping the screw, by accident or by design; and stopping the screw meant that, almost certainly, the strain on the anchor and cable would be too great. And if the strain became too great, then either the cable would break or the anchor would drag—one or the other. If the former, then the ship would be ashore within a short time; if the latter, she would be ashore in a slightly longer time. The only practical difference the time factor would make would be to alter the geographical location at which she went ashore. That might be important, but no one could calculate her exact point of arrival in either event.

There was one other consideration which must have weighed with Captain Taylor, and that was the possible damage which might be caused to the *Royal Charter* by cutting away her masts at the height of a hurricane. Both foremast and mainmast were nearly four feet thick, the mizzenmast nearly three feet, and the yards heavy in proportion. Even the upper yards weighed five tons. They might all fall neatly overboard, but again, they might not; and a five-ton yard, falling downwards like a spear, could perhaps penetrate the passenger accommodation and cause havoc.

On the other hand, if the masts were not cut away, the strain they caused on the remaining cable might also serve to break it. There was no certain way out; there was only a weighing of chances. The chance Captain Taylor took after his discussion with the two other shipmasters, was to rely on the screw and the anchor to outlast the storm. It may have been that the deciding factor was his understandable reluctance to ruin his beautiful ship and thereby to confess failure to his passengers. It seemed so short a time ago that he had promised them to have the *Royal Charter* safe in the Mersey that very night.

For an hour the *Royal Charter* rolled and pitched at her one remaining anchor. Now and then the screw would thrust her forward a little, so that the chain cable hung down in an arc; then a fresh gust would come scream-ing out of the night, and the ship would lose ground, until the cable brought her up like a savagely bridled horse, grating and groaning. The working party had taken nearly an hour to get the stream anchor up on deck from its stowage in the after orlop. But they never got it over the side.

At about 2.30 am, almost exactly an hour after the port chain had parted, the starboard cable proved unequal to the terrible strain. When it broke, the *Royal Charter* heeled over, turned right round, and drove towards the land, unseen in the black night and driving rain.

Suaicar, standing near the wheel, called out to Andrew Cowie, the Second Officer, to ask if anything was to be done to cut away the rigging. Captain Taylor heard him, and called back, 'Not yet, my boy.'

Down below, James Russell, dozing in the cabin he shared with his wife and two little girls, became aware of the change in the motion of the ship. She was no longer fighting the storm. Bleary-eyed and unshaven, he got up and went out into the passageway. He heard his friend, Mr Watson, talking to another passenger, Mr Smith, in the opposite cabin, and heard

The disaster scene at high water, September, 1960. By dire chance, the *Royal Charter* went ashore on the rock ledges off the headland instead of in the white shingle bay, where she might have survived until morning. *Photo: Alexander McKee*

Smith say, 'Oh, we are drifting!' Too alarmed to waste time questioning them, he rushed back and frantically helped his wife to dress the two children. The little girl of ten was able to help herself, but the baby of two-and-a-half had to be helped into everything.

There were a number of rather tousled passengers in the saloon already, mostly those who had stayed up the best part of the night; the majority, however, were still in their beds, sleeping, dozing fitfully, or so seasick as to be beyond caring whether they lived or died. From the deck above their heads came the bang of a distress gun, as a fresh burst of signals was made. Rockets soared skywards, blue lights were shown, and improvised torches made of oakum dipped in turpentine were lit. No one at sea or on land saw anything of them; if they had, there was nothing they could have done to help.

It was probably at about 3 am that Captain Taylor, facing the final ruin of his fine ship, told the Chief Officer, W. B. Stephens, to have the masts cut away. Stephens, a Scotsman like Cowie, the Second Officer, had already survived two wrecks and the Crimean War; he was a very quiet, cool man. He passed on the order to William Foster, the carpenter. The mainmast was to go first. It was very heavily rigged and it took some time to cut the ropes with the axes and knives available, particularly when the men had to balance on a heaving deck. Because of the damage the falling yards might cause, the Captain ordered all passengers to be kept below, and for the second class passengers to be got out of their cabins and into the lower saloon, out of the way of danger. Mr Allan, chief steward of the second class saloon, began to knock up his passengers and get them out of their cabins. Those passengers already on deck now began to come down below; they included Russell and four of his friends. After dressing his children, he had left his cabin, met Captain Adams, who told him that there was great danger, and had at once gone up to see the nature of it. But there was nothing to be seen in the black tunnel of the night but a rain-blurred picture of part of the deck, and of heaving waves. There was no sight of land. Visibility did not extend for even half the length of the ship.

It was this inability to estimate the danger which caused so many passengers throughout the night to badger any sailor they saw, and particularly their fellow passengers, Adams and Withers, for an explanation of their plight, and to ask what was going to happen now. Adams had always been blunt, but it was Withers who took the initiative at this moment. He ran along the passageways, opening cabin doors and rousing the passengers. He did not stop to consider the embarrassment of the ladies, possibly half-dressed, but ran on and banged at the next door.

Thomas Gundry was awake at the time. He was the saloon passenger who had gone to bed at 10 pm, believing that all was well. He had dozed for a while, but had been unable to sleep properly for the motion of the ship and the noise of the storm. In his mind, Gundry had a mental picture of the *Royal Charter* ploughing through the gale at about one knot towards Liverpool. That impression was brutally dissipated when his cabin door was flung open and he heard Captain Withers call out, 'Come directly, we are all lost!' Then he heard the bang of another cabin door opening, and Captain Withers saying to someone across the passageway, 'I will take your child. Come along directly.'

Gundry jumped out of bed and looked down the passageway, but Captain Withers had gone on. He put on a few clothes and ran towards the saloon, from where a gangway led to the deck.

Henry Carew Taylor was awakened in the same way. He stayed up late, until the Captain's gesture of ordering coffee had convinced him that there could be nothing to worry about, at which he had gone to bed. What he remembered Captain Withers as saying was, 'Come directly, there's no time to be lost.' And then there was a woman's voice, which Taylor recognised as that of the handsome Mrs Woodruffe, companion of Mrs Foster, and Withers telling her that he would take her child. Just as Gundry had done, he jumped out of bed, went to the door, looked down the passageway, and saw no one. Captain Withers had either gone on, or bustled Mrs Woodruffe up on deck.

Like Gundry, Taylor also had to make a mental adjustment, from complete confidence in the safety of the ship to the realisation of mortal danger for them all. As he stood there, worrying in his mind as to what he should do about his small daughter, who was sleeping in another cabin with her nurse, there was a slight tremor under his feet. Then there was a definite shudder and thump, which shook the whole frame of the ship, and he had to put out a hand to save himself from over-balancing. The vessel appeared to ride forward a little, and then there were two more heavy thumps, as two waves close together struck her in succession. She was ashore, beating on some unknown beach. He scrambled into trousers, coat, and slippers, flung a greatcoat over his shoulders, and ran for the saloon on the heels of Gundry.

Gundry's first impression was of a mass of milling people, trying to keep their feet when, at intervals of a minute or so, the hull thumped and shuddered violently, and they all swayed from side to side. 'It was,' he said, 'crowded with ladies and gentlemen in the utmost state of tremor. Families were all clinging to each other; children were crying out piteously, whilst parents were endeavouring to soothe them with cheering hopes.'

Gundry had more than himself to think of, for he was returning with the girl he was to marry and her family. Taylor had his child—and there was no sign of her, or of the nurse. The saloon was a hundred feet long, with the mizzenmast passing through the centre of it, and it was now packed, as Taylor described it, 'by ladies and gentlemen who were in a state of great consternation, crying and praying, and Mr Hodge, a clergyman, praying extemporaneously. I went to seek my nurse and child at the other end; but I found the lobby of the saloon so crammed that I could not go through. The thumping went on more violently, and quicker than at first.' Desperate with anxiety, Taylor elbowed his way about, and at last found his own child.

The wind still roared at hurricane force and the booming of the breakers made an incessant accompaniment; and, as here and there skylights shattered, water began to come down into the saloons and cabins. Mr Allan was still urging the second class passengers into the lower saloon, as the mainmast had still not fallen, but was due to go any minute now. The delay, he found, was due to the heel of the ship, which had caused the entrance doors of the saloon to jam, so that the passengers crowded the passageway, unable to get through. Those nearest the doors eventually decided to break them open and, when this was done, all of them trooped through, very quietly, with no hurrying or crushing, and silently took their seats.

What was happening lower down in the ship and forward, in the packed steerage accommodation, we do not know. Those steerage passengers who survived were not very articulate, where reporters were concerned, and still less so during the official inquiries. They did not describe what they saw, but merely what happened to them. But it is clear that they became intermingled, and that some groups made an attempt to get on deck. An Able Seaman, Edward Wilson, described the scene at this time as, 'Nothing but confusion on deck, fore and aft passengers, saloon, cabin, and steerage all mixed together, fathers and mothers clasping their children in their arms, wives clinging to their husbands, shrieking, and crying, "Save me, save me," "Don't leave me," and so on.' As the masts were due to go over the side any moment now, a mass rush on deck could be disastrous.

Captain Taylor immediately sent down an apprentice boy, Charley, to tell the passengers to be calm, and that the Captain had said that all was well, they were only on a sandbank. The voice of young Charley did not carry much weight, and there was still great alarm.

In the saloon, the women passengers crowded around Henry Carew Taylor, and implored him to go to the Captain and ask on their behalf what the situation was. Perhaps they chose him because he had a child to whom he had to be both mother and father, but being a man, could get a straight answer to a sensible question, instead of being brushed aside as an excitable female. But as Taylor was leaving the saloon, he met Cap-

The wreck site at high water, September, 1960. It is flat calm, with hardly a ripple as the sea laps the rock edges. On 26 October, 1859, winds stronger than 100 mph were driving tremendous seas right over the ledges, turning the scene to a boiling white fury in which few swimmers stood a chance. *Photo : Alexander McKee*

tain Withers, on his way with a message from the Captain, and radiating confidence. Taylor told him that the women were anxious about the state of the ship, so Withers, raising his voice, gave them the Captain's message.

'Ladies,' he began, 'we are on shore, and I hope on a sandy beach, and I hope to God we shall all go on shore when it becomes light.' There was a note of confidence in his voice, possibly forced, which was at odds with his choice of words. But he had hardly finished speaking before Captain Taylor came hurrying in on his heels. He stood for a moment, looking around him, calm, collected, confident, the very picture of a clipper captain. His voice rang out. 'Now ladies, you need not be at all afraid. We are on a sandy beach, and embedded in the sand. We are not ten paces from the shore, and the tide will leave us dry, and in ten minutes you will all be safe.' There were breathless gasps of relief and happiness, and people smiled at each other reassuringly, as if their fears had been but a dream. Taylor saw a friend of his, Mrs Fenwick, gathering her children around her, and giving out clean stockings and shoes to them so that they should be neatly dressed for going ashore.

*   *   *

In the short time that had elapsed since the ship had struck, a great deal had been done, both on deck and below, at the Captain's orders. He had only left the deck, to speak to the saloon passengers, because it was but a short step away and because, presumably, if he could get the first class passengers to set an example of order and discipline, the rest might follow. How much he himself believed in what he said, no one will ever know. Some of it was true, but it was not the whole truth.

At 3.30 am, the *Royal Charter* had struck the shore; as Mr Gapper expressed it later, 'the fact is, she was driven ashore like a log of wood.' She had then swung round, broadside on to the booming surf, with a list to starboard—which was the seaward side. As she had a freeboard of about eight feet only, her deck was a dangerous place. The shock of her arrival had thrown Captain Taylor to the deck, but he had quickly recovered. He sent Foster to take soundings in the hold—and the carpenter came back to report that there was hardly any water, a mere six inches or so; and that the Scottish Chief Engineer, John Rogers, had told him he was ready to give steam if required. The hull had not been shattered. He sent Strongman to take soundings outside the hull—and the quartermaster came back to report 2 fathoms forward, $3\frac{1}{2}$ fathoms aft. The ship drew 18 feet 5 inches forward, 20 feet 6 inches aft—therefore her bows were higher than her stern. She was firmly aground forward. Captain Taylor judged, rightly, that she was on a sandy beach; and, in order to take her beyond the reach of the worst of the breakers, he ordered the engine to go full speed ahead, so as to 'harden her on'. What he did not know was the nature of the coast he was on, because the only sign of it was the booming of the breakers.

He thought he knew—or so it seems—that the tide was about to go out and leave the great iron ship high and dry. Certainly, the tide was now on the turn. It was slack low water—the tide was about to come in, with high water shortly before 10 am. And it was to spell the doom of the *Royal Charter*.

Now, the mainmast was nearly cut away. On the swaying deck, shifting and vibrating as the hull was beaten and bumped on the sand, the men fought to sever the lee rigging. Often, they were buried in water from a bursting wave; often, they slipped or fell, or their blows missed. But at last the rigging was cut. After that they cleared away all the running gear and anything else likely to hold the masts. And finally, the weather rigging was cut. Then the hurricane itself came to their aid, and the mainmast went over the side, snapped off like a pipestem, falling clear of the hull and taking the heavy yards with it.

The passengers, huddled below, heard it go and felt the ship shiver and lighten. Then there was a pause, and a renewed commotion on the deck above, as the party hastened to cut down the equally heavy foremast. This went on for some time, possibly an hour; then the foremast also fell. Massive, iron-banded, it slanted out over the port side and crashed into the sea abeam, clear of the ship. Now, only the funnel and the mizzenmast reared high above the deck. The mizzen, which had already been weakened by the cutting away of some of the other rigging, was the thinnest of the masts and went down to the keel through the saloon. Before much work could be done to cut it away properly, the hurricane took charge; the mizzenmast, swaying violently as the ship was beaten in the breakers, broke half-way up its length, and the top of it came plunging down. One of the heavy yards, in falling, struck the deck and a hole appeared in the deckhead of the saloon, through which, as the waves washed over the ship, the water cascaded onto the frightened passengers.

Throughout this phase, distress signals were being fired; two guns banged away and rockets roared upwards. The sound of the distress signals, the crashing as the masts were hacked away, the violent pounding of the ship on the ground, the lurching that sent passengers reeling and staggering, and the water that came in through broken skylights and the holes in the deckhead, produced terrible scenes below, particularly among the families with small and helpless children. By themselves, the children might have been brave enough, but upset by the communicated fear of their parents, they clung to their mothers' skirts in desperation, while the mothers turned to their husbands for the security they were powerless to give. Not the least alarming factor was the passage through the saloon, on several occasions, of a working party from the crew on their way to get fresh powder for the signal guns, and additional flares. They were led by Andrew Cowie, the Scottish Second Officer, and John Lewis, the Purser, a much-liked man from Bristol. All were grim-faced, sweating, and stripped down to trousers and shirt, their obvious haste and preoccupation belying the evasive and reassuring answers to the questions the passengers called out to them.

John Bradbury, the Manchester man, had come into the saloon early with many of the second class passengers, and had heard the Captain's reassuring words; in spite of them, he said afterwards, 'those few hours

The wreck site of the *Royal Charter* at low water, looking towards the Moelfre headland and Ynys Moelfre. Those who tried to swim ashore were driven onto these rocks by mountainous waves. *Photo: RCSE Ltd/Ken Jones*

of darkness seemed to me longer than all the previous years of my life.' A strong swimmer, he badly wanted to get up on deck, not liking the idea of being trapped like a rat down below, but he had been restrained by a rumour that one of the ship's officers had already been killed by falling spars.

The signal guns did not remain much longer in action, for it became impossible, on the wave-swept deck, to keep them sufficiently dry. A litter of wreckage lay across it, entangling some of the four life-boats in a mass of fallen cordage. Under the direction of Mr Stephens, the Chief Officer, a party led by Suaicar began to cut away the obstructions from one of the boats. Another boat and its davits had become similarly entangled by the falling of the mizzen stay; Rodgers was one of the party ordered by the Captain to clear it. All the life-boats had previously been prepared for launching, but had not been swung out; nor had men been told off to man them. The reason was that, even in these circumstances, the hull of the *Royal Charter* was still their best protection.

None of the seamen aboard even considered the life-boats as a possibility. In particular, the party of eleven riggers who had boarded the *Royal Charter* from the steam tug off Bardsey Island the previous day, had given up any idea of trying to use them. First of all, said one of them, William Barton, 'It was as dark as pitch; we could not see our hands before us. We were in total ignorance as to what sort of coast it was. And the sea was so rough that no boat could have lasted five minutes in it. Instead, we made up a tar barrel, ready to set fire to, to send ashore to light the coast and let us know what kind of place it was. But the ship thumped so heavily, and danger was so imminent, that the idea was not carried out.'

It was a dreadful dawn, tense with expectation, that began to break at about 6 am. The darkness, thick with blown spray, slowly became diffused by a thin, grey light. Sea and sky were still one, mingled in a doubtful haze; is was still hard to say where the water ended and the low, scudding clouds began. Shoreward, in the frothing water, the fallen masts and yards leaped in the breakers like live things, tangled together with the maze of rigging. And, as the booming darkness all around them lightened further, those standing on the deck of the *Royal Charter* stared shorewards with uncomprehending amazement.

The were barely 25 yards from land.

Beyond the stern, the high headland of Moelfre loomed indistinctly, like a heavy fog bank; it might have been a fog bank, but for the breakers surging up 100 feet into the air, as they burst in thunder on the limestone cliffs. The waves, as they reared above the stranded ship, were the colour of muddy, half-thawed snow, stained by the sediment stirred up on the seabed, and reflecting a whitish glare on the clouds above, as if the very laws of nature had been reversed, and the light came from below.

And as each wave sucked back into the depths with a harsh, grating roar, it made the land seem so near that you could toss a coin onto it. Directly opposite the *Royal Charter* was a low, wave-swept plateau of grey rock, reaching out towards them from the base of a hill which was neither steep nor high. And standing on the highest rocks, just out of reach of the waves, a man was standing; staring out at the great, beating ship as if he could not believe his eyes.

71

Chapter 7

'RODGERS OF THE ROYAL CHARTER'

The villagers of Moelfre lived mainly from the sea. Some were quarrymen, but most were inshore fishermen. The herring season was at its height, and, if they were not disturbed, good catches now would see them through the winter. This night, however, they knew well that the only harvest to be reaped would be from the wreckage cast ashore. The village of Moelfre clung to the slope of the hillside where the headland broadened out to the east to form the shingle beach of Moelfre Bay; the tremendous surf beating into the bay was pushing up the shingle to a height many feet above its previous level, and the wind was plucking at the roofs of the little cottages built of whitened stone. The walls seemed to tremble, the sound could have been heard down in the cellars, under the trapdoors; but the villagers slept snug.

The only cottage to suffer serious damage was that called Cocyn Uchaf, which stood some fields away from the others, higher on the headland, and overlooking that other bay to the west, beyond which was Point Lynas. The roof of this cottage seemed about to fly off, and so the occupant, Mesach Williams, went to get help from another cottager, Thomas Hughes, and together they set about securing it. The night was still very dark. The cottage overlooked a small shingle beach, rarely marked on maps, which was known as Porth Helaeth; it occupied, west of the headland, much the same position as did Moelfre Bay to the east. The headland itself was rock, with a number of flat ledges running out under water; then came the curve of grey shingle that was Porth Helaeth; and to the west of that the coastline, for a few hundred yards, was rock again—a confused mass of low rock platforms. It was just off this point, as the sky became lighter between 5.30 and 6 am, that Mesach Williams happened to glance in that direction, and saw something new and strange by the shore.

In the uncertain light of the stormy dawn, masked by blown spume, the shape took on the appearance of a ship—or rather, of a ship's hull, for only the funnel and the stumps of three masts stuck up above the deck. It was a great ship, by the standards of the day; a fine, rich clipper ship, an ocean greyhound of the nineteenth century; and it was beating heavily

The village of Moelfre, with the hills of Snowdonia in the background, September, 1985. *Photo: Alexander McKee*

and helplessly in the surf a stone's throw out from the rocks.

Both men scrambled down from the roof, debating what to do. It was Thomas Hughes who went for help, stumbling over the headland, leaning forward against the gusts, through the fields, and over the low stone walls towards the village. Mesach Williams went down towards the wreck, keeping well away from the cliff edge—not only because of the danger of being blown over by the wind but because the earth was liable to subsidence. At one point of his journey there was a sheer drop of one hundred feet. Then he breasted the little hill where the *Royal Charter* memorial stands today, and went down the other side towards the semi-circular sweep of jumbled rock platforms, now a mass of seething, broken water, where the *Royal Charter* lay aground, broadside on, her bow pointing to the west.

Roller after roller struck her. Sometimes, when one wave sequence over-ran another, there was just a mass of jumbled water seething and pushing around her, shooting up spray. Then a great roller would arise and, building up, reach a height twice that of the preceding wave and strike her starboard side with frightful force, sluicing over it in a welter of foam. Where these unexpectedly large waves struck the rocks, unbroken by the breakwater of the iron hull, they were forced upwards and, at the point of breaking, seemed to be trying to rear bodily into the air and surge over the cliff. Some may well have been sixty feet high. There was nothing

73

that Mesach Williams could do but stand there, an impotent spectator. Nothing, it seemed, could bridge that gap of roaring water between wreck and shore.

* * *

Until some time before dawn, and long before Mesach Williams had got down on to the rocks, George Suaicar had been with the Chief Boatswain on top of the deckhouse, which was the highest available point on deck. There they were out of reach of the worst of the seas, which were making a complete breach over the ship; but even so, they had been sitting on a spar, gripping it with their legs. Then Suaicar climbed down and, holding on grimly, made his way forward in the now lightening darkness; when he was quite clear that those darker shadows some thirty yards away were rocks, he reported the fact to Mr Stephens on the poop. Stephens must have known what the real state of the tide was, for he replied, 'We will loose the foretopmast staysail, and, when the tide makes up, run her up.' Suaicar suggested that they should give her the foresail as well, to make sure she did ride up the beach with the incoming tide. With the rocks so near, it seemed the obvious thing to do. They appeared to rise straight up out of the water. Only one man aboard might have been able to tell them just what sort of coast this was. That was the seaman, Isaac Lewis, whose home lay less than half-a-mile away over the headland, in Moelfre. We do not know when the realisation came to him that he had been cast up almost on his own doorstep; we do know that his father was one of those who were presently to come struggling over the hill towards this strange wreck.

The waves on deck were too much for Suaicar, so he went down into the comparative shelter of the forecastle. There he found many of the crew and some of the passengers, waiting for full daylight. Among them were Joseph Rodgers, David Strongman, and Edward Wilson. 'What are we going to do?' asked Rodgers.

'Try to get a line ashore,' replied Suaicar.

'I'll go,' said Rodgers at once. Strongman, the quartermaster, and Wilson, the able seaman, also agreed to make an attempt.

There was no doubt in the mind of Rodgers what had to be done. That dire gap had to be swum by a man with a light line tied round his waist. He was going to be that man. Once the line was ashore, it could be used to pull across a hawser, which would be secured to a rock; and on the hawser a bosun's chair would be rigged, by which every man, woman and child aboard could come safely to shore. Everyone knew what had to be done, but it was only Rodgers who was determined to do it. He

Able Seaman Joseph Rodgers
(Joie Rodriguez), hero of the
Royal Charter, born Malta, 1830,
died 1897. *Photo: Ken Jones (by
permission of Mr Noel Platt)*

stood there now, working out the details of the attempt, while he looked around for a line.

He found one, being held by another man who did not seem to know what to do with it, took it off him, tied one end of it round his waist, and went clattering up on deck, preoccupied with the details of his task. He found the Chief Officer, Mr Stephens, reported to him what he was going to do, and brushed aside the offer of a lifebelt. 'No, I am a Maltese. I can swim ashore.'

In that remark lay all his quiet pride at being a man who was at home in the water, and really knew the sea—compared to the ordinary sailor, who merely floated about on the surface of it. Then he stood a moment, his glance going rapidly between ship and shore, estimating, weighing courses of action. With complete certainty, he made his decision—get as clear of the ship as possible before dropping into the water. He went forward, climbed out on the flying jib-boom, which stretched far out from the hull over the bow; caught hold of the guy, which had been carried away and was dangling; judged his moment, and lowered himself into the seething torrent below. Then he was gone, the top of his head occasionally visible amid the muddy breakers and flying spray, but most often hidden from sight. Gone for ever, thought Suaicar, with a sick feeling.

The sight and sound of that terrible sea was enough to chill the boldest man. Strongman and Wilson, although they had said they would go, made no attempt whatever. Mr Stephens, the Chief Officer, actually had a line in his hand; he was holding it reluctantly, and watching the incoming breakers that reared up and came racing down upon the ship, hearing first the boom as they struck the rocks and then the grating roar as hundreds of tons of water poured back into the sea. He turned to Suaicar, who was standing beside him, staring overboard as though mesmerised by the sight. 'I'm quite willing to take this line ashore, Suaicar, but I can't swim. Can you swim?'

Suaicar was suffering from a bad attack of the 'Stares'. He had spoken up so boldly when down below, had so obviously made the first suggestion himself, that he was irrevocably committed now. But he did not want to go. Anything to delay it, to postpone the terrible test. Something might happen to make it unnecessary.

'Yes,' he said.

'Will you swim ashore with this line?' prompted Stephens.

'Yes, sir, anything I can do to save life,' answered Suaicar doubtfully.

'Then come forward with me.'

There was a pause. Neither of them moved.

'Can I have a few moments to put on a lifebelt, sir?'

A few minutes later, Suaicar was stumbling forward, encumbered by a lifebelt, wondering what he was doing there at all. Had he gone quite out of his mind? But by the time he had got right forward to the bow he had seen a way of escape. Standing on the rocks opposite, tantalisingly close, were three men, obviously villagers. It would be foolhardy to enter the boiling surf with a line, when it might easily be thrown ashore and caught by one of these men. Cupping his hands, he called out to them to come as close to the edge of the rocks as they could. He was going to heave a line over to them. He was to regret that sensible decision for ever afterwards.

The three Welshmen linked hands and advanced cautiously. They were very brave, for the highest of the waves were going right over the rock; and, without warning, some monster wave two or three times higher than the rest might submerge them entirely, tear them from the rock and suck them back with it into the wreck-littered sea. There was no telling when such a wave might strike, but they knew the sea, they knew such things did happen.

76

Eight or nine times Suaicar and the others threw the line. Each time it fell short. The three soaked figures, shuffling forward on the slippery surface, just failed to catch it.

Suaicar's eyes went blank. He still had one end of the line round his waist, people were looking at him, he had to do something. He had to get into the sea. Instead, he turned and went amidships, saying that it looked easier from there.

When he got there, he was still surrounded by other members of the crew. He asked for a volunteer to hold the spare end of the line when he swam ashore. No one was very anxious to hold it, for he did not seem very anxious to go. The Chief Boatswain came to his rescue, saying that the attempt was madness, the waves were running altogether too high. A seaman then said that, if Suaicar would go, he would take the end of the line. Suaicar gave it to him and turned to get over the side. He got across the rail, a strangely laboured proceeding, and then looked down. The waves, as they rolled back, repulsed from their assault on the shore, were violently striking the swaying side of the ship, and gurgling and roaring under the hull. A tiny portion of Suaicar's brain told him with cold certainty, that if he dropped in there he would die.

He pushed away the rail with his hand, and fell.

The water was cold, malevolent; it seized hold of him as if he was a straw. Then there was shouting up above, and a sudden, painful tightening round his waist. Miraculously, he was rising out of the water. As he was drawn up again the eight feet or so to the rail, he heard Captain Withers shouting. Withers was hauling on the line, helped by some of the seamen. Withers was telling him that if he got in at that place, he must be lost, owing to the suction under the ship. Suaicar heard himself saying that, nevertheless, he would risk it. He was being lowered down again, when there was a shout from forward. 'Man ashore!'

Joseph Rodgers was on the rocks, being helped up by a crowd of villagers, which was growing in size every moment as more people scrambled over the hill towards the wreck. George Suaicar had lost his chance of immortality.

*   *   *

By a swim of some thirty yards plain Able Seaman Rodgers had beome 'Rodgers of the *Royal Charter*'; it was the most famous swim of the century. The feat lingered even into the twentieth century; an early motion picture featured a life-saving exploit based on that of Rodgers. But, in reality, it could hardly be called a swim at all. Certainly, Rodgers did not say so. On the only occasion on which he did publicly mention it—and there he had to because he was being questioned at the Board of Trade Inquiry—he said simply, 'The sea between the ship and the rocks was very heavy. I partly swam and partly was washed ashore. I was three times washed back to the ship.'

In the motion picture, the swimmer hero ploughed through the breakers in a terrific crawl, master of his element, and at length hauled himself out on the rocks. Nothing of the sort happened at Moelfre. David Strongman, the would-be swimmer, who watched closely, said that Rodgers was 'washed about for some time', before he succeeded in getting the line ashore. It is easy to understand what happened.

There is, on the north coast of Anglesey, even in calm weather, a curious 'slip' in the water, a kind of swaying, to-and-fro movement. This may be due to that coast being directly in the path of the tide as it comes down the Irish Sea from around the tip of Ulster. In the English Channel the tide does not in fact 'come in', it travels along like a wave in a bath. The top of the wave is high tide, the trough low tide. But at the Anglesey coast, the tide meets a shore head on. It cannot push the land out of the way, therefore it recoils, and then comes on again. The effect of any wave, driven against any coast, is similar; the effect in a gale is extremely violent and rapid, so that it is very nearly possible to be seasick in the sea. The swimmer is literally 'rocked in the cradle of the deep'.

This oscillation makes it possible for him to approach, in a heavy sea, a line of rocks, a breakwater, or a promenade, and put out his hand and touch them, without the least danger of being driven against them—so long as the object is high enough to prevent the waves from sweeping right over it. The actual movement of the water can best be seen right down on the bottom, perhaps twenty feet below the surface. The smaller and lighter types of seaweed can be seen executing a grotesque dance—first bending in and then bending out—marking time exactly to the rhythm of the sea. Above, with each bursting wave, the point where the rock meets the surface is momentarily flecked with foam—like a cloud streaming from a mountain peak.

It was this rhythm, magnified many times by the tremendous power of the hurricane, which swept Rodgers back and forth between the shore and the ship. There was little danger of his actually drowning. The giant waves with their white crests lifted him up at their approach, the broken water bubbling round his head; they passed on, towing a hissing spray behind them. As soon as that was gone, he could kick his head up for an easy gulp of air.

But they were frightening to look at, discoloured with suspended sand and an almost solid mass of seaweed fragments, torn from the bottom like leaves from the trees in autumn; mixed with the floating bodies of small dead crabs, and other waste life plucked from the seabed. Dangerous, too, with a mast sticking up through the curtain of a bursting wave, a broken, bobbing yard or spar, and a mass of splintered gear and trailing rigging cut away from the deck. To fight a way through this deadly driftwood was to court a risk unnecessarily; Rodgers let himself go, and the sea which moved the wreckage moved him at the same pace. Back and forth he was swept, until a larger wave picked him up as it moved thunderously in towards the rocks. The moment had come.

The danger for Rodgers lay actually on the shore line. The swimming was nothing, the rocks everything. For they were in no convenient plan, stopping the sea like a barricade. That coast was made up of many shelves of rock, with a flat but abrasive surface which had the feel of a bared razor blade—harsh, bone-cracking rocks, intimidating even to look at. Some rose up above the highest wave crests; from them, the sea fell back, baffled. Others were below even the troughs of the waves, just beneath the swimmer's feet. And some, dripping as the waves receded, would be used as an anvil by the next breaker, vast masses of water plunging downwards with the weight of many tons, spurting and swirling in different directions before roaring backwards off the flat surface, pouring off into the sea, boiling in little bays and re-entrants. Such a breaker, rearing high, picked up Rodgers like a toy, bearing him on the arc of its crest, and broke with shattering force on the rocks of Moelfre.

He was spewed out on to a rock platform, driven forward over it to the uttermost extremity of the wave, ripped, bruised, and breathless; left gripping desperately, half-entangled in the line, at little tufts of seaweed,

The rocks exposed at low water under the Royal Charter monument on the cliff above, September, 1985. *Photo: Alexander McKee*

which broke away in his grasp, and at the slippery green sea-growth which slid under his fingers like polished moss, as the mass of water began to pour back into the ocean. He was surprised at the ease with which the wave had put him ashore; if only he could hold on now. He did hold on. And behind him, the next wave built up. This was the one that would do the damage, would finish him.

He had ridden the crest of the other; he would be underneath the crest of this one. Hundreds of tons of water began to heave slowly upwards, as the wave neared the shallows and began to rear in protest at the curb on its speed. Higher and higher it mounted, taking its slow, inexorable time. Rodgers was tired now, exhausted by his exertions, the weight of the sodden line tied to his waist and stretching back to the *Royal Charter*, drained of body warmth by the shocking coldness of the sea. He tried to get up, but the line was holding him back; he called out to a little group of villagers for help, and they began to move down the rocks towards him.

They had time to reach him, no time to get back. They knew that. Even if this next wave was only of average height, they could not completely escape it. And they all knew of those monster waves which arise mysteriously out of the deep, to sweep anglers off rocks into the sea. Once in every two or three days, on the edge of a storm, there comes to shore a wave four times higher than the normal. One wave in 1,175 waves is three times higher than the normal. And one wave in every 23 is twice the height of the normal wave. There is no warning of when it will come. They did not know the exact figures, but they were mostly fishermen, and they knew the facts. They linked hands together and, slipping and sliding over the rocks, went down to where Rodgers lay. The wave reared up. Grabbing Rodgers under the armpits, the leading man hauled him to his feet and then, hands linked together, so that if engulfed, there might still be a chance of some keeping their feet, though one or two fell, they went slithering back up the rocks.

The roller burst, and surging water drove over their boots, swirled round their legs, so that they staggered; the man lowest down the rocks was waist deep in it. But the chain held, and Rodgers was dragged up to safety. And after him, the line that led across the stretch of tormented sea to the fore part of the *Royal Charter*. Rodgers was afterwards very reluctant to talk publicly about his exploit; but he spoke freely to these men, admitting that, but for them, he would have drowned.

Aboard the *Royal Charter* a 10-inch manila hawser was being made fast to the shipboard end of the line Rodgers had carried ashore; and the villagers began to make preparations to haul it in and fasten it securely round a rock. By this time, Rodgers, exhausted by his efforts and the savage cold of the sea, and shivering uncontrollably in the bitter wind, his soaked cloth-

The wrecking of the *Royal Charter*, a contemporary impression from the *Illustrated London News*, 5 November, 1859. *Photo : British Library*

ing fluttering around him, was drawing concerned looks from the villagers. He had been up all the previous day, then spent half the night high up the masts of the clipper in a hurricane, fighting the bellying canvas, and had topped it off by making the epic swim of the century. Despite his protests that he wanted to stay and watch the rescue operations, they said he must not; and Rodgers was helped away up the hill to a cottage, to get dry and warm again.

It remained only to draw the hawser ashore, fasten it to a rock, and rig the bosun's chair. Then the evacuation of the passengers could begin. The hawser would be submerged in the wave crests, there were children and heavily over-dressed women to be got across it, in an age when the female was fragile. But, on the other hand, the *Royal Charter* was bumping higher and higher up the sand with the now rising tide; the distance between the wave-lashed hull and the rocks was growing appreciably smaller. Safety was in sight, and the men on the forecastle worked hard to get ready the rescue apparatus; soon, the bosun's chair was rigged.

The danger that lay in wait was unseen, some twenty feet down under the foaming water. Up to now the *Royal Charter's* hull had been beating on sand. What no one knew was the nature of the bottom immediately to seaward of the rock ledges. Captain Taylor assumed that it was sand. It was not. The jumbled rock ledges of the shore were repeated under water. Shafts and boulders of rock stood in the undersea gloom, just under the surface; a sloping shelf lay below, covered with green algae, and at its edge a fringe of small weed like a skirt; and beyond the ledge a further fall still, almost vertical, into still greater depths. It was a fantastic jumble of stone streaked with green weed, a dreadful ship trap; and onto this, as the tide rose, the thin iron hull of the *Royal Charter* presently drove, the midships section right above one of the massive blocks which reared up from the seabed. The next tumultuous breaker flung her hard down upon it.

It was at this moment that the Reverend Charles Vere Hodge began to pray, and all the passengers in the saloon joined him. As the hull creaked and groaned under repeated impacts, and a foot of water sluiced about the deck to every roll and heel of the wreck, they urged their God to save them; or to take them with a quiet mind. Very soon now, many hundreds of men, women and children would attempt that swim to shore, which Rodgers had made. The glory of Rodgers was, that he went first, when he did not have to—carrying the weight of the line which might have saved them all.

Chapter 8

A MAN OF GOD MEETS HIS GOD

The survivors of the *Royal Charter* did not tell the whole story; there were a number of points they missed. Perhaps they did not notice them, or thought them unimportant. Strangely, often enough, it was the dead who spoke most eloquently.

They tell us with apparent certainty that the passengers got dressed in a very great hurry, snatching up in their cabins the first article that came to hand, often belonging to someone else. Women, particularly distracted women with children, were likely to do this. Mrs Hogarth, who had a son to get ready, too, dressed herself in clothes marked 'G Pringle'. (Understandably, because her maiden name was Pringle.) Another woman put on one leg a stocking marked 'Lewis', and on the other leg a stocking marked 'Robinson'. A well-made, middle-aged woman put a patent elastic garter with a brass clasp on her left leg, while on the right leg she put a black tape garter. She put on her stays, with steel springs; and knitted flannel vest; and a black silk top to a dress. Presumably she put on a skirt and underwear, but none was afterwards found on her, perhaps because the waves had removed them. But she had put on black Jean boots, laced at the sides, with patent leather toes, and wore under them white cotton stockings. Yet another woman had not bothered apparently to put on her clothes, and was wearing only a chemise; this was sensible enough, in view of the fact that she was soon going into the water, but she had her stays on and, worse, a heavy money belt holding £36 in coins.

The height of unsuitability was reached, so far as we know, by a Mr Matthew Scott, who tried to carry with him the sum of £320 in gold. Doctor Hatch, of Farnham Royal, had £150, and Mr Edwin Fowler £35 in gold; others, picked at random, had £58, £63, £40, and £44. 19s. One man had ten guineas in a money belt, £1. 6s. in his pockets. Another had £44. 10s. in gold, 9s. in silver, and four gold rings; he was wearing a fancy blue shirt, flannel drawers and Blucher boots. John Maule was fully dressed in grey coat, plaid vest, duck trousers, red scarf, and Blucher boots; and so was another man who was wearing a black frock coat, white drill trousers, fancy yachting shirt, and the inevitable Blucher boots. Curiously

Matthew Scott (centre) who
went into the sea carrying
£320 in gold coins and was
drowned. This family
photograph, taken perhaps
150 years ago, survived
despite damage during the
bombing of Liverpool in
1941. *Photo: courtesy of Miss
M. Scott and the Royal Charter
Salvage Expedition*

enough, one of the few wearing Wellington boots was apparently a German, for he carried a German memorandum book on him with two names
written in it, A. Weyrawitz and Heinrich Brandes. A powerful man of
fifty, he was fully clothed in mackintosh, monkey jacket, waistcoat, red
shirt and fustian trousers, with flannel underwear and woollen socks; over
his shoulder he carried a leather belt with a purse containing six and a
half sovereigns and a bag with two to three ounces of nuggets and gold
dust. He may well have had more—there were ample opportunities for
a corpse to lose all, or part, of its wealth; as was soon to become apparent.

Even Captain Withers, who certainly knew what he was in for, carried
on him £36 in gold and was fully dressed except for his coat. He was wearing his watch. It stopped at precisely 7.30. Some watches stopped as early
as 7.20. None stopped later than at eight o'clock on the morning of Wednesday, 26 October.

The Board of Trade decided that the *Royal Charter* got on the rocks at
about 5 am, but this is not in accordance with the weight of the evidence.
It seems much more likely that this occurred some time between 6.30 and
7 am. At all events, once her hull was being beaten onto the rocks by the
hurricane, her end was not long delayed. It was a matter of only half-an-
hour, perhaps forty-five minutes at the outside.

84

Just after the masts had been cut down, there had been a rush of passengers on deck; but the waves sweeping the ship had washed some overboard and made it hard for the remainder to keep their feet, for the hull was lurching violently from side to side under the impact. Nevertheless, a number of them were now crowded aft on the poop, together with some members of the crew. Other passengers, particularly those with families, were waiting under cover in the saloon, for something to be done to get them ashore. Captain Taylor had promised that they would be safe on land soon after daylight. Their numbers were now increased by second class passengers coming up from the lower saloon, who also chose to wait under cover. It was not dry, indeed most of them were wet through from the water that poured in, but the hundred-foot long, luxurious apartment gave the impression of security and civilisation; it was some bulwark against the hurricane howling outside. One of the ladies had just fainted, a Miss Murray; anxious relatives had taken her to her cabin, and she was now lying down. A third class passenger, soaking wet, then came to the doorway and shouted out that he had come from the forecastle; the bows were almost touching land, he said, they could all wade ashore. Stripped down to trousers only, and shaking with excitement, he produced a great impression. But, in fact, a crisis was building up on the forecastle.

It was being cleared of passengers, to allow the bosun's chair to be got out and tested, which was why this man, naked to the waist, had come aft. But most people had gone below into the forecastle, to wait there. There was only one on deck, and she was a pretty young woman—the third class passenger who had grown so fond of William Bean, the Third Officer. And it was William Bean who was in charge of the men working to bring into action the escape route by the hawser. It was ready now, but it was surrounded by a group of Liverpool riggers, jostling everyone in their haste to be first into the bosun's chair. White-faced with fury, Bean drove them back. He beckoned to the girl, shouting 'Passengers first!' She moved forward nervously, then stopped.

Not only was it not possible to wade on shore, but anyone who went in the bosun's chair was bound to be half-drowned by the giant combers that rolled against the rocks, submerging half the length of the sagging hawser. Bean spoke to her urgently, knowing, as he must have done, that no orders had yet been given to start putting the passengers on shore. He was in fact 'jumping the gun', in trying to sneak his girl friend ashore in front of everyone else. But nothing would be lost by it, except the time lost in persuading her. He pleaded, he implored, he put his arm round her and almost pushed her into the chair, but she sprang away with a scream, half-hysterical with panic. Breathless with tension, angry at himself and with her, he began to bully.

Around the squabbling pair the crew stood silently, the minutes of their lives ticking away. There was no other hawser, since the failure of Suaicar's attempt to take a line from amidships. Amid muffled curses from the baffled riggers, Bean made one more effort to persuade her. But she was sobbing now. It was no good.

Two men, an unnamed seaman and an unnamed rigger, described the scene from their point of view. 'Sixty or seventy women and children, who had been ordered up from below, were standing on one side of the forecastle, waiting for a favourable opportunity to be passed ashore by the hawser. The seaman saw Bean engaged in giving orders and doing his utmost to save the passengers. While so engaged, several of the riggers rushed forward and got into the hawser, and Bean, with the gallantry of the British sailor, reproached one of them and ordered him back, telling him that he and the other riggers had only come on board the day before, and that the women and passengers must be saved first. The rigger replied that he had a soul to be saved as well as any other person, and urged his way on to the hawser and was hauled on to the rocks.' Almost immediately 'a mighty sea broke over the vessel'; and Bean was swept to his death off the forecastle, together with the sixty or seventy women and children who were waiting to be saved.

How long Bean's frightened sweetheart delayed the evacuation of the passengers is uncertain. To William Foster, the carpenter, who was impatient to go, it seemed like half-an-hour. Another estimate was ten minutes, and that is probably more accurate. Certainly, it cost an unknown number of lives. The testimony of John Bradbury, who was then in the saloon, gives us our only definite clue. He had heard an order given for the ladies to go on deck, and watched them as they began to pass down between the groups of men towards the doors forward, which opened out onto the Captain's bridge. But before any actually reached the deck, Bradbury heard the order countermanded—'Would the ladies please remain below for another ten or twenty minutes before going ashore?' Bradbury was at a loss to understand the reason, but almost certainly the delay was caused by the angry scenes around the hawser, between Bean, the girl, and the Liverpool riggers. If a young girl was afraid to face the ordeal—it was a very real one—the older women and the mothers with children might equally refuse; and perhaps the Captain was still waiting for the tide to go down. In any event, the girl's hysteria was only a result of Captain Taylor's mistaken attempt to prevent panic by assuring his passengers that there was no danger. Had she understood how serious the danger was, she might not have baulked.

After a delay which Bradbury estimated at fifteen minutes, he heard a second order given for the ladies to go on deck, and saw the saloon doors

86

flung open to let them through. The Chief Officer, Mr Stephens, had now taken over on the forecastle and was ready to begin disembarkation of the passengers. Probably he gave a hand signal to those on the bridge aft, who relayed the order Bradbury heard. We know for certain that he turned to Owen Williams, the quartermaster from Caernarvon, telling him to go aft and get the women passengers up on deck, and then lead them forward to the hawser. Williams began to walk aft, with the hull rocking and grinding ominously under him; down by the bow, canted over to port, obviously badly holed. He moved slowly, for he had to elbow his way through a group of sixty or seventy passengers. Equally slowly, for the saloon was packed, and many of the women did not to want to leave their husbands, a group of females began to make their way to the doors.

Meanwhile, a few members of the crew were scrambling ashore by the bosun's chair. Edward Wilson, the would-be swimmer, claimed to be, not the first man on it, but the first man who used it to reach the shore alive. Several others who went ashore ahead of him were washed off and lost, he said. He may have been mistaken about this—it may merely have seemed that they had vanished—but it was no easy ride. Certainly Foster, in his narrative, seems to imply that he was first, for he said, 'The female refused to go, and then I went along the hawser and was thus saved; about three of the crew came on shore in the same way after me.' Suaicar, who was ashore very early, was probably one of them; once on the rocks, he was foremost in organising the party already ashore for further rescue. Therefore, within a few minutes, there were working parties of seamen at both ends of the hawser, one party on the rocks and another on the ship's forecastle, ready to run a shuttle-service with the bosun's chair. It now remained only for Owen Williams to reach the saloon and call the women passengers forward, with their children. It would have been useless, and would have caused unnecessary loss of life, to have kept them marshalled on deck before the bosun's chair was actually in action.

Thomas Gundry, who was below in the saloon at the time, could hardly keep his feet; several times he was thrown against the side of the ship. 'The screams were dreadful,' he said. Samuel Grenfell, the Cornish goldminer, recollected men and women clinging together in despair at the late realisation that they were about to lose each other; he saw mothers frantic for their children's safety; and husbands, raging and helpless, or broken down with grief. A friend of his, whose family were clutching at him for the strength and support he could no longer give, had the tears running down his face. 'Sam!' he called, 'what will I do with my wife and children? We shall be lost, lost. Try and save us.' One man alone would be hard put to it to save himself; for a father to take care of his family was impossible. Muttering that he would do what he could, but he was afraid it was no use, Grenfell joined a group of passengers who were beginning to scramble on deck. 'The sea was breaking over the ship in an awful manner, carrying everything before it; no one could keep his feet, and most of them were washed overboard.' Gundry, too, joined the rush for the deck, and found that the ship was bumping so much that he could hardly stand. He still had some money with him—35 golden sovereigns in a bag.

Mr Gapper and Mrs Rose were still in the saloon, but James Russell, much alarmed, began to lead his family through the throng. James M'Cappin, an upholsterer and cabinetmaker from St Kilda, was one of those who remained to the end and witnessed what followed. Many of the women passengers began to turn to God, in the shape of His representative in the *Royal Charter*, the pathetic Reverend Charles Vere Hodge. 'He was surrounded by a group of females,' testified M'Cappin, 'wringing their hands and piteously bewailing their impending fate.' None knew the poor man's secret, that he was a hen-pecked husband disdained by his wife and being bullied home by his Bishop. He certainly feared these two, and he may have feared God; but he did not fear death. Unlike the tough sea captains, Taylor and Withers, the old clergyman did not tell these people that they were going to walk ashore when the tide went out. He told them they were going to die. There was very little time left to them on earth, perhaps a few minutes only. Would they, with him, spend that time in prayer?

One or two only, at first, joined him in the solemn words; then more began to pray. Mr Gapper and Mrs Rose, standing side by side, bowed their heads silently. Carl Bartel, the Prussian musician, could not understand all the words, but inclined his head in silent respect to the will of God. The screaming stopped, slowly the sobs died away. The ship lurched suddenly, but not as she had before, there was a grating, groaning roar as iron plates twisted and rent, men and women fell to the deck, and a swirling, foaming wave of water roared down into the saloon. People ran madly for the gangway, but Bartel was up to his waist in water by the time he reached it. The Russells were just outside, and were on deck in a moment. There, they stood, staring about them like lost souls.

*   *   *

Thomas Gundry had been on deck at the time and seen the enormous wave which had completed the damage begun by the pounding of the iron hull on the rocks. 'A great sea came against the broadside, and divided the ship in two, just at the engine house, as one would smash a pipe stem, and the sea washed quite through her. People were carried down by the debris, and as many must have been killed as drowned.' James Russell

The wreck site at high water, September, 1960. *Photo: Alexander McKee*

led his family on deck at this moment, and they clung to the rail at the
top of the stairs. 'We found we were on the stern part of the vessel, separated from the fore part by a yawning chasm, into which every moment
human beings were dropping, or being driven by the waves.' James Dean,
the goldminer from Wigan, was also on deck; and he was a very good,
thoroughly rested witness. He slept through the hurricane, he slept when
the ship struck the sand, he slept when she got on the rocks—and he only
woke up when another passenger shook him violently, with a bellow of,
'I think we're lost!' He dressed, spent a minute or two in prayer, and had
just now gained the deck. 'She broke like the snapping of a tobacco stump,'
he said, echoing a simile which occurred to many people; it was apt, for
she was a long, narrow vessel. 'The people on board stood petrified at
the catastrophe, seemingly unable to make the slightest struggle for their
lives, whilst the terror was increased by the awful scenes as unfortunate
creatures fell and were crushed to atoms between the chasm separating

89

the two sides of the ship.' He was the only witness to notice that preliminary hushed pause, most of the passengers remembered only the terrible screaming which succeeded it.

One of those who went down with the rain of debris as the ship broke was Walter Hughes, an apprentice. The hull buckled under his feet, the plates tearing away from the beams and frames like the skin of a peeled banana, the heavy gear and machinery on deck cascading into the foaming waters. Hughes was crushed, cut, bruised, hurt internally, and half drowned; all he could say afterwards was, 'I felt as if I were being killed.' Seared into his brain was his last memory of the *Royal Charter*—'three little children, standing on deck, holding each other's hands, screaming.'

As Hughes was being washed about in the sea, in agony from his injuries, to be cast within minutes on the rocks, and repeatedly hammered there until his hands and face were bloodied from these fresh impacts, a steerage passenger was washed clear out of the ship from below decks. This was John Judge, an Irishman of enormous size and strength, who had been biding his time quietly below in the forecastle. 'I saw hundreds of people closed up in the jaws of death around me,' he said. There were at least a hundred people in the water now, washed to and fro by the enormous rollers, but most of them had been on the upper deck. Those below had had their lives snuffed out almost at once, as the two broken ends of the giant clipper swung slowly round, presenting their jagged wounds to the pounding seas, and were instantly swept through from end to end by waves forty or sixty feet high.

Young Miss Murray, who had fainted and been carried to her cabin by relatives; Samuel Henry, the Adelaide jeweller, said to be a lunatic and confined below under guard; the unfortunate miner James Potts, whose broken thigh would not mend properly—they had as little chance as the tiny children and the old lady of eighty whose husband had been shot at Ballarat. Darkness fell upon them in seconds. In the chilly shock as the masses of cold, discoloured water grasped and took them, then pinned them up alive against a deckhead by the little air in their lungs, they struggled for perhaps half a minute and were then engulfed by a blackness that came quickly. In minutes after they had ceased to struggle, they were dead.

Of the scenes in the water between the ship and the shore, James Dean is once again our best witness. There was that tidy mind of his, always taking precautions, shown in the way he kept his money—a cheque in a waterproof belt round his waist—and the sharp detail he always gives, where others present only a picture of blurred horror. In this first moment of utter disaster, as the ship broke and hundreds fell into the sea, he stood there, briefly, at the rail, taking in various 'distracting incidents' going on all around him—clearly, there were too many for any one man even to note, let alone remember. He makes that point, where no one else does. Then Dean turned and looked shoreward, concentrating his interest on those who were trying to reach land. Hughes was there, and so was Judge. The tossing water was covered with the wreckage of the fallen masts and all sorts of gear torn off, or washed out of, the ship. Judge got hold of a spar and, holding on grimly, let himself be washed ashore, bruised and lacerated from head to foot. Hughes was simply pitched onto the rocks, where the villagers got hold of him and hauled him beyond reach of the sea. He had to be carried all the way up the cliff and over the headland to Moelfre, so badly was he injured.

Dean watched these struggles with a critical eye. He saw that most of the people in the water, floundering about in their heavy clothing, some with boots on, many unable to swim, made towards the heavier floating portions of wreckage, such as the masts, and—what no one else recorded— that this was often fatal to them. 'They were crushed to death,' he noted, 'the bodies dreadfully mutilated against the rocks by the great weight of these materials. Mangled corpses, arms, legs, and even heads were discern- ible on the crest of many a retreating wave.' Those who grasped lighter pieces of wreckage, as Judge had done, appeared to be more fortunate. The reason for Dean's critical interest in the fate of those who grasped wreckage for support in the water was that he was a non-swimmer.

This, of course, made his self-possession the more remarkable. For he assumed, as most non-swimmers do, that the sea is a suffocating medium. Taking off most of his clothes, and discarding with them the small amount of ready cash he had, Dean went overboard without hesitation, his mind quite made up, and seized hold of a wooden box which was neither too large nor too light. But no sooner had he done so than a head was thrust up under one of his arms, nearly loosening his grip, and this desperate, drowning person—he does not say whether it was a man or a woman— fought him for sole possession of the wooden box. Dean resisted, but when he saw another floating box nearby, he ceased to waste his strength in the struggle and grasped hold of that.

He never realised just how right he had been to take off his clothes, nor the real reason why so many people were having strange difficulty in hauling themselves out of the water. They were dying all along the line of the rocks by the score, whereas few were actually drowning, despite the layers of clothing they wore. Where a man or a woman went down almost at once, it was because they were carrying, so to speak, weight-belts of solid gold; and women with tight, constricting stays, or men with wide, floppy boots, found themselves floundering about in fatally unsuitable clothing—the stays prevented proper breathing, the boots acted as drogues. But the weight of the clothing was nothing—because they were in water and buoyed up by it. The moment of truth came when they were thrown onto the rocks and tried to stand up—they literally staggered under what felt like the ton-weight of sodden greatcoats, trousers, coats, waistcoats, and flannel underwear. It was no coincidence that all who survived complained of being thrown ashore 'nearly naked'. It was a main factor in their survival. Another was the presence of the villagers.

Dean, still clinging to the box, was washed right up on the rocks, virtually without injury; but he could not get clear of the danger area in time. He staggered to his feet, in his underwear, and began to haul himself up; he was not quite quick enough, and the following wave, striking him in the back, knocked him over and sucked him out to sea once more. He found himself threshing desperately among a tangled mass of floating wreckage and ropes. Exhausted by only those few minutes in the cold water, he had difficulty in freeing himself. His movements seemed strangely feeble and slowed down. In this state, gasping, nearly beaten, he was twice washed up on the rocks and twice washed back. Again, he was thrown up, and this time he held on to the rock and when a rope was thrown to him by the villagers, was able to scramble up and grasp it. 'By it,' he said, 'I was finally drawn out of danger, without experiencing any injuries or bruises other than of a very trifling description.' Very satisfied with the success of his theories—and not realising just how lucky he had been—he was taken off to Moelfre to get dry, his cheque still safe in the waterproof waistbelt.

Of those hundreds pitched into the sea when the ship broke, or caught below, or washed overboard at once, or who, like James Dean, jumped into the water almost immediately afterwards, only a handful survived. We know only of three; some of the survivors never told their stories, so there may have been one or two more. While they were tossing in the surf, or struggling on the rocks, a few more members of the crew, and some of the riggers, were passed safely across in the bosun's chair. But the tragedy was that most of the surviving passengers, and almost all the women and children, were in the stern section, where they had been sheltering in the saloon, while the hawser carrying the bosun's chair was secured to the forecastle, which was in the bow section. And between these two parts of the shattered clipper was an unbridgeable gap of foaming water, spouting fury, where the waves struck the sunken, tangled structure on the seabed which had once been the machinery in the midships section of the *Royal Charter*, and was now a tomb.

Owen Williams, the quartermaster from Caernarvon, had never delivered to the female passengers the Chief Officer's message that they were to come forward to the hawser to begin evacuation. He had still been elbowing his way aft, when the deck buckled in front of him and the way aft was cut off. He had turned and stumbled back along the bow section, now beating frightfully, and reported to the Chief Officer, who was standing on the forecastle, ready to control the going ashore of the women and children. Mr Stephens had seemed very worried about the fate of the women passengers, and was not satisfied that nothing could be done for them, until he had seen for himself. The two surviving hull sections were now swinging round, their severed ends pointing seawards, so that they were almost parallel, separated bow and separated stern both facing the rocks. The last sight Williams had of the Chief Officer was of Stephens walking aft, towards the rollers sweeping the bow section. The quiet, cheerful Scotsman had a wife and two children of his own; probably he was thinking of them now, certainly he was not thinking of himself. 'Neither Mr Stephens nor Mr Bean made any effort to save their own lives,' Williams afterwards testified.

But the moment Stephens had gone, Williams turned his mind to the bosun's chair. There was obviously no chance for the women and children, so he might just as well save himself while there was still time. The bow of the *Royal Charter*, nearest the shore, highest on the rocks, and lightest—because the engine was in the stern—was still substantially above water; but the giant breakers were still striking it incessantly, and there was great scrambling for a chance on the hawser; the whole iron structure was fast breaking up and subsiding, in spite of its watertight compartments, ripped open by the rocks. The two halves of the ship were literally coming apart under the battering ram force of the breakers; they made short work of the remains of the iron hull now, hammering and flailing them on the rocky seabed. And still the wind screamed at hurricane force, gusts of one hundred miles an hour driving on the giant waves, urging them to complete their task.

Williams got his chance at the bosun's chair, half-way down the queue, and was soon sitting, sodden and dejected, on the rocks overlooking the wreck. David Strongman, another quartermaster, was one of the last to cross. One man in the queue, who never made it, was Isaac Lewis of Moelfre. The distance to shore was so short that he could recognise his own father standing on one of the rocks, and the old man recognised him. They cried out to each other, their words carried away as incomprehensible sounds in the fury of the roaring sea and gale. He got into the bosun's chair to make the attempt, but was swept completely away by a giant wave—so possibly he preceded the seaman Edward Wilson, who claimed to have been the first man actually to reach shore by the hawser, 'several others who tried to do so having been washed off and lost'.

This was the sort of story which, basically true, tends to become changed by much telling. Contemporary newspaper accounts report that, while standing on the forecastle, young Lewis cried out to his father, 'Oh, I am come home to die!' Mr W. F. Peacock, who visited Moelfre the following summer, was told by the villagers that the young man actually reached the rocks, but was swept back into the sea; that his father got to within a few feet of him and heard him say, 'Oh, father, I've come home to be drowned.' One thing is deadly sure—the young sailor's body was washed up that day, half a mile from his father's house.

When he got ashore, Wilson simply sat down. His main feeling was of utter weariness and helplessness, now that the strain of personal survival was over; he had to sit there and watch his shipmates die, the two portions of the wreck dissolving, with their human cargo, into the sea before his eyes. 'It was dreadful,' he said, 'dreadful. There were mangled bodies floating about in the water; men, women and children standing up on the deck and shrieking for assistance; others on their knees, praying; others being washed overboard. There was a large number of passengers huddled on deck to the end; the shrieks of the poor creatures as they met their death was absolutely appalling.'

Among these people were James Russell with his wife and two little girls, Mr Gapper and Mrs Rose, Henry Carew Taylor and his child, W. Henry Morse, the magistrate, Second Steward Thomas Cormick, Captain Taylor, and many others. Their story takes longer to tell than it did to enact in reality, for in a few minutes there was nothing whatever left above water of the *Royal Charter* but the stumps of her masts.

Chapter 9

THE BITTER END

Of all those left aboard the *Royal Charter* at this moment, few can have had less chance of survival than John Bradbury. Gritting his teeth in a dull agony, he lay trapped among the wreckage of the hull where it had broken in two. He could hardly realise yet that this had happened, and that it must be the end of him. His right foot and ankle were trapped, twisted; the pain, when he tried to free himself, was sickening. As the deck sank down almost to the water level, and each wave went over his head, leaving Bradbury choking and spluttering, he writhed and wrenched madly in a final attempt to get loose. There was a snap, almost audible. A shock wave of agony shot up his right leg. Abruptly, he stopped moving. He felt sick, weak, but the overpowering sensation was of astonishment. Breathing heavily, he lay there, trying to recover his nerve.

He had broken his leg. There was no doubt about it. When you really did it, you knew, yes, you knew. It was not like a sprained ankle. But so easily! The bone had snapped like a rotten stick. He could see now, when he looked back at his right leg, that it seemed no longer straight; it was—he looked away. No doubt about it, the foot and lower leg were twisted away at an angle to the rest of his body. Bradbury half-raised himself on hands and elbows and shouted, in a voice strangely weak and hysterical, 'Help!' And again, 'Help!'

His voice died away, without effect. He could attract the attention of no one. Once more, he called, in a cracked voice. No one noticed what had happened to him, or if they had, were too distracted by their own peril to take any notice. It was up to him. Bradbury could think quite clearly. He was calm, probably the calmest man aboard. His brain began to tick over, regularly, precisely, like a machine. There was not much pain as long as he remained still. It was hardly pain at all—nothing like the dentist's chair, for instance. Really, it was quite peaceful, restful, to lie flat and do nothing. But he could have done with a cup of tea, to ease the shock that he felt. If he went on thinking like that, giving in, he would die. He must get to the side, and into the water.

The yawing motions of the torn hull, as the waves struck, and the scouring breakers themselves, seemed to have disturbed the wreckage, even washed some of it off him. Bradbury curled his body round, breathless with the anticipation of agony, and tried to shift the remainder. Although he was very careful, moving only above the waist, there were one or two black moments before he could drag himself clear; they were literally black, for consciousness flowed almost away, but never completely. He knew what he was doing, he still had hold of himself. Bradbury lay back, let the dark curtain slowly ebb from his eyes.

When he was stronger, he summoned up all his resources, all his will for the attempt to get into the water. It would have to be quick. One supreme effort. Bradbury pulled himself up on hands and knees, and crawled, a savage, grinding agony in his right leg where the broken bones grated together. Helped by a wave, he slithered in one mighty burst to the edge of the deck, and slumped head first overboard, the world darkening before his eyes.

He hung, strangely comforted and restful, in the waves; the sea supporting his broken limb, the cold water reviving him. Bradbury grasped the first piece of wood he saw, and hung on limply, recovering, letting the waves wash him where they would, surrendering to the sea, breathing deeply, heavily, in shuddering gasps.

Soon, he saw a solid piece of wreckage rocking nearby, with a man on it whom he knew, a Mr Lewis. Bradbury let go and began to pull himself with his arms through the water, kicking with his left leg, but letting the right leg trail limply behind. He reached the spar and gasped out, 'Are you hurt?' Lewis replied that he was not. At that moment an enormous breaker picked them up and the spar came down on the rocks with a violent thump. Lewis disappeared, and never came up again, probably knocked on the head. Bradbury fell off, too, but lay washing in the waves, quite helpless, as they picked him up again, dashed him on the rocks and drew him back once more. At last, as he lay stranded, three brave men came stumbling down the rocks towards him and, holding onto each other, began to carry him to safety. Bradbury tried to gasp out that his leg was broken; but this was the least of his injuries now.

Bradbury's hurts were so terrible that he was not considered out of danger until a month later; and it was not possible to move him from Moelfre for some time after that. Not the least of his trials was that no doctor was immediately available. His escape, with its elements of sheer will power and sheer chance, was probably the most miraculous of all.

A little group of people, with among them most of the women and children, were trapped on the stern section. Some dropped into the water quite early; others, including the Russells, stayed very nearly until the end, trying to devise some way of getting ashore. The time factor involved, however, was only a matter of minutes either way. James M'Cappin, a

The *Great Britain* at sea,
probably off Lundy Island,
powered by both steam and
sail. *Photo : The National
Maritime Museum, London*

The forward deck of the
Great Britain, now back in
her home port of Bristol.
Photo : Ilse McKee

Panorama of the wreck scene, with the Bestspeed boats marking the remains of the *Royal Charter*. Low water in September, 1985. *Photo: Ilse McKee*

The old, abandoned life-boat house at Moelfre, from which it was impossible to launch on the night of the '*Royal Charter* Gale'. *Photo: Ilse McKee*

The rock ledges where the *Royal Charter* struck, looking towards the site of the *Hindlea* wreck. *Photo: Alexander McKee*

Passengers from the *Royal Charter* were battered mercilessly on this jumble of rocks. *Photo: Alexander McKee*

Llanallgo Church, where the bodies of the wreck victims were brought and where many of them are buried. *Photo: Ilse McKee*

Inside the tiny church, September, 1985. In October and November, 1859, the corpses were laid here for identification by grieving relatives. Most had been horribly mutilated on the rocks. *Photo: Alexander McKee*

A porthole recovered from the wreck site, before cleaning. *Photo: RCSE Ltd/ John Russum*

The porthole after cleaning. *Photo: RCSE Ltd/John Russum*

The Royal Charter Salvage Expedition at work on their pontoons above the wreck site. *Photo : RCSE Ltd/John Russum*

A gold eternity ring, showing the design on the outside edge. *Photo : RCSE Ltd/John Russum*

The inside edge of the ring, engraved with the words: 'From W Newlove to M Davis 4th Feb 1856'. *Photo : RCSE Ltd/John Russum*

Early finds. The Ovens ring
and a sovereign from the
Sydney mint, 1859. The
Ovens River valley was a
prime recovery site for gold,
using dredges. *Photo: RCSE
Ltd/John Russum*

A Sydney mint sovereign.
*Photo: RCSE Ltd/John
Russum*

A gold nugget on a pin.
*Photo: copyright RCSE Ltd/
John Russum*

Diving on the *Hindlea*; the frame and a plate show dimly through the typical pea soup of British waters. *Photo: Alexander McKee*

The author swimming back to the boat after surfacing from the *Hindlea*. *Photo: Ilse McKee*

second class passenger, who had been on deck before the ship broke, saw the Captain hurled by one wave right across the deck and pinned to the rails, and then, as he staggered to his feet, hurled by a monstrous breaker against the structure of the saloon near the companionway. He became entangled in the wreckage of the fretted woodwork which decorated it, and 'lay there for some time, exposed to every wave that broke over the ship'.

He had only just fallen when the second steward, Thomas Cormick, bursting up from below, was caught at the head of the companionway by a wave, and rolled down to the lee side of the deck, where he saw Captain Taylor lying down, and one of the women passengers also. Both Thomas Gundry and Henry Carew Taylor saw him there, before they got into the water almost together. Gundry called out, 'Captain, this is a fearful state of things,' then made for the lee side, seized a rope which was hanging down, and tried to lower himself into the water, losing his hold in the procsss. He went down into water cold, dark, and writhing with weed and particles of sand, the dim, metallic light of the surface many feet above his head. As he kicked up towards the air, Gundry felt a jarring blow. 'My head,' he said, wryly, 'had to open a passage, for the water here was thickly strewn with timber.'

Half stunned, but a good swimmer, he was able to make for a piece of timber, and hang on. There were many other people tossing in the waves around him; one of them, a man wearing a lifebelt, was astride a large spar and looked to have a good chance until a drowning person reached up and clutched at him, and the spar rolled over, taking both of them down with it. One of the yards was sticking out of the water a few feet to seaward of Gundry, with each roller rising high above his head and threatening to brain him. 'But strange to say, it was carried over me, and we were both pitched on shore for a moment together.' Both went back into the sea with the surge of the retreating surf. A second time Gundry was thrown on to the rocks, grasping desperately at the slippery, moss-like weed, but went slithering back, ripped and bruised, into deep water. But he had now been seen and marked by the villagers, and as he was thrown up on the rocks again, a rush of helpers came down the dangerous slopes and dragged him out, virtually unconscious. He still had his moneybag on him, but there was only ten pounds in it. Twenty-five golden sovereigns were lost in the sea.

Thomas Bowden, the Devonshire miner, was unluckier still, for he had been returning to his 'old woman' with £200 in gold. A non-swimmer, he lost all in the sea except his life, being thrown onto the rocks with such violence that his shoulder was nearly smashed. W. Henry Morse, the New South Wales Magistrate, was washed off the poop and had no clear recollection of how he got ashore, retaining only a confused memory of being left lying on a rock by a receding wave. Carl Bartel, the Prussian musician, jumped from the poop and seized a piece of wreckage; a little later, his face streaming blood, he, too, was dragged to safety.

Some twenty-eight villagers, with Suaicar leading a party of them, were making attempt after desperate attempt to seize hold of the battered bodies that the sea sent swirling in; some alive, but most of them not. Many times he led a chain of men forward at the run, as a great wave receded; nine times he seized a sodden, bloodied body which still kicked feebly, and dragged it up the rocks in time to escape the next wave, rearing up majestically and moving fast upon them as they ran back, breaking in fury, and sending a swirling surge of foam round their legs, sometimes drenching them to their waists. One man alone would have been dragged back, over the dripping edge of rock, as tons of water poured off it; but the chain held, the men further up the rocks leaning their weight against the pull of the sea on the men half-engulfed in it. There was no let-up whatever on the part of the hurricane. The wind was still as strong, although a little more to the north-east; the onslaught of the breakers was as irresistible as ever. The water was full of wreckage, brought thundering on the shore, to be left dry or dragged back; it was a fantastic jumble, for the sea was pouring right through the two hulks which had once been a great ship, sweeping everything out. The wool cargo was coming ashore, blown over the water with the sleet and spray, littering the rocks, a strange debris. Afterwards, when part of the wreck was salvaged, a solid gold ingot was found embedded in an iron plate from the ship's side, hard evidence of the titanic force of the breakers. The copper cargo was torn out of the shattered hull, the strongroom broken up, and the ingots scattered, mixed with gold coins from the pockets of the passengers. Like a shower of golden seashells, gold sovereigns were thrown up by the sea, gleaming in the crevices of the rocks. They lay there for the picking up, a fantastic harvest that grey morning, a harvest of gold and of death. Poor men saw before their eyes more wealth cast up by the sea than they could earn from the sea in many hard years of toil.

Henry Carew Taylor went into the water several minutes after Gundry; he had been knocked down by the waves while on deck, and had seen the Captain similarly knocked down. He had called out to him much as Gundry had, 'Oh, Captain Taylor, what a fearful scene this is.' There was no reply from the Captain, and when another wave swept over the deck, Henry Carew Taylor jumped overboard. This was for him the last resort, because he had seen a number of people attempt the short swim to the land that seemed so near. Watching closely, he noted that only one was able to get up on the rocks. Now, in the last minutes of the *Royal*

Charter, there were, he said, 'masses of people in the water on the lee side of the two halves of the ship, clustered as thickly together as grapes'. He had to clear them to stand any chance of survival. Among them were 17-year-old Jane Fowler and her best friend, Sophia Davis; the two impetuous young girls had rushed on deck as soon as the ship broke in two, and Taylor had seen them almost instantly swept overboard by a wave. Hampered by the bulky lifebelt he had prudently put on, Taylor seized a rope hanging from the side of the wreck and gave a great spring outwards to clear the heads of the wildly agitated mass of men, women and children in the water below him. 'The struggle was so desperate that I had not the slightest hope of being saved,' he recalled. Taylor had on trousers and coat, but no shoes; prudent again, he had put on slippers, because they would be easy to kick off.

Held up by the lifebelt, he laid hold of a baulk of timber; but as there was another man on it already, he changed over to a spar floating nearby. In a moment, he and the spar were thrown fairly high up the rocks, and he managed to hold on by gripping some seaweed. Two villagers, Robert Lewis and another man, got hold of him by the fingers just in time; 'Just as another wave was going to nip me back,' he said. His clothes had been torn to rags and were held in place only by a belt; his money had been lost in the sea, apart from ten sovereigns, but he still had his gold watch. Lewis took him to his cottage, put Taylor in his own bed, and gave him some of his own clothes to wear; he was later to take Russell there also. Tight-lipped, Henry Carew Tayor never said how his child and her nurse had met their deaths; or whether they were washed overboard.

Samuel Edward Gapper, the New Zealand farmer, had held young Mrs Rose in his arms to the last. She was very calm, he said, down below in the saloon and afterwards on the wave-lashed poop. Close alongside them, a studding-sail boom was tossing in the water. Mrs Rose allowed Gapper to lower her down from the deck into the water, so that she had only to stretch out her arms to grasp it. Then he dropped into the foam with a splash and swam over to her. With one arm round the 23-year-old girl, and the other round the boom, he was clinging tightly when an enormous roller broke right over their heads. The cruel power of the cold sea tore them apart, drove them under, whirling them like rag dolls; when at last Gapper came gasping and spluttering to the surface, there was no sign of Mrs Rose. A minute or two later he was thrown onto the rocks and, terribly battered, found himself being dragged out of reach of the waves by a villager. He looked back, but Mrs Rose had gone.

For the elderly, for the young children, and for their almost demented parents, the monstrous bursting seas were an overwhelming terror, a nightmare too harsh to surmount. The waves sweeping the little group of people

99

who remained to the end were powerful beyond the power of the strongest man; strong men were swept overboard by them like straws, or pulped on the vicious rocks, or smothered in the surf with open mouths. With horror and dread, they began to realise that many, many bodies tossing in the surf were no longer alive. Some were not even human any more. They lacked an arm, or a leg, or a head. Splintered bones protruded through the flesh, skulls had been split clean open, and the top of one man's head had been taken off clear down to the chin. This horrible, inhuman flotsam rocked and tossed between the ship and the shore, washed back and forth, bundled in the breaking waves, and dashed once more upon the land in a slow, satanic rhythm, with occasionally a lifeless limb thrust up out of a falling breaker, to mark a dead man's return to shore.

In their terrible hysteria, some people jumped overboard and tried to fight the sea, to thrust it down and away from them, to hold frightened, screaming, writhing children above its suffocating surface; others huddled on deck, hoping that something of the ship would remain above water. Even the most courageous man, if he had a family, was numbed by grief and fear.

When the Russells, with their two little girls of 10 and $2\frac{1}{2}$ years respectively, had first come up from the saloon, to find that the ship had broken, they had been comparatively calm; they were horrified mainly by the fate of the people falling into the yawning chasm between the two riven sections of the hull. 'It was a moment of the intensest anguish,' said Russell. 'As we all clung to the rail at the top of the stairs, hurried farewells were spoken. Then we awaited death.' Two of the friends Russell had made on the voyage were holding on to the binnacle—Mr Henderson, a Melbourne merchant, and the Mr Watson who had formed a successful mining company and was now returning to England to marry. Henderson called out, 'Oh, Watson, all is gone!' Trite words, perhaps, in other circumstances, they imprinted themselves on Russell's memory as part of a scene he never forgot. 'Time could never obliterate it—they were the last glimpses of fellow-voyagers, the dying expressions of old companions.' He remembered, too, a man named Welsh, standing there with two black canvas bags tied round his neck, bulging heavily with gold. Russell had seen Welsh fetch them from his cabin to the saloon, and spend his last few minutes on earth tying them securely in place around him, so that nothing would get them free. It was merely the unthinking gesture of a man who had slaved to get a little comfort for himself, and had perhaps believed what he had been told, that he would walk ashore when the tide went out.

Near the Scottish family, a Jewish couple, also with two children, were clinging to the rail. Mr and Mrs Marks had made their money at the gold fields, but were more elderly than the Russells. As another wave rocked the hull and burst over the deck, one of the children was torn away and Mrs Marks was swept into a corner of the wrecked stern and trapped there. A sailor rescued the child while Mr Marks, frantic with grief, rushed towards his wife, pulling and tearing at her clothes in trying to get a grip and so wrench her free. 'He tore her clothes to rags,' testified Russell, who then became too preoccupied with means of saving his own family to notice any more.

One of the last to leave the wreck was James Ferris, who had been a storekeeper at Ballarat. He did not see what happened to Mrs Marks and one child, but he was a witness of the fate of the husband and the other child. He saw Marks swim away desperately from the side of the ship; he was making, in the boiling water, curious beating, downward strokes, splashing terribly, with his mouth under water most of the time and fighting for air. On his back sat a terrified child, clinging chokingly to its father's neck, it hands tight around his throat. A wave, the great, foaming crest rearing high above them, struck the struggling pair. In the bubbling water behind it, only the father could be seen, looking around with desperate eyes. After the next wave had passed, he, too, was gone.

Ferris slipped overboard and struck out for the rocks. He was a swimmer; he knew that the sea is a supporting, not a suffocating medium— unless you fight it. He let himself be carried, buoyant, towards the rocks, hardly bothering actually to swim, forcing his head up only a few inches for an occasional breath of air. He did not try to rise unnaturally high nor did he panic at the breakers, but let himself go limp, so that when he was thrown onto the rocks, still riding the upper curve of the wave, he was unhurt. Only as the undertow roared back into the sea did he suffer injury, for he clung on grimly with arms and legs, forcing himself to embrace that razor-sharp bone-cracking surface as if it had been a mistress, and, as he slid back a few feet, suffered long gashes, which smarted and bled. Then, unhampered by sodden clothing, for he was, he said, 'as naked as the day I was born,' he scrambled unaided out of reach of the sea.

Ferris was immediately given clothing by a villager, Captain Copeland, who was distributing clothes to survivors. He saw washed ashore a child whose father, the man who went under the false name of S. Perry, had also tried to swim ashore with it on his back. 'Perry' was a much younger man than Mr Marks, but he had no better luck; the child was dead and its father somewhere deep in the raging surf. Possibly it was the failure of these attempts which prompted Russell to try a better method of escape; besides, even if he did succeed in bringing one little girl to shore, he must necessarily leave his wife and his other daughter behind to die. There was no chance of bridging the gap between the stern section and the bow, where the hawser was and where a few last members of the crew were making their escape. But it gave him an idea. Shouting to his family to hold fast to the rail, and pushing the two frightened little girls even closer to their mother, he began to unfasten some ropes which were tangled on the deck and bulwarks. His plan was to free a long length of rope, tie one end round his family, and throw the other on the rocks, so that the villagers could grasp it amd draw them ashore. With the rising of the tide, the wreck was nearer to the rocks than when Suaicar had attempted this, and Russell might have succeeded. He tried several ropes and found that, although it was easy to free one end, the other remained secured on board; and he had no knife. White-faced, he went back to his wife. 'We are all gone,' he said.

The whole family were clinging desperately together, determined not to be parted, even by death, when a gigantic roller burst over them. Catherine Margaret, ten years old, was torn from them by the impact, carried across the deck and left lying by the rails, with a box across her legs, pinning her down. As the wave subsided, James Russell saw her, and ran across the slanting deck; he heaved the box off and dragged her back to join the others, the deck groaning and shifting under their feet, rolling from side to side. Another enormous breaker lifted it bodily and smashed upon them with the shock of many tons of cold water. Mrs Russell and her daughters were carried right across the deck and pinned against the bulwarks; but James Russell himself was taken clean overboard.

He was swept towards the rocks in the wake of the boiling water, then washed back to the hull as the wave recoiled from the shore. Seeing his chance, Russell leaped half out of the water and grabbed at a piece of iron wreckage which projected over the side. Succeeding in this, he then got his hands round a dangling rope, and was able, breathless with exhaustion, to haul himself on board again. His wife still had hold of Catherine Margaret, but the little girl of two-and-a-half had been washed out of her grasp and was lying on the deck, sobbing. And yet another wave was building up to seaward. James Russell made a frantic dive for his little daughter, his hand held out; he had just touched her shoulder when the wave burst upon them with all its appalling fury. The little girl was swept out of his grasp like a leaf in a mountain stream, buried under the crushing weight of water; and Russell found himself once more carried clean over the side into the sea.

The waves swept him backwards and forwards, in spite of his useless struggles; he clutched out desperately at something he felt in the water, but it was only a piece of canvas, and would not support him. Then he felt seaweed under his feet, the receding wave leaving him face down on the rock a moment afterwards, spluttering out some of the water he had gulped, and feeling sick. A man was running down towards him, with outstretched hands, in a rescue attempt, but as he grasped Russell's fingers the next wave burst and separated them. Behind it came an even mightier wave, which picked him up and washed him higher. Again his hand was grasped, and this time held. Limp, unresisting, James Russell was drawn up to safety.

When, after a minute or two, he was able to force himself up to a sitting position, Russell found that he was on a rock high above the waves. His eyes turned desperately seaward towards the half-buried stern of the *Royal Charter*, on which the seas were breaking and bursting high. There was not a living soul on it.

In that minute when Russell had been washing between ship and shore, the few figures still huddled on the stern section had been either washed overboard or made an attempt to reach the rocks. Samuel Grenfell, the Cornish goldminer, dropped off into the water only when 'the deck was down to the water's edge.' With two other miners, both friends of his, he had been hanging from a rope dangling from an empty davit; as they hung there, swaying, they were arguing about what to do. Captain Taylor was only a few feet from them, and they heard him say to the few passengers left, 'The *Royal Charter* is all right; you will soon be saved.' Then a wave struck them all, completely burying them, tearing Grenfell from the rope and from his companions, whom he never saw again. The violent back-wash sucked him in under the overhang of the hull, and Grenfell pushed frantically at the iron plates in an effort to avoid being trapped.

He had a hard struggle to the shore, impeded by floating wreckage which, as it bobbed up and down, got in his way and struck him about the head and shoulders; he records that the surf was full of this wreckage and of struggling people. He grasped a rope which was thrown out to him from the rocks, and was hauled up. Under him, at that moment, he saw scores of passengers struggling in the surf on the edge of the rocks. One of these people was certainly Russell, for there now took place the final act of the drama, unseen by Russell, as he was being dragged out of the water semi-conscious.

It was witnessed, however, by the Reverend Stephen Roose Hughes, rector of Llanallgo Church, who had just come hurrying down to the site of the wreck to render assistance. Standing at the scene of the disaster two months later, with Charles Dickens, the novelist, who was also one of the finest reporters of the century, the Rector gave his version of the last minutes of the *Royal Charter*; and Dickens subsequently recorded it in his book, *The Uncommercial Traveller*. 'As they stood in the leaden morning, stricken with pity, leaning hard against the wind, their breath and

The Rev Stephen Roose Hughes. *Photo : courtesy of Mrs Fraser, of Altrincham*

104

vision often failing as the sleet and spray rushed at them from the ever forming and dissolving mountains of sea, and as the wool which was part of the vessel's cargo blew in with the salt foam and remained upon the land when the foam melted, they saw the ship's life-boat put off from one of the heaps of wreck; first, there were three men in her and in a moment she capsized, and there were but two; and again, she was struck by a vast mass of water, and there was but one; and again, she was thrown bottom upward, and that one, with his arm stuck through the broken planks, and waving as if for the help that could never reach him, went down into the deep.'

What he was witnessing was the death of Captain Taylor. But, doubtless because of the low visibility, and because there was so much to see, going on simultaneously, in front of him, the Rector presented no very coherent picture. At that moment, two people who had been in the boat, second steward Thomas Cormick and James M'Cappin, second class passenger, were still alive, very close under the rocks in the raging surf, and probably invisible from where the Rector stood. Their narratives, taken together, tell us exactly what happened.

Cormick's arrival on deck had coincided with a wave which had rolled him down to the lee side, where he saw Captain Taylor and a lady, possibly Mrs Marks, lying prostrate and trapped. Cormick went to the stern of the forward boat on the poop, abreast of the stump of the mizzenmast, got hold of a belaying pin, put a rope round it, and let himself down slowly into the water. He climbed up onto some spars and for several minutes rode them astride as waves washed him back and forth on the lee side of the hull.

Captain Taylor lay trapped for a time, 'exposed to every wave that broke over the ship,' according to M'Cappin. When he was freed, the Captain called out to Andrew Cowie, the Second Officer, 'I won't go ashore without you.' Cowie then began to lower a boat on the port side, telling Captain Taylor to get in and that he would be safe enough. 'Captain Taylor was shedding tears at the time, and was much excited,' said M'Cappin. He had reason to be. Apart from a captain being automatically responsible for what happens to his ship, he had promised his passengers that they would all walk safe ashore, and he had just watched hundreds of them drown. Tragically, it was not his fault, merely an evil run of bad luck from start to finish, with every decision, however sound, leading inexorably to this terrible ending on the rocks of Moelfre. His ship and his career alike ruined, the last thing Captain Taylor was thinking of was his own personal survival.

M'Cappin, however, was very much concerned to save his life; he went and held the thwarts of the boat as Cowie and Captain Taylor got into it. Another wave, passing right over the wreck, struck them at this moment and totally disorganised the launching. The deck by then must have been almost submerged, for the wave carried overboard, not merely M'Cappin, Cowie and the Captain, but the boat as well. As they kicked up to the surface, Captain Taylor rose almost alongside Thomas Cormick, who was still riding the piece of wreckage. The steward seized him and pulled him onto one of the spars. One of them, it seems to have been Captain Taylor, gasped out, 'There's hope yet.' Then the next wave knocked him off his hold, and he fell back into the water. Cormick grabbed him again, and then saw that the boat, now torn loose from the davits, was riding empty towards them.

Cormick hauled himself over the gunwale, then leaned over the side to grasp Andrew Cowie, pulling him in as well. M'Cappin was next to come aboard; after him, Captain Taylor. They were only a few yards from the rocks, with Cormick up in the bow and Cowie sitting in the stern; probably, Captain Taylor was lying exhausted on the floorboards, which would explain why the Rector thought he saw only three people in the boat. Right ahead of them, washing in the surf, M'Cappin saw a young man, a fellow-passenger he knew well; three times the young man was thrown up on the rocks, and three times he was drawn back by the tumultuous sea. Then the lurching, waterlogged boat, sluggishly riding a giant wave, was dashed down, bow first upon that iron shore.

It shattered instantly. Cormick, in the bow, was thrown out towards the rocks; his last view of it was as the wreckage went back down the slope, in the boiling surf, with Cowie still in it. M'Cappin saw Captain Taylor and Cowie struck by the wreckage, as the boat came apart under them; 'both of them,' he said, 'instantly disappeared.' For several minutes more, Cormick and M'Cappin were washed about, up and down the jagged rock face, until, one after the other, they were grabbed by George Suaicar, the boatswain's mate, leading a little group of rescuers.

The after part of the *Royal Charter*, weighed down by the engines and machinery, had been the first to go under. The forepart of the ship, which was lighter, and to which the hawser was secured, was the last to go, and one of the last to escape from there was a passenger from Bradford, Christopher Anderson. 'At this moment the forepart broke up lengthways on the deck. As the deck inclined to the sea the side of the ship was resorted to by a great number of passengers, it being more easy to hold on to, because the position was nearly horizontal. This side of the ship split lengthways, and the whole of the remaining part was carried back into the water and thrown up by the waves onto the stationary piece, and both sank immediately.

'Every soul was now in the water!

'Preparatory to the breaking up of this last portion, I, with a few others, prepared for the final struggle by throwing off all our spare clothing. After struggling for some time, amongst fragments of the ship, I was thrown onto the rocks, and three times over was borne back by the waves. The fourth time I was rescued by a kind old man, who had waited the opportunity of laying hold of me, and who had secured me from the force of the returning wave.

'Those passengers who were swept from the vessel early, or who, in despair, threw themselves into the water, were dashed by the violence of the waves against the face of the rocks and fearfully mutilated, the water being too low to allow of their being thrown onto the top of it.'

Anderson was probably among the last to be saved, but there were at least a dozen still to die. M'Cappin saw them clustered thickly round a single spar which was bobbing in the water over the spot where the *Royal Charter* had been. The shattered hulk was now visible only when a wave receded, when it took on the shape of two huge, half-tide rocks. It was against one of these that they met their end. 'A wave,' said M'Cappin, 'dashed them with terrible violence against the side of the ship; there were masses of timber heaped above them.' The spar and its human cargo vanished in the frothing water and welter of wreckage. When the wave subsided, the wreckage was still there, but the human heads were not.

*   *   *

All who were going to be saved had now been saved. The bodies still rolling in the surf were lifeless, obviously so; although one child, a little girl, did reach the shore with breath still in her body, only to die within minutes from her injuries. It was Catherine Margaret Russell, elder daughter of James Russell. There was nothing now to do but identify the dead. James Ferris helped to do so, once he had put on the dry clothes brought down to the beach by the kindly villager, Captain Copeland. M'Cappin was another who was re-clothed on the spot by these poor people. While he was dressing, Ferris walked along the rocks, looking at the bodies. Many were unrecognisable. 'Some were minus the head, arms, or legs; in other instances the skull had been dashed in, the brains protruding, or the limbs had been frightfully crushed.' But Ferris was able to identify a Mr King, of Hull; Thomas Taylor, of Stockport, another passenger; and the old lady whose husband had been killed in a gunfight at the gold diggings.

It was with a slowly dawning horror that the little group of survivors on the rocks looked at each other, or made enquiries about those who had already been carried away, because of their injuries, to the cottages over the hill in Moelfre. Could there really be so few? Were they really

The disaster scene at high water, September, 1960. Had the *Royal Charter* grounded in the white shingle bay, almost everyone might have got safely ashore in the morning. Instead, she struck on the rocky headland, dooming the ship and nearly all aboard. *Photo : Alexander McKee*

all that were left alive from the *Royal Charter*?

It was never exactly established how many passengers the clipper had carried that October night. The ship's papers had perished with her. The crew numbered more than 100, without including the 11 riggers taken on board off Bardsey Island. Probably some 390 passengers embarked in Australia, of whom about 14 got off at Queenstown. At the end, in all there must have been aboard almost 500 men, women, and children of whom around 40 survived. All of them men.

Not a woman survived, not a single child was still alive. The officers had been wiped out. The only two remaining members of the crew who held any rank at all were George Suaicar, boatswain's mate, and William Foster, the carpenter.

But of all the terrible scenes enacted that morning, none matched the moment when James Russell, stumbling about the shore in despair, came across the body of his elder child. 'It was a heartrending sight to witness that bereaved father carrying in his arms his dead offspring up the rocky heights to Moelfre,' wrote A. and J. K. 'We saw the little innocent in one of the cottages, carefully wrapped in a white sheet; it looked as if sleeping peacefully.'

But it was only as the survivors, one by one, were led away up the hill, and looked backwards to the wreck, that they saw the real irony of the tragedy. Two hundred yards to the eastward of that dreadful shelf of rock which had taken so many lives, was a small shingle beach. Had the *Royal Charter* struck at that point, instead of where she did, she would most probably not have broken up, but would have remained intact until the hurricane had passed and all aboard could indeed have walked ashore. Even if, by some chance, she had broken up, passengers and crew would have been washed up onto a gently sloping shingle beach, and been able to pull themselves beyond reach of the sea; probably almost all would have survived. If the existence of that beach had even been known, some of the swimmers at any rate might have been able to reach it, for the current was flowing in that direction.

As a local historian, R. R. Williams, has written in his study *Anglesey and the Loss of the 'Royal Charter'*,

> . . . the tragedy appeared inexplicable to the public and uncanny in its circumstance. In her final struggle for survival every command that her master gave, every turn of the wheel and every stroke of the engine only brought her on to a track and into a position expertly calculated, as it were, for her utter destruction and the death of all who sailed in her.

But above all, it was the complete wiping out of every woman and child aboard that sent a chill through the nation, and caused furious questions to be asked; that, and the terrible suspicion that the tiny village of Moelfre was grown suddenly rich with gold pilfered from the hundreds so pitifully drowned.

Chapter 10

THE VILLAGE THAT BECAME RICH

The *Royal Charter* was down and finished, but the hurricane was not. It was a day of storm and wreck over large parts of the British Isles. The London mail was five hours late in reaching Plymouth; the South Devon railway was impassable, in four places; between Bexhill and Hastings, in Sussex, 250 yards of the line had been washed away, and the sea had broken into the town of Worthing, reaching the town hall; at Flint, a brand new chemical works had been destroyed, a tall chimney being felled like a tree and the buildings themselves crumpling up; off Hartlepool, 45 ships were driven ashore, five of them a total loss.

But it was in the west that the damage was worst, marking the direct northward track of the '*Royal Charter* Gale'. Rail communications in Devon were disrupted for weeks afterwards, and there was severe flooding. Where the line from Teignmouth to Exeter skirted the sea, it was protected by a wall three feet across at the top which sloped down to a massive base faced with granite blocks; the hurricane treated it like shingle, strewing the railway tracks with blocks of granite weighing many tons. The river Teign overflowed, so that farms became islands in an inland sea, with ricks and barns sticking out of the raging water; and road traffic was almost entirely suspended. The sea wall near Dawlish was virtually dismantled by the breakers, its height being lowered by some five or six feet; slabs of over a ton in weight were flung inland contemptuously, like pebbles. At Totnes the streets in the lower part of the town became rivers navigable only by boats, while real rivers, like the Dart, swelled to unimaginable proportions.

Moving north over Devon and Cornwall, the hurricane struck Wales. List after list came in, of stricken vessels lost or damaged—not only at sea, but in harbour, or even on the stocks. The *Pride of Anglesey*, of Amlwch, damaged; the *Margaret*, of Bangor, damaged; the *Alma*, of Aberystwyth, much damaged; the *Elizabeth*, of Hull, very much damaged, her stern completely beaten in; the *Nell*, of Aberystwyth, stranded and much damaged, mate drowned; the *Equity*, of Amlwch, sunk, and almost a complete wreck; the *Messenger*, of Caernarvon, foundered, crew and boat missing; the *Ann and Susan*, of Bangor, ashore; unknown schooner, off Porthor, sunk, all hands lost. There were many such lists, 20, 30, 40 ships in every one. They were known, but what of those which had gone down during the night, out of sight of land, or on some desolate beach? The coasts were strewn with timber and wreckage from lost vessels. In many homes that day, and even more during the night that followed, women wondered if they would ever see their husbands or brothers again.

By 8 am the *Royal Charter* had gone from sight and, soon after, the shocked, shivering survivors, many of them streaming blood, some of them desperately injured, had been dispersed among the cottages of Moelfre. Outside, the sea thundered on the beach and the hurricane screamed overhead with unabated fury; indeed, the worst had yet to come, with the high tide at about 10 am. At nearby Llandudno, a reporter who worked for the *Caernarvon and Denbigh Herald* was struggling into his 'dreadnought' coat before venturing outside. He expected that the unusual combination of an NNE gale running directly into Liverpool Bay with the last quarter flow of the tide, would produce damage worth writing about; and he was not disappointed, as his subsequent report shows.

At 9.45 am, part of the railway, with a large proportion of the roadway of the New Pier erected this year, was carried away by a heavy wave; and shortly after this, about 10 o'clock, one grand wave swept over the pier from one end to the other, which for a second or two was completely concealed from view, and struck the timber with such violence as to cause a report like distant thunder, and to shake the earth under my feet, at a distance of nearly quarter of a mile. In another moment, piles, 30 feet long, sprang with great violence into the air, and the sea had made a complete breach through about one-third of the pier. At about high tide another wave swept over the inshore portion, and carried away about one-third more, with equal, if not greater force. The whole of the beach is covered with wreckage and the Esplanade with hundreds of tons of shingle and large pieces of rock. There is a vessel at this moment lying at anchor, about four miles from shore, without masts or rigging, with two men and a boy on board, and we have no life-boat or any craft fit to go out to them.

In Red Wharf Bay a few of the crew of the schooner which had stranded there during the night were still clinging to the rigging. No boat could put out to them, either. The cox of Moelfre life-boat, Rowland Hughes, saw the wreck being pounded there at 6.30 am, but could do nothing; an old villager of 81 told Hughes that never in his life had he seen such a sea as this. The men were saved only when the gale had abated and the tide had gone out, leaving the vessel half-beaten into the sand.

Had the *Royal Charter* struck there, or on any part of that wide stretch

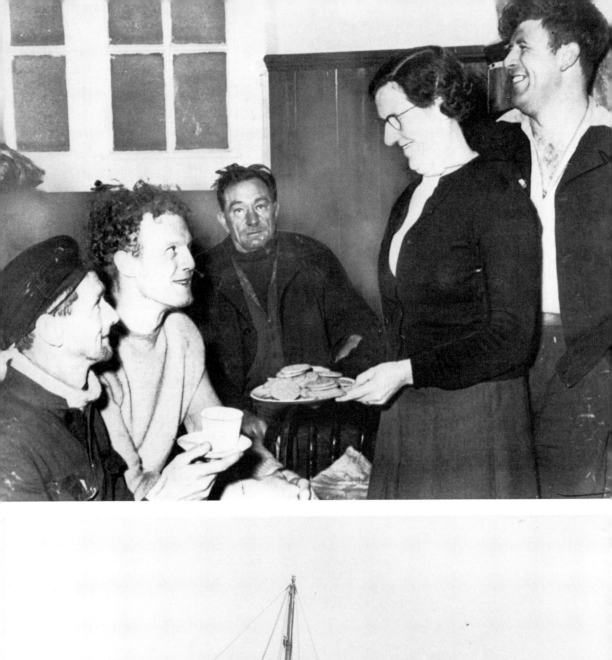

of sand, she might have become a constructive total loss, but all aboard would have survived. As it was, only one thing might have saved more lives—had the cutting away of the masts been delayed until she was driven up close to the rocks, they might have fallen ashore, bridging the gap. It was only a thin chance, for the hull had been pounding violently and they might have gone right overboard; but, because Captain Taylor was wrongly informed as to the tide and was unaware of the nature of the seabed, it was apparently not considered.

However, a much greater disaster even than that of the *Royal Charter* now seemed imminent. The 19,000-ton monster *Great Eastern*, anchored in open sea off Holyhead but partly protected by the lie of the land, had been uncoverd by the steady shift round of the wind to the north; by 9 am she was rolling wildly in a heavy sea from the beam. At 10 am her master, Captain Harrison, decided that there was no alternative but to raise the starboard anchor and then to re-lay it in a position nearer the breakwater, keeping the port anchor down meanwhile.

The great iron ship began to move ahead through the wreck-strewn water, the screw thrashing astern and the anchor cable rattling in through the hawse hole at the bow. Abruptly, the screw stopped, fouled by wreck-age. Captain Harrison ordered the steam power to be transmitted to the paddles instead, in spite of the risk of damage, and the starboard anchor was eventually let go again in a more suitable position. She was now held by one anchor and by the screw which had been re-started and was forcing her forward and so easing the strain on the single cable. But the beam sea, which was sweeping over and past the breakwater with irresistible force, was making the great ship roll violently and uncontrollably. The sea was nothing like so terrible as that encountered by the *Royal Charter*, a sea which had nothing to obstruct its progress for 140 miles; but, even in the lee of Anglesey, it was still powerful enough to nullify the effect of the *Great Eastern's* engine, to overcome it, and to force her bodily astern. The port anchor cable kept tautening more and more. 'At about 10.30 am,' recorded the correspondent of *The Times*,' it sprang up like a

Survivors from the *Hindlea*, after rescue by Dick Evans and his crew on 27 October, 1959, with winds gusting to 104 mph. At one point, the life-boat was swept up onto the deck of the 506-ton ship. For his success, Dick was awarded the gold medal of the RNLI, the lifeboatmen's VC. The faces of the survivors mirror the ordeal they had all endured. *Photo: Liverpool Daily Post & Echo*

The old reserve life-boat, the *Edmund and Mary Robinson*, in which Dick Evans carried out the *Hindlea* rescue, far better able to cope with fierce seas than the rowing boat of a hundred years earlier. *Photo: courtesy RNLI.*

cord out of the water, and in another moment the *Great Eastern* was adrift, rolling and tumbling like a drunken ship towards the shore.'

Like Captain Taylor before him, Captain Harrison was forward, personally supervising the work at the anchors. But he had a trump card to play. Lower starboard anchor and go full steam ahead with the screw, he ordered. This was done, but even so, it seemed for several minutes that nothing could stop the *Great Eastern* on her road to destruction. Then the screw began to take effect and, as it did so, it was fouled by an immense mass of wreckwood, and the machinery came to a shuddering stop. There was no time to wait for the waves to wash away the wood; the steam power was instantly diverted to turn the paddle wheels. They churned up the wreck-strewn water; the floats were damaged, the iron work of the wheels bent, but they continued to revolve. As soon as the screw was cleared, the paddles were stopped, and the screw restarted; when the screw stopped again, the paddles were brought into action . . . the whole exhausting process was continually repeated until about noon, when the force of the gale moderated and the *Great Eastern*, once more secured by two anchors, was riding with her head to the sea, but still pulling and tugging like a nervous horse.

'In this last struggle,' wrote the man from *The Times*, 'some of the links of the chain were actually dragged out one-third longer, and one which passed under the sharp bows of the vessel was bent nearly double. The cable on the port bow was then hove in, when it was found that the shank of the anchor, after bending considerably, had been torn in half about a foot below the crown, showing both good anchor and good holding ground.' It needs little imagination to visualise what had happened to the anchor cables of the unfortunate *Royal Charter*, exposed to forces still more monstrous and elemental.

At 12.30 the Rhyl life-boat was alerted for one of the few successful rescue attempts of the day. Coastguards sighted an unknown schooner driving onshore with the gale, only a topsail set and no flag flying; ignoring signals indicating the entrance to the river and safety, she drove straight on to the beach, her crew taking to the rigging as fearful seas swept over her deck. The wreck signal was flown from the Coastguard Station and the Life-boat house, where a crowd assembled to help in the launching. The life-boat, on its wheeled carriage, was driven out behind a team of horses and taken down to the beach opposite the wreck; and the horses were driven into the breakers, until the boat floated off. By 1.30 pm she was tossing alongside the wreck, rising on the wave crests high above the vessel's rail. The ship was the *Oriental*, 84 tons, of Lancaster, and her crew of five men and a boy were all saved; but when the gale subsided, there was nothing left of her above water.

In the foreground, the stony bay where the *Royal Charter* might have survived
long enough for the passengers to escape in daylight. Off the headland, the
salvage craft of the 1985 expedition moored over the wreck. And beyond, the
sandy bay of Traeth Lligwy where the clipper could have run aground safely.
Low water in September, 1985. *Photo: Alexander McKee*

Even in the Mersey the storm was felt with extraordinary violence. Here
it did not reach its height until between 11 am and 12.30, later than at
Moelfre and Holyhead. Then the river became a sheet of spray with
visibility reduced at times to half a mile. The blind force of the wind drove
up the tide four feet beyond its expected level and maintained it there,
despite the ebb, for three-quarters of an hour. Liverpool Observatory
recorded a wind force of 28 lbs to the square foot. This exceeded anything
previously recorded, the nearest being 27 lbs pressure during a gale the
previous July; the nearest to that was 24 lbs, registered in December, 1855.
The ferry service across the river was suspended, and tenders serving the
ships were unable to venture out to them. Two large vessels were prevented
from sailing—the screw-steamer *North American*, bound for Canada with
90 passengers, mail and cargo; and the screw-steamer *City of Baltimore*,
bound for New York with 225 passengers and mail. There was another
large vessel in port, the Australian clipper *White Star*, which was lying,
deeply laden, off Prince's pier. As early as 10 am she began to drag her
anchors. Rolling heavily, she was driven up-river to Bromborough and
then beyond the tail of the Devil's Bank. In the course of her wild and

uncontrollable ride she smashed into the *Gladiator*, a Bombay-bound ship, carrying away bulwarks, anchors, and chain, and brought up alongside HMS *Hastings*, the Mersey guardship, lying off Rock Ferry, both ships being damaged in the process. Captain Mends, of HMS *Hastings*, who was very soon to be involved in the *Royal Charter* affair, recorded the wind in the Mersey as Force 10 at this time, approximately 1.15 pm.

There was no news yet, in Liverpool, of the fate of the *Royal Charter*, hourly expected in the Mersey. North Wales was cut off, both the railway and the telegraph line having been broken in a number of places; at several points on that low-lying coast trains were at a standstill, finding the line ahead obstructed or washed away altogether. The looming mountains of the interior were white with snow, and passengers from coaches trapped in the drifts were struggling on foot towards the nearest shelter. The telegraph was restored later in the day, but it took some time to repair the railway. At one point, there was graphic evidence of the fury of the gale, for a small sailing ship was lying wrecked in a field to the south of the railway track, having been washed clean over the line.

* * *

In Anglesey itself, however, the news spread fairly rapidly. Mr Wagstaffe, a Liverpool Councillor, was in Beaumaris that morning when he heard a rumour of a large vessel ashore near Moelfre, some twelve miles distant by road. He called on the Customs-house agent and was shown a message which had just been received—'The *Royal Charter* is on shore; 400 passengers drowned.' By 1 pm, together with some friends, he was on his way to Moelfre. It must have taken him some hours to get there, for the village lies off the beaten track, and even today there is no road anywhere near the wreck, the nearest being a rough path leading down to a caravan site. They dismounted in the village and went by footpaths over the back of the headland, clambering over stiles and low walls of weathered grey stones until they were in view of the cliff edge on the other side—a terrible journey for the badly injured who had been carried up this path a few hours before. As they walked along the cliff edge, looking down, there was still no sight of any large vessel by the shore. So they went across the fields behind the shingle beach of Porth Helaeth, and up a little hill, and in the last field before the rock ledges began, they found their first sign of the disaster—the body of a man dressed in corduroy trousers and a pea jacket, the head matted with blood under a piece of cloth which had been laid over the dead face. There was one last stile to scramble over, and, as he jumped down on the other side, Mr Wagstaffe found that his hands had become smeared with blood—mute evidence of the human wreckage which the villagers had so recently carried that way. Then he was standing on the rocks above the wreck.

There were only a few twisted fragments showing above the surface, at that state of the tide, but they were so near the shore that Mr Wagstaffe felt that he could have thrown a coin over them. Nor was he mistaken. When, two months afterwards, Charles Dickens came down to the same spot, he did actually toss a coin over the remnants of what had been one of the finest fast passenger liners afloat.

The rocks were crowded with people, all working busily, digging into crevices, shifting the wreckage strewn there, and the piles of clothing. Virtually the whole population of Moelfre was there, together with visitors from villages and towns within a radius of ten miles or so. Mr Wagstaffe did not notice them particularly at that moment, for he was too impressed by the air of tragedy and disaster. One man, however, caught his attention, for he 'was rambling about the shore more like a maniac than anything else'. Wagstaffe spoke to him and found that he was one of the passengers; although the man did not give his name, it is clear from what he said that it was James Russell, nearly demented at the sudden, unbearable sweeping out of existence of his wife and two little girls. He had taken the body of his daughter to the cottage of Mr and Mrs Robert Lewis, who were also looking after Henry Carew Taylor, and had now returned

The wreck of the *Royal Charter* at low water, with iron plating littering the rocks on which the hurricane smashed the hull as if on an anvil. *Photo: source unknown*

to the scene where he had lost his loved ones. His blind grief was to have its repercussions in the village that night, and later, at the Coroner's Inquest. Penniless, wifeless, childless, all in one stroke, there had to be a cause. Somebody must have been at fault.

Wagstaffe then spoke to two men whom he described as Cornish miners—presumably the two friends, Samuel Grenfell, of St Ives, and Thomas Bowden, of Torquay—and to another man who described himself as William John Ferris, storekeeper from Ballarat. From what was to happen later, we can well imagine the note of complaint in Ferris' voice, as he told how those on board 'set the bay on fire' with signals of distress, in the hope of obtaining assistance from the shore; and yet they had received no help. Here was someone else looking for a scapegoat. The only attempt at rescue, went on Ferris, was made by a coloured man who swam ashore with a hawser—and he pointed to a heavy manila rope lying on the rocks, one end submerged in the sea.

Sticking out of the waves was what appeared to be a portion of the screw and something else nearby, which was pointed out to Wagstaffe as being the bullion chest containing the gold. All these details were highly fanciful, no doubt, but it was obvious that the hundreds of people thronging the shore knew that the wreck was of a treasure ship, literally rich with gold. Lying high and dry on shore were the masts and twisted fragments of iron, distorted by the hammer blows of the sea; and a part of the deck, about five yards square, was lying in a pool of water. Indeed, there was so much scattered detail to take in that Mr Wagstaffe became a little confused, but it was soon clear to him and his friends that many of the villagers were definitely searching for something. 'We saw a number of people busily looking amongst the stones, and when we asked what they were looking for, they replied: "For gold." We were told that one man had picked up a bag containing 100 sovereigns, and that altogether £200 or £300 in gold had been recovered.'

This must have been a masterly understatement, for the villagers had been on the scene since daybreak, eight or nine hours ago. The Rector, Stephen Roose Hughes, had been there fairly early, but he could not look everywhere at once on that jumbled, rocky shore.

The Customs-house agent from Beaumaris, Mr W. H. Smith, had now arrived at the site of the wreck, possibly a little before Mr Wagstaffe, who recognised him. Mr Smith was standing a little apart, making notes, taking the names of those people who brought him gold or articles of value which they had picked up; superficially, it was a picture of order and propriety. But when Mr Wagstaffe looked closely at the actors in each little drama, instead of, impossibly, trying to grasp the whole scene at once, he saw something very different. 'I saw a man bringing two sovereigns, and he seemed to part with the money very unwillingly. A photograph likeness was picked up by a man who was about to appropriate it to himself, when he was observed, and he was obliged to hand it over to the Customs-house agent.' Wagstaffe then saw that about twenty men, all villagers, were being employed by Mr Smith, who was Receiver of Wreck as well as Collector of Customs for the Port of Beaumaris, to take charge of the property which had been washed up; but the gold was taken only to Mr Smith, who gave a receipt for it.

Even at this late hour, and under the eyes of Mr Smith, the collection of sodden clothing amid the rocks gave excellent cover for the unnoticed pilfering of gold, as well as excuse for the search, and anyway, the pockets might contain gold. Another responsible witness, who must have come down to the shore on the heels of Mr Wagstaffe, also thought that, while Mr Smith was doing all that one man could do, it was not nearly enough. This new visitor was Mr J. H. Gregory, a solicitor, also from Liverpool. 'It is to be hoped,' he wrote that evening, 'that a competent staff of either coastguard or military will be immediately despatched to the scene of the disaster, to protect as much as possible so valuable a cargo, which, so far as the passengers' gold is concerned, is very much scattered about. I saw men picking sovereigns out of the holes of the rocks, as they would shellfish.'

Gregory closely examined a photograph picked up, probably the same one which was so nearly appropriated by the finder. 'In the midst of fragments of massive ironwork, with fearful evidence of violence and death all around, there was found perfect and unbroken on the rocks a small photograph, the portrait of a lady and gentleman, both young and evidently of superior position. The Collector of Customs at Beaumaris, who, today, is the principal person in authority at the wreck, carries the photograph in his hand, and compares it with the lineaments of the dead washed up, but as yet without having succeeded in establishing the identity of either of the originals.'

Mr Wagstaffe, soon oppressed by the atmosphere of despair and utter waste that clung to the rocks, began to stumble up the hill away from the wreck; on his way, he passed again by the dead man lying in the field. There were now a few people standing by the body, doing nothing. Wagstaffe spoke to one of them, who said he was the church warden of the parish, asking what they intended. 'I cannot get the people here to do anything,' replied the warden, adding viciously, 'It is not likely you will get them to assist you unless they are paid for it.' The reason for the body's lying so strangely where it was, as if suddenly abandoned, now became less hard to seek. Judging by the fresh blood on the stile, the man had probably been alive when taken from the sea but had died in the villagers' arms as they carried him up the hill. So they had left him there. It was

A portrait photograph found, still in its frame, by the Royal Charter Salvage Expedition in the 1970s. The photograph itself had reverted to a negative image, but after conservation work the positive print on the right was achieved. *Photos: RCSE Ltd/Ken Jones*

no light matter to carry a heavy man up from the scene of the wreck to Moelfre; it might take a number of men an hour's hard work. For an injured survivor, the villagers were only too willing to work their hearts out, and to surrender even their beds and their scanty stock of spare clothes; the inhabitants of almost any fishing village would have done the same, it was traditional. But a corpse was only an encumbrance, beyond all earthly help. It could hardly weigh against the second, unspoken tradition of a fishing village—that everything thrown up by the sea is theirs by right. So when the man died, they had left him and gone down again to the rocks, where the treasure was.

Not all, however, had done this, for at that moment Wagstaffe saw a party of villagers struggling up the path with a corpse. 'Of all the frightful sights I ever witnessed I never saw anything like this,' he wrote. 'Both legs were broken about a foot above the ankle; and his feet, which hung only by the skin, had been bent backwards, and tied to keep them together. The bones were visible, his head was twisted round, and his bowels protruded. Another body we noticed with half the head off. One ear was hanging down, and the brain had been washed out.' When doctors at last arrived and carried out post mortems, they began slowly to realise the horrifying fact that very few indeed of the *Royal Charter's* passengers and crew had been drowned; they had been pounded to death on the rocks.

But there was no doctor on the scene yet. The first doctor to arrive did not reach Moelfre until midnight; he was Mr A. Hughes, surgeon, of Menai Bridge. Until then the badly injured, with broken bones, writhed in their beds, groaning for skilled help and for drugs, tended by the villagers as best they could.

Many bodies were coming ashore, not in the vicinity of the wreck, but along the line of the headland, carried there by the current running eastward into Liverpool Bay, or by the eddy of the outgoing stream. They had been found at once by the villagers, who knew by experience where to look. Noticing this, Wagstaffe and his companion went down to the beach. The first body they saw was of a young girl, clad in a black jacket and petticoat, 'her face very much cut with being knocked about among the rocks'. They judged the child's age as fourteen or fifteen, but there are indications that it was Jane Fowler, seventeen years old. The villagers were at that moment pulling ashore another body. 'It was identified to be that of the sailmaker—a fine, powerful fellow, who presented no marks of injury. There were some four or five bodies further on, but we did not go near them; in fact, our feelings were so harrowed that we would go no further, and we came away.'

The little party returned to Beaumaris, embarked in the steamer *Druid*, which was delayed several times by large masses of wreckage drifting about in the bay, and reached Liverpool at 8 pm with their sensational news of the disaster. But, while they had still been wandering about the rocks, the first official message had been telegraphed to Liverpool. It was from Commander M'Gregor, of the Anglesey Coast Guard, and it was addressed, for action, to Captain Mends, of HMS *Hastings*, the Mersey guard ship. Reports reaching M'Gregor admitted of no delay—'The inhabitants of the district are stripping and plundering the bodies to a shocking extent.' Mr Smith, Collector of Customs, had responsibility at the scene of the wreck, but no power. Captain Mends was to supply him with the necessary force to cordon off the area and control the operations. He at once packed a party of coastguardmen, with their kit, into a steam tender, and sent them direct to Moelfre, which they reached that evening. When subsequent developments showed this force to be insufficient, two days later a party of thirty Marines, under a lieutenant, were sent by rail to reinforce them. Commander M'Gregor called in also the local Coastguards and a party of Militia from Beaumaris; and very shortly after, an Army detachment from Chester was also called upon. Martial law was impending, in fact, if not in name.

As an afterthought, late that Wednesday evening, Commander M'Gregor telegraphed to Gibbs, Bright that their fine ship was a total loss; the owners were, therefore, unable to take any measures of their own until Thursday morning, when they sent their Marine Superintendent, Captain William Martin. Meanwhile, the press had already got hold of the story, reporters having reached Moelfre at about the same time as Mr Wagstaffe. They were local men from local papers, serving a seafaring area; they had to be clear and accurate, and they were.

At high water, they recorded, only the stumps of the masts were visible; but at low tide most of the wreck could be seen. It was in three sections, the largest being perhaps thirty or forty feet long. One section was obviously the bow—identified by the riding bitts, around which the broken anchor cables were still twisted. Another section, equally obviously, was the stern—identified by the wheel, now hanging upside down. The third portion lay between these—it was hardly more than a pile of ballast and iron a few feet high. This was where the hull had not merely split in two, but had shattered and crumbled up for some distance on either side of the break, trapping at least a hundred passengers in the wreckage, many of them women from the second class cabins. It was widely believed that most of them were still there, and the correspondent of the *Liverpool Courier* was told that several bodies had been seen tangled in the twisted ironwork.

But the first duty of the reporters was to find out what had happened, and why. They were presented with a confusing picture, because not a single officer remained alive to tell them of the reasons for the various decisions made during the gale; even the two ship captains aboard as passengers were among the missing. They sat up late that night, in the cottages where the survivors were being housed, and took statements. Joseph Rodgers, the hero of the hour, would hardly talk at all. Suaicar, also Maltese, talked at great length, but he was speaking a foreign language; they may have misunderstood him. James Russell was half-crazed with grief; he had heard someone say that the Captain was drunk, and now he furiously repeated it. They noted that, with some reservations; and some of them heard, or thought they heard, a murmur of agreement from Suaicar and the carpenter, Foster. The survivors were, of course, all tremendously shocked and excited, having passed through a staggering experience; and a number of them had been fortifying themselves at the Talyfron Inn, Moelfre's solitary pub. The rooms where the interviews took place were packed with dozens of people, with several often talking at once, too fast for a reporter to get it down, or even to note who said what;

Captain Thomas Hughes, of Cocyn Newydd, one of the heroic 'twenty-eight men' at the wreck site. *Photo: Gwynedd Archives Service*

and in the background a babble of Welsh from the equally excited villagers, few of whom could speak English. Confusion was not only possible, but inevitable.

Because of the language barrier, one story which they failed to get was that of the heroism of the twenty-eight villagers, drawn from the great crowd down by the shore, who had at the risk of their lives carried out the rescues and without whom perhaps no more than two or three people would have survived. They also failed to appreciate, at first, the really big question being pondered all around them—the fate of the bullion room.

The gold that had been picked up on the shore, declared or not declared, was a mere bagatelle compared to the worth of the ingots and coin that had been there—over £322,000 of consigned gold and bags holding many thousands of pounds deposited for safe keeping by the wealthier passengers. Was it, or was it not, torn open to the sea? What had been so far washed up was enough to make poor villagers rich for a few years; but what lay in the strongroom went beyond all this. The aftermath of the storm might that day, or that night, or on succeeding days and nights, shower that desolate shore with wealth. For every lobster they had been accustomed to catch, the fishermen might now draw up a gold bar—and every gold bar was worth more than £100. The gold fever that drew men out to the Australian diggings was as nothing compared to the excitement that swept Moelfre that Wednesday night. For it was the men of Moelfre who knew, as no stranger could, just where the sea was likely to bring forth its glittering harvest.

They knew where wreckwood always came ashore, where bodies would be likely to come ashore; where gold might lie in shallow water or in rock crevices exposed as the tide went down; and those places where the shingle had been piled high by the storm. They knew, and no one else did. Some of these were not obvious places, they were not in the semi-guarded vicinity of the wreck, but half-a-mile and more away. We may be sure that that was where they went during the night and in the early morning; and later, ten to fourteen days later, when the bloated corpses were likely to rise from the seabed and drift with the currents into the places, the secret places, where the driftwood was always to be found.

We cannot know just how successful they were, but it is a fact that when, in after years, some puzzled youngster would ask why old captain so-and-so owned so many cottages, when his own dad was so poor, the reply would be a wink, and a grin, and the knowing words, 'Ah, that's the *Royal Charter*, me boy.'

Chapter 11

'SO STRANGELY BROUGHT TOGETHER'

By Thursday morning it was known in Liverpool that the *Royal Charter* was lost; crowds thronged all likely centres of information—the Underwriters' Room, the Exchange News-room, the offices of Gibbs, Bright. But until 1 pm there was not even a list of survivors. The owners themselves did not know; they had despatched Captain Martin to Moelfre in a steam-tug that morning to find out. The first list held only ten names—Ferris, Capper, Gundry, Taylor, Bradbury, Grenfell, Gapper, Judge, Russell, Dean. Later in the day came a fairly full list of the surviving members of the crew, including some of the Liverpool riggers who had boarded the ship off Bardsey Island. People who had never expected to be touched personally by the disaster found, to their horror, that they were involved.

The wife of James White, a surviving rigger, received a letter from him that day. 'Out of 500 there are only twenty saved,' he wrote, pessimistically. 'I am very much afraid that poor brother Henry is among the missing. My dear wife, kiss the children for me, and thank the Lord for his kindness and mercy. God help poor Sarah Ann if poor Henry does not turn up. Console her, my dear wife, as a sister can do. May God help the bereaved, and be all in all to them in need.'

When incomplete passenger lists were issued soon after, Mrs Bakewell of Manchester noticed a 'T. Bakewell' among them—her son's initial. Her first thought was to go to the scene of the wreck, to find out if it was indeed her son; John Bradbury was able to tell her that it was, and that he had not survived. The boy had intended to give his parents a surprise, by returning home unexpectedly; he could not have guessed how terrible the shock would be.

The lost gold caused nearly as much consternation as the lost lives, among the firms which had insured it; a Mr Thomas L. Pelling was deputed to take charge of it, when salvaged, and he was soon on the way to Moelfre. Meanwhile the Marine Superintendent of Gibbs, Bright, Captain William Martin, 'a bluff, out-spoken, well-informed jolly captain, evidently respected by those under his command,' according to Mr W. F. Peacock, who saw him during the salvage operations, was already standing on the rocks above the wreck. He had just seen to the welfare of the survivors, especially the badly hurt men, and was now surveying the beach. But he was not looking particularly jolly at this moment. There on the shore for all to see, washed up during Wednesday night, was an empty wooden box addressed to the 'Union Bank, London'. All speculation was ended. It was proof irrefutable that the strongroom had been torn open by the blind fury of the sea. It was possible, however, he told a reporter, that most of the gold boxes were still under the wreckage of the stern, where they might be recovered by diving operations. The unspoken question was, had the gold from the empty box been strewn over the seabed or was it now in some cellar in Moelfre?

Mr Pelling was afterwards to receive striking evidence of the demoniac strength of the storm, in the shape of a two-foot square of iron plate studded with golden sovereigns and half-sovereigns, which he delivered to Lloyd's at the Royal Exchange, London. 'The plate had quite the appearance of a quoiting pitch, all the coins being driven to a greater or less depth,' he wrote, unable to explain how the soft coins had been driven into the hard iron.

Captain Martin returned to Liverpool with his report at six o'clock that evening, bringing with him in the steam-tug *Reliance* those of the survivors who wished to go to Liverpool and were in a fit state to do so. There was an anxious crowd standing on the dock to greet them, scanning their faces in the hope of recognition. The tug had not even tied up when there was an outburst of sobbing from the quayside; 'the outbursts of grief were heart-rending,' wrote a local reporter. As the dozen or so ill-kempt men stumbled down the gangway, incongruous in borrowed clothing and with hardly a penny in their pockets, they were surrounded and jostled by a mass of people demanding to know the fate of relatives and friends. A well-dressed man and woman were brandishing portraits of a Mr Glover and his wife, asking if anyone knew them. One by one, they shook their heads. Then one man stopped and looked closely—'Mrs Glover! Yes, I knew her.' The couple's eyes lit up with hope. But the survivor shook his head. 'She's missing. But Mr Glover's all right, he wasn't on the ship. Stayed behind in Melbourne, so she told me.' Amid a sea of stricken faces, which included the relatives of Captain Taylor, the pitifully small group of survivors walked into the night.

Among them was James Ferris, who afterwards complained bitterly that Captain Martin left them stranded and destitute on the dock in the rain; a dock-gateman, however, took them to the Sailors' Home and a hospitable welcome. There may or may not have been truth in his accusation. A number of the passengers certainly harboured a grudge against the owners, and intended to make trouble.

Miss Stephens, sister of the Chief Officer, W. B. Stephens, was married in Liverpool that day; the news of the wreck was brought to the wedding breakfast.

Hope was not yet quite extinguished for the relatives, however. It was speedily obvious that this small group of survivors did not know exactly who had come safe ashore and who had not—for they were dispersed among various cottages in Moelfre, and a number had been left behind: the injured, and those who stayed of their own free will because they were waiting for their loved ones to be returned to them by the sea.

Next day, Friday, 28 October, the storm broke. The 'stripping and plundering of the bodies' was reported, and so were the emergency measures to guard the wreck. A reporter of the *North Wales Chronicle* had already seen proof enough to convince him. 'We have no doubt that there were many robberies perpetrated at this wreck,' he wrote. 'Yesterday (Thursday), we were shown some bills of exchange, printed in red ink, and drawn on the Union Bank of Australia, which had been taken from a drunken man, on the coach from Amlwch to Menai Bridge, which had evidently been stolen from the *Royal Charter*. There was one, 13 August, 1859, for £10, in favour of Henry Collings, and three, issued at Melbourne, on 20 August, 1859, in favour of William Hughes, for £200. The person who had them stated he had not been in Australia for three years.' The drunken man was unlucky, he was caught, presumably because he was drunk, during his getaway from Moelfre; but, although a stranger, visiting the wreck only for a short time, he had been able to rob two corpses undetected at the scene of the crime.

There was never any love lost between the English and the Welsh; when the English press, both national and local, got hold of the story, they wrote about 'plunderers of the wreck', 'horrible pilferers of corpses'; the *Daily Telegraph* demanded the death penalty for the 'greedy Cambro-British thieves'.

The effect of these sensational revelations on the relatives of the dead

How the news of the disaster reached the public. Headline from the *Liverpool Courier*, 29 October, 1859. *Photo: British Library*

TOTAL LOSS OF THE
ROYAL CHARTER,
AND 454 LIVES.

was appalling. They conjured up the possibility, perhaps probability, of the dear one as a corpse, white in the breakers, feverishly dragged to shore by thieving, pawing hands. There followed an almost insane rush to get to Moelfre, to see the worst, to know what had really happened there to daughter, son, husband, or wife, or whether—perhaps—they were not dead at all, but miraculously safe somewhere. To the groups of Coast-guards, Marines, and Militia proceeding with full kit to help in controlling the area, there was now added this rush of frantic mourners. The atmo-sphere at the last railway station, Bangor, was gloomy enough; it became sadder still as each train added to the crowds seeking road transport. 'Cabs, phaetons, and vehicles of every description were in great demand, and such a throng of people on the road to Moelfre was probably never before seen,' wrote the correspondent of a Liverpool paper, who travelled down on the Saturday.

Impatient as they were, a short journey would have been far too long; but the way to Moelfre was far longer than any of them had ever expected. The Liverpool reporter complained bitterly:

> We had to travel at least 15 miles, and that, too, over one of the most narrow, uneven, zig-zag roads that can well be imagined. Indeed, so hilly is this thoroughfare, that a great portion of it has to be walked over to save the horses from being over-fatigued. About midway between Bangor and Moelfre is situate the small village of Pentraeth, where there is a small inn, at which the weary traveller will be glad to stop a few minutes to refresh himself and his horse. On the route, a few pretty nooks are to be seen, but the country is almost devoid of trees to relieve the monotony of a somewhat flat, inhospitable-looking district, where the population is thin, and the houses of an exceedingly humble character, many of them being mere huts.

On they trudged, with the great hills of Snowdonia looming in the back-ground, across the other side of the Menai Strait, in Wales; but it was not until this day that they began to arrive at Moelfre in numbers, and to make for the church of Llanallgo, where most of the bodies were now being brought for identification and burial. As the days went on people came, not only from Liverpool, but from all over the British Isles, converg-ing on that little stone church above the sea. It seated about 100 people and was overshadowed by a rather formidable building, the home of the Rector, Stephen Roose Hughes. His brother, The Reverend Hugh Robert Hughes, was Perpetual Curate of Penrhoslligwy, a neighbouring parish. Llanallgo Church was even then very old, built on a site which had prob-ably been used for worship for a thousand years; to the Liverpool reporter it appeared little better than 'a barn, with a small belfry at one end supplying the place of a tower or spire'. The congregation had departed, and held their services in the school building nearby; even the pulpit had been moved out of the way. The floor of the church had now been given over to a silent company.

When Charles Dickens came there two months afterwards, the stones were still stained with the salt and sand of the sea; it was still possible for him to see where a head had lain, or a foot. When the Liverpool reporter arrived, they were there in fact—30 of them; with many more still to be brought up the steep paths from the sea, the Rector paying the villagers 10 shillings for each body.

A carriage clattered to a halt outside the church, and two men, obviously father and son, got out; the elder appeared to be about 70. They went slowly into the church, the reporter following behind. Clearly, they did not know if the person they were looking for would be there or not; they walked right in upon the bodies, and then stopped abruptly, as they saw what lay before them. A cry from the old man rang through the church. 'Oh, my son! Oh, my son, my son!'

After a quick glance had shown him that none of these pitiful remnants in the least resembled the son he sought, the old man turned round and stumbled out of the church, tears streaming down his face. There were murmurs of sympathy from the other mourners, some of whom began to sob. Even the reporter felt a quickly-stifled impulse to tears.

To avoid such scenes, the Rector and his wife soon began to adopt the practice of meeting the relatives outside the church and, obtaining a description of the man, woman or child they were looking for, make the search themselves; if successful, they would lead in the relatives blindfolded, letting them uncover only when they were standing by the body they sought. Even so, some fainted.

Worst of all was trying to answer the guileless letters sent to the Rector by relatives who could not afford to come to Moelfre, but asked him to identify a loved one for them by some all too human characteristic. 'My dearest brother had bright grey eyes and a pleasant smile,' wrote one young girl, her heart full of trust.

That Saturday afternoon, however, one very poor couple had made the journey all the way from Everton; the man explained that he was an unemployed seaman, looking for his son, John Plair, aged 22, a steward. 'Oh, sir,' exclaimed Mrs Plair to the reporter, 'he was a good and devoted boy. He sent a letter from Melbourne, stating that he had made £25 on the passage out, and expected to make about that sum on the passage home. Oh, he was a good boy, and always left us his half-pay.' The reporter scribbled it down, while the embarrassed husband tried to hush his wife,

The Rev Hugh Robert
Hughes. *Photo: courtesy of
Mrs Fraser, of Altrincham*

Llanallgo Church and
Rectory. The numbered
graves include Edwin
Fowler (1) and his daughter
Jane (2), Mr Russell's
daughter Catherine
Margaret (6), and the
Misses Davis, Sophia (8)
and Florence (69). From *The
Wreck of the Royal Charter* by
A. & J.K., Dublin, 1860.
*Photo: The National Maritime
Museum, London*

muttering, 'The Lord gave, and the Lord has taken away.' But she was not to be denied. 'Oh, he was a good boy, and his loss is fit to make my old heart break. The night before he was lost, I said–"Oh, I have two children in Heaven," but little did I think that the Lord had taken to himself my third and only son.' When Mr Plair explained that he had been a steward in the *Great Britain*, but was now looking for employment, his wife burst out with a cry of, 'Oh, dear, I'd rather you only got three shillings a week ashore than go to sea after this.' They were eventually comforted by finding, not the body, but a box belonging to their dead boy, with his name written on it.

Another mourner was Mrs Cowie, wife of the Second Officer, who had travelled from Ayrshire to be in Liverpool on Wednesday morning in time to meet her husband; the news of the disaster had come on her, she said, 'like a thunderclap'. The couple had two young children, five-year-old Peter and a baby, Jemima, of only three months. Accompanying her was James Cowie, her brother-in-law, serving as a seaman in HMS *Hastings*, who was later to die at sea of yellow fever and be buried at the Cape of Good Hope. His sister's husband, Captain Beamer, was to sail from Liverpool and, with his ship, disappear without trace. Mr Foster, proprietor of the Shakespeare Hotel in Manchester, was there also; the merry party held in the hotel to celebrate his wife's imminent return, had been blighted by reports of the loss of the ship. The body of Mrs Foster was not lying in the church, but her travelling companion, the handsome Mrs Woodruffe, was there, rigid and bruised, but 'lovely even in death'.

'Behind the pulpit and reading desk, under the belfry, as if too appalling for public gaze, lay two or three dreadfully mangled corpses, with the limbs torn away from their bodies, all covered over with hay and rugs washed from the wreck,' noted the reporter. 'The male adults were stretched in front of the pulpit, whilst the women and children were lying close to the communion rails. The head of the man, Samuel Henry, said to have been a maniac, was swollen to a most extraordinary shape and size, and was frightful to behold. Another body had the head completely torn away.' Among this mass of pulped humanity was the old Irish widow from Ballarat; Isaac Lewis, seaman, of Moelfre; Mrs Fenwick, who had given new shoes and stockings to her children to go ashore in; Mrs Marks, the Jewess who had been trapped on deck; John Smith, a boy of four whose parents were still missing; and Catherine Margaret Russell, one of James Russell's two young daughters. With set face, exhausted by grief, James Russell formally identified his own dead, and then turned to young John Smith and Mrs Woodruffe, both of whom he had known well. There would be a reckoning for this, he was determined.

His opportunity would come when the Inquest began on the following

131

Wednesday, 2 November. The formal opening had already taken place, in this church, the previous day. The Coroner of Anglesey, Mr William Jones, had stood at the communion table, beside the dead, while the jury were sworn; he had then gone to Penrhos Church, where he had charged the jury with the investigation into the circumstances of the bodies lying in that place also. All this had been in Welsh, and Russell had understood nothing of it, but an interpreter would be present from Wednesday on.

Meanwhile, the identification of the bodies, so far as was possible, proceeded. John O'Brien, a seaman who had got ashore by the hawser, recognised the body of the joiner, who had lent an axe to cut down the masts. The reporter could get little out of O'Brien, as he seemed 'quite oppressed with grief'.

Inside the church also was Samuel Edward Gapper, the New Zealand farmer, surrounded by a crowd of people anxious to hear about their relatives and the details of the disaster; many of them could not be restrained from talking at once, and Mr Gapper was turning this way and that before the barrage of questions.

'Yes, yes, I knew Mr Jenkins, he was a saloon passenger, a tall gentleman, who was accompanied by his wife and four children.'

'Yes, I knew Mrs Fenwick.'

'I knew Mr and Mrs Master, and the Misses Davis. I knew the Misses Davis very well; they were very fond of dancing. I knew the Reverend Mr Hodge; I saw him at the last prayer meeting. I attended it.'

'Yes, the ship would do nothing; in fact she was driven ashore like a log of wood.'

And then a personal question. 'How did you get saved?' a bystander asked him.

'By the interposition of Providence. I had Mrs Rose in my arms, determined to hold her to the last, when a tremendous sea broke over us, and we were separated. I was driven on the rocks, she was buried in the foaming waters. I intended to go back to New Zealand in three months; I cannot. I am so unnerved. My brain is all in a whirl. I am waiting to see if that lady will turn up, for I looked upon her as a sister.'

So Gapper stood inside the church, waiting for his lost love to come back to him from the sea, while from outside, instead of the ringing of bells, there was only the ring of spades on hard earth as the new graves were dug.

Gapper's waiting was not long. At that moment the young body of Mrs Rose, only 23 years old, was being brought up from the waves and laid on the shore, to await the villager's cart which would take her on her last ride to that churchyard where 'so many were so strangely brought together'.

Salvage operations on the wreck at high water. In the foreground are the three masts of the *Royal Charter*, and behind them a steam tug and three diving boats, with one diver about to go down. Compare with the photograph of the same scene taken at low water (page 117), with parts of the wreck fully exposed. From the *Illustrated Times*, 12 November, 1859. *Photo: British Library*

The whole area around the wreck was now sealed off, guarded day and night. There were Coastguards from Amlwch and Bangor, Militia from Beaumaris, and some Anglesey Police; but the bulk of the force was made up of the Coastguards and Marines from HMS *Hastings*, together with English Militia. There were now more English voices than Welsh. It was not merely martial law, but invasion, which the villagers took with dignity and unfailing politeness, in spite of the fact that their fishing, at the height of the season, had been disrupted. During the daytime, some 20 of them were employed in helping the military to guard the wreck; they were distinguished from ordinary civilians by bands of black cloth worn round one arm. For several days after the wreck, they could be seen collecting the gold, and bringing it up to the cottages by the bucketful to be officially handed in and counted. On Friday, 28 October, one of the guards, a man from HMS *Seamew*, made a significant find on the beach—a $7\frac{1}{2}$ lb bar of gold, worth nearly £300. It was further proof of the fate of the strongroom. Next day, Saturday, a tug, with divers aboard, anchored close to the wreck, and salvage operations began. In the evenings, Jenkins the diver became a familiar figure at the Talyfron Inn, distinctive with his heavy black beard and rich velvet vest. There, too, were usually to be found Captain Martin, in charge of salvage operations, Mr Smith, Receiver of Wreck, and a number of the crew of the *Royal Charter*, as well as some of the passengers, who were waiting to give evidence at the Inquest.

On the shore, half a mile away over the headland, a rough hut had been constructed out of the shattered timbers lying on the rocks; it had makeshift tables and seats, also fashioned from the remnants of the *Royal Charter*, and it served the invaders as a guardhouse. At night the glow of watch fires cast a strange light over the ill-fated spot, and gusts of boisterous laughter echoed among the rocks, as the men patrolling the shore kept up their courage by inventing stories, funny, fanciful, and fearful, to while away the time. The best of them they would relate to the villagers in the morning—tales of hearing screams from the sea and unearthly moanings in the night. For, the truth was, they were afraid.

So many had died here that every lap of the waves against the rocks reminded them of what lay in the sea at their feet. They could imagine shadows in the water, which were not shadows; and occasionally, indeed, some horrible thing would ground gently, bobbing, sodden and weed-strewn, at the edge of the tide. It was not hard to imagine that gaunt place haunted by the souls of the dead, saturated with violent grief. The feeling was intensified by the crowds of sobbing women and white-faced men who, by daylight, would toil over the headland and down to the rocks to seek some sign of their lost ones. The dead were not faceless here, but remembered by the living; and so remembered, still lived, not least in the imaginations of the men whose fate it was to guard that dreadful shore by night.

The number of military drafted to the spot was necessary, not only to guard the wreck, but to control the hordes of relatives and other sightseers who flocked down to the shore, and to check the opportunities for looting which the situation presented. Four persons only were caught and success-fully prosecuted. There was the drunken man caught red-handed on the coach from Amlwch with non-negotiable bills of exchange which were of no value to him, but did represent proof of what he had been doing. A villager from Penrhoslligwy was found taking away a coat which was not his, and another person from Llanfihangel Tre Beirdd had pocketed a gold watch. In all these cases the stolen goods were evident proof of guilt. The fourth person, a casual visitor from Beaumaris, had picked up 12 pounds at the scene of the wreck; and his case was the most significant. If a brief visit to the scene by a stranger could net him 12 pounds, what opportunities must have been open to those who lived at Moelfre, particu-larly those whose cottages overlooked the actual spot and were early on the scene. Apart from this, the authorities had reason to believe that those guarding or collecting the gold were themselves not above temptation. They set on foot enquiries by Mr Smith, and they ordered house-to-house searches to be made by the Coastguards.

Of course, those living nearest to the wreck had the best opportunities, not only of laying their hands on some of the gold, but of hiding it in places secure from any casual search. All the snap checks in Moelfre drew blank, and the story is still told with glee of how one family—which had done particularly well out of the *Royal Charter*, owing to the fortunate position of their cottage—were actually engaged one evening in counting the day's 'takings', when a searching party of Coastguards marched up and hammered on the door. With one swift, decisive movement the lady of the house swept the hoard of glittering gold coins into her apron and then poured them in a flashing stream into the teapot. When, a moment later, the door was reluctantly opened to the searchers they saw nothing but the poorly lit interior of a humble home, crowded by polite, dignified villagers whom the English, privately, thought of as furtive, secretive and suspicious. They made a cursory search, without much hope of finding gold which, unlike stolen clothing, can be easily concealed; and then went on to the next cottage.

The villagers had set the pace, but other people were soon to try to get in on the act; as if the very mention of treasure in the sea had made men mad. Indeed, it still does, to judge by the number of expeditions which search for it on insufficient evidence and with no idea of the difficulties involved. And the treasure of the *Royal Charter* was very real and exceedingly evident. The humbler inhabitants of Anglesey were forced to rely on their wits in their contest with the Coastguards, but the fourth Lord Boston, lord of the manor of Penrhos, decided on a frontal attack which would sweep them bodily from the field. The *Royal Charter* had been wrecked on a corner of the Lligwy estate—his estate—and the Receiver of Wreck, Mr Smith, had no business to be there at all. He was a trespasser. Further, in so far as he was collecting treasure from the shore, he was a thief. The consigned bullion was, of course, the property of the Underwriters and he did not contest the ownership of gold coins found on the bodies. He did claim, however, in a macabre, unintentional pun, that, 'by virtue of certain Royal Charters', he was lawfully entitled to all unclaimed property thrown up by the sea on to his manor. He was, of course, not merely challenging the hapless Mr Smith, but the authority of the Crown. It may have been that he intended only to chasten Mr Smith, who had failed to notify him officially of what he was doing on Lord Boston's property; in any event, when legal difficulties appeared, Lord Boston dropped the case.

135

There were other ripples, too. The wreck was not merely an Anglesey disaster, but a disaster for Anglesey. There was the cost of burying the bodies and, above all, the cost of many separate inquests which had to be held as corpses were washed ashore at increasingly scattered points all around the coast. As this went on the Chairman of the Quarter Sessions, John Williams, suggested to the parish officials that, in effect, they should conveniently forget to notify the coroner when a body was washed up, as his services were both costly and superfluous. This was to advise them, flatly, to break the law. But he had good reason for, in the event, even with a grant from the Board of Trade, financed by the money found in the pockets of corpses, the wreck of the treasure ship cost Anglesey a sum equal to an annual rate of a penny in the pound—nearly a quarter of the County's expenditure for the whole year.

The surface politeness and deference natural to the Welsh concealed from their English visitors the fact that Moelfre was seething with rage. They had not appreciated the demands made in the English press, that they be instantly hanged. A group of villagers met together to plan a suitably subtle reply, which the Welsh newspapers would be sure to publish. They first established among themselves who had actively participated in the dangerous rescues on the rocks. There turned out to be 28 in all, so that, as the correspondence presently began to run its vituperous course, it became known as *achos yr wyth ar hugain*—the cause of the 28 men.

They made the valid point that there would have been virtually no survivors but for the '28,' and, to support their case, they canvassed those survivors. Samuel Edward Gapper duly certified that he owed his life to them, and John Bradbury went further, stating, 'I believe that these men were the means of saving all that were saved.' They then went on to attack the Rodgers myth, with arguments which were valid but dangerous, because, in England, 'Rodgers of the *Royal Charter*' was the hero of the hour, shortly to be publicly fêted in Liverpool and rewarded in cash. Myths, once established, are hard to destroy. Cautiously, they hammered out a phrase which would not offend. 'The courage and gallantry of Joseph Rodgers are worthy of attention,' scribbled their spokesman. 'But had it not been for the assistance we rendered him, he would have been among the drowned, according to his own statement. Most of us were in very dangerous positions. There were five or six of us hand-in-hand in the water; and we were in danger of being swept off by the furious billows.' This was no idle exaggeration. Their positions would have appalled most of those Englishmen who were calling them thieves, which some of them were. Perhaps in order to combat this, and to suggest that, far from having grown rich on the wreck, they were really very much in need, they decided to add the sentence, 'We wish to state that we have received no remunera-

The names of known survivors, as they appeared in the *Bradford Observer* of 3 November, 1859. *Photo: courtesy of the Bradford Telegraph & Argus*

tion for what your paper may call bravery.' This was a tactical error; in the circumstances, it sounded petty and mean, echoing the bitter words of their own church warden on the day of the disaster, 'You will not get them to do anything unless they are paid for it.' Also, it was a form of boasting unacceptable in England, where a form of calculated understatement, very difficult to counterfeit, is normally used.

The counter-blast by the villagers was bound to fail, except perhaps in Wales. It was out-of-tune with the great wave of horror that had swept the country as a whole at the news of the disaster. It had the same mesmeric force as the loss of the *Birkenhead*, seven years before. But there, although there was sadness, there was also cause for pride, and a tightening of the throat; the Emperor of Prussia himself had commended that story to his sternly disciplined soldiers. The picture of the British redcoats standing fast in ranks as the ship went down, so as to let the women and children get clear in the boats, was something that every Englishman hugged to his breast; he himself might not do so well, but that was the ideal. But this! Why, the story of the *Royal Charter* was the direct reversal of the *Birkenhead*. More crew than passengers saved—and not a single woman or child!

What a disgraceful panic there must have been. And why had it happened at all? What terrible blunder had been committed to cause such a modern, luxury vessel, fast and splendidly equipped, to be cast away upon a barren coast so far from her course? Was it perhaps true that her Captain was drunk at the time? And then this business of the thieving, barbarous Welsh falling like wolves upon the bloody corpses and robbing them. Really!

In the week that elapsed between the disaster and the first hearing of the witnesses at the main Coroner's Inquest, when the newspaper information available was fragmentary and not entirely accurate, speculation ran wild. The wreck of the *Royal Charter* was in the headlines daily, a topic of conversation everywhere; but the proceedings at the Inquest served only to intensify the drama.

Chapter 12

MR MELLOR'S BOMBSHELL

The inquest was to be held in the school building near Llanallgo Church, a mile from Moelfre, at noon on Wednesday, 2 November, but the crowd was kept waiting an hour for the Coroner, Mr W. Jones. He had been called to Penrhos Church to view two bodies washed up that morning. Was there anyone present to represent the owners of the vessel? was his first question.

Mr Tyndall Bright got up to say that he was representing Gibbs, Bright & Co. The company had made every effort to prepare as much evidence as possible. He would presently call three witnesses who were first class passengers—Messrs Morse, Taylor, and Gundry. Of the crew, there were Foster, Suaicar, John O'Brien, and Thomas Cormick. There was also, he said as an afterthought, James Russell, second class passenger. There was a reason for his hesitation at that point. Evidence might also be taken, he added, from two injured survivors who were being treated nearby— Bradbury and Hughes.

The Coroner then gave the usual, very necessary, warning to the jury that they were to lay aside everything they had seen or heard of the affair, and to consider the evidence only. Mr Robert Pritchard, of Bangor, was then sworn in as interpreter. The Coroner apologised for being unable to get an entirely English-speaking jury; they were, however, the most respectable farmers of the district he could find.

The first witness was W. Henry Morse, Magistrate, of New South Wales. He said little of his own escape, and confined himself to the story of the last hours of the *Royal Charter*. It was the tale we already know, but nothing like so complete, because it was the experience of one man only. There was a stir of interest when Mr Morse stated that he had seen the Captain during the storm and that no one had attempted to remonstrate with him. Wise with knowledge afterwards, a number of people had claimed to have known better than Captain Taylor and had either themselves advised a different course of action to him, or had heard other people do so. Consequently, the correspondence columns of the press had been filled with criticism from retired sea captains; a little premature, as the facts had not then been established. After the vessel struck, said Mr Morse, he had heard the Captain tell the ladies that there was no danger, they would soon walk on shore. In that courtroom, filled with relatives, and with the sea-stained bodies of the dead lying stark in the church nearby, the statement possessed an inconceivably morbid irony; there was an angry muttering here and there. Mr Morse went straight on, meeting directly the ugly suspicion in their minds.

'The Captain was perfectly sober at the time.' Slowly and firmly, Mr Morse continued. 'I did not see the Captain or any of the officers once intoxicated during the passage. Everything went favourably until the storm.'

Obviously Mr Morse, with his prestige as a Magistrate and a first class passenger, was going to be the star witness for the owners. Mr Bright got to his feet to question the witness, as he was entitled to do. Had a testimonial been given to Captain Taylor? Yes, replied Mr Morse, there was such a testimonial, and it had been signed by all but two of the first class passengers. But some of the second and third class passengers had harboured a grudge against the Captain; some trifling matter—he had not allowed them to dance on the poop, reserved to the first class. This

The little church of Llanallgo in September, 1985. *Photo: Alexander McKee*

was to discredit in advance the testimony of the second class passenger, James Russell, and to show malice in the accusations of drunkenness. The witness rubbed it in. He had observed the Captain to be calm and collected at all times; and he had come down several times to speak calmly to the ladies, and once to order a cup of coffee for them. Mr Morse had had a cup, too.

There was an interruption. A recent visitor to the village was on his feet, speaking excitedly. He was, he said Mr John William Mellor, of Oldham. He was a solicitor. He was representing professionally some of the families who had lost relatives and friends in the disaster. In his manner there was a hint of suppressed tension which was uncomfortable. Sensing the highly charged atmosphere of the court, he asked them to bear with him if he at times would appear somewhat excited. His brother and cousin had died in the *Royal Charter*.

The Coroner looked hard at Mr Mellor, then turned to the court. If there were any more solicitors present representing families, would they please nominate one spokesman only. It would facilitate business. Meanwhile, Mr Mellor might examine the witness.

Mr Mellor did, and Mr Morse was soon in trouble. How had he known this, that, or the other? By hearsay, was the answer. He had been below at the time, had only heard so. Mr Morse had heard correctly, as it happened, but the solicitor managed to make it sound like carelessness. Then he led the Magistrate into making a fatal admission. He had hardly been on deck at all and had seen the Captain only briefly, three times, at very long intervals. However, he *had* seen the Captain in the saloon, at the time the anchors broke.

The Captain in the saloon at a time of crisis? asked Mr Mellor, mildly. Mr Morse stammered that it was unusual to see the Captain in the saloon; indeed he had not dined with them that day, having been up the two or three previous nights.

Mr Mellor pounced. If everything had gone well before, why did the Captain remain up the two or three previous nights?

The Coroner jumped in to save Mr Morse, by asking the question which was in everyone's mind: Had anyone asked the Captain to turn in to Holyhead for safety, or to any other harbour? Carefully, Mr Morse explained that, if so, he was not aware of it—no one, in his hearing, had made any such suggestion.

Mr Bright then put a pertinent question. What had Captain Taylor done when it was reported to him in the saloon that an anchor cable had parted? He had immediately gone on deck, replied Mr Morse. The damage done by Mr Mellor's insinuations was repaired a little, but before anything further could be said, there was another interruption. James Russell was on his feet, trying to say something about the differences the second class passengers had had with the Captain. But before he could even complete one sentence, Captain Martin, Marine Superintendent for the owners, was also on his feet, angrily demanding that no evidence be taken except on oath. The Coroner agreed, and Mr Russell sat down reluctantly. The next witness was called.

This was Henry Carew Taylor, first class passenger, who had lost his daughter and the nurse who had charge of her. He said that he generally agreed with what Mr Morse had said. He had been so convinced, by the demeanours of Captains Taylor and Withers, that all was well, that he had gone to bed at 11 o'clock. He then told his story, finishing firmly with a strong defence of Captain Taylor. 'I saw Captain Taylor with Captain Withers after the vessel struck. He had lashed himself to the ship. He was as sober as any man could be. Indeed, I never saw him in the least degree intoxicated, or anything approaching it. He always appeared the reverse.' Then he made a telling point. 'If I had thought him drunk I would not have gone to bed, but gone and got some valuables I had on board.' And in reply to questions, 'No it is not true that I remonstrated with Captain Taylor; no, I did not hear any other person say anything to him about going into some harbour.'

Mr Mellor kept up the attack, firing question after question, most of them irrelevant, taking the witness to and fro in time without getting any contradictions or damaging admissions. But Mr Taylor became more and more angry.

'No, I do not know whether the tide was ebbing or flowing. No, I cannot say if the vessel could have been got out to sea before the port anchor was let out.' And then, raising his voice in exasperation, so that it rang through the courtroom. 'I know nothing more about it than my little daughter did!'

As the solicitor's nautical knowledge was of a comparable standard, Mr Taylor had reason to be annoyed. But, as a lawyer, Mr Mellor knew what he was doing. He had Mr Taylor rattled. And the admissions came. Taylor blurted out that he had heard Captains Withers and Adams say that the ship would not wear. He had not heard the Captain say so. But he had heard Captain Withers voice that opinion two or three times during the passage. There was a hush in court. The previous rumours hinted that there was something wrong with the Captain; this looked as if there was something wrong with the ship.

Mr Taylor went on, with transparent honesty, to describe again that scene in the saloon, with Captains Taylor and Withers saying that all was well. 'The ladies remained there and became pacified—and Mrs Fenwick gave clean stockings and shoes to put on her children to go ashore. I felt both ways. I did not know what to think—whether it was right or wrong—but when I saw the ship divide, I knew it was all wrong.'

In the deadly silence that followed, Mr Taylor sat down.

The next witness was called. This was Thomas Gundry, another first class passenger, who also testified in favour of the Captain. He was not drunk; he was perfectly competent, and giving orders. Nobody had remonstrated with him, or asked him to put into any port. Mr Gundry had, however, heard someone say that the masts ought to have been cut down earlier, as the ship might then have ridden safely to her anchors.

This was Mr Mellor's cue to pounce on another witness who was honestly trying to say what had happened, but was without technical knowledge. A newspaper reporter described it as 'a severe cross-examination'. 'Could anything more have been done to save the passengers?' he snapped at Mr Gundry. 'Why did the Captain not take action earlier?' Mr Gundry hesitated, thinking it over. 'We were waiting for daylight,' he replied at last. 'It was pitch dark.' Sweeping aside this inadequate attempt to describe the fury and horror of the scene, Mr Mellor pressed his advantage, to gain another damaging admission. Under a flurry of suggestions, Gundry admitted, hesitantly, because he was not really sure, 'Yes, the hawser might have been taken on shore earlier.' But it would not have fallen to Mr Gundry to take the line, and certainly not to Mr Mellor. What the solicitor was demanding, with a great show of indignation, was that someone should have committed suicide in a good cause. Even Joseph Rodgers, brave seaman though he was, waited for daylight before he volunteered.

But the court did not know that, and on a note damaging to the Captain and to the owners, the Inquest was adjourned to the next day.

*   *   *

The Coroner opened the proceedings on Thursday, 3 November, by asking Mr Bright if he had any nautical gentleman present who was prepared to give evidence, as he himself knew nothing of such matters. Mr Bright said he had. The modern equivalent would not be a seaman, but an engineer, for it was factors affecting the main motive power of the *Royal Charter*, her sails, which would be discussed. At this point, a policeman was so unwise as to walk into the courtroom. The Coroner, incensed by the interruptions of the day before, told him sharply that the least assistance he expected from the Police was to keep order; yesterday, either they had been absent altogether or they had disturbed the proceedings by walking in and out. On this acid note, Samuel Edward Gapper was called to the witness stand.

143

He explained that he was not a mariner but a farmer from New Zealand, and a second class passenger on the *Royal Charter*. He gave a brief summary of events as far as Holyhead, then stated that at 8 pm he saw signals made for a pilot. On being taken up on that point, he admitted that he did not know the difference between these and distress signals. He declared that he had seen the Captain, perfectly sober, walking up and down with a telescope under his arm, and occasionally looking at Point Lynas Light. His version of what the Captain had said to the ladies in the saloon was— 'Ladies, we are on shore, it is a sandy beach, with the help of God I hope we shall get on shore when daylight appears.' He may have been confusing Captain Taylor's statement with that of Captain Withers, made in much the same terms only a moment or two before. In any case, this was a much more reasonable statement than the words attributed to Captain Taylor by Mr Morse, and created a better impression. It was becoming clear that the ship had indeed struck on sand and that, in the darkness, no one could have known about the rocks lying closer inshore.

The other main cause of the disaster—the reason why the clipper went ashore in the first place—was now made by Mr Gapper, in response to promptings by Mr Bright. The wind had shifted, he said, about 10 pm, when they were east of Point Lynas, and had simultaneously increased in violence. In short, the *Royal Charter* had been overtaken by the north-west quadrant of the hurricane; instead of moderate winds blowing them out to sea, hurricane-force winds sent them on to the Anglesey coast. In endeavouring to make his point, Mr Gapper recalled that Captain Adams had shown him the ship's position on a chart, and told him that he would not be surprised if they were on shore by morning. But, as far as the court was concerned, the point was not made; instead, there was alarm and consternation. Whyever had Captain Taylor allowed his ship to get into such a dangerous position? And why did he not then stand out to sea? Why didn't he put into port earlier?

But before Mr Mellor had a chance to rattle the witness, there was yet another interruption. Mr Pitcher, shipbuilder of Northfleet, who had lost a sister-in-law and her two children in the wreck, was on his feet, asking a question. 'Was it not a fact that people on board had desired Captain Taylor to put in to Holyhead?'

No, it was not a fact, replied Mr Gapper. True, there was a message sent to the Captain. But it was only to ask if they might go near enough to Holyhead to see the *Great Eastern*. The message sent back by the Captain was that they might sight the *Great Eastern* at Holyhead, but that he would not turn from his course for that purpose, as he wanted to get home.

This answer only made matters worse. There had been plenty of speculation as to the cause of the disaster, and many people had hinted that it

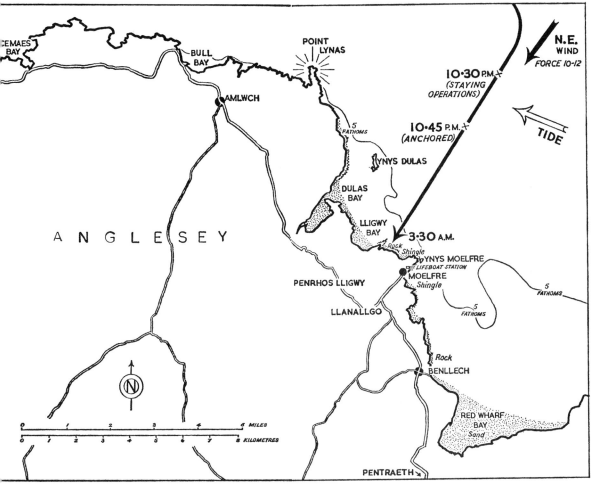

Map 2. The last hours of the *Royal Charter* and the coastline where she met her fate.

was because Captain Taylor had knowingly risked his ship in an attempt to make a record run.

Mr Pitcher was on his feet again. 'What was the wind direction off Point Lynas?'

'It was on the port bow,' said Mr Gapper, not quite sure.

'Did the Captain give orders to head the ship out to sea?' demanded Mr Pitcher.

'No. At least, I heard none given.'

Mr Mellor struck. 'You said, Mr Gapper, that the wind shifted at ten o'clock. How did you know it was ten o'clock?'

Gapper hesitated, then said he knew the times by the change-over of the watch. The first signals he knew of were at eight o'clock. He examined the chart three or four times with Captain Adams, both before and after ten o'clock. At ten o'clock Captain Adams said she was on course.

'And yet Captain Adams said you were likely to be on shore by daylight?' rapped out Mr Mellor.

'I don't know what time he said that,' replied Gapper, nervous now and muddled, 'but he did say it.' Then the New Zealander pulled himself together. 'It was after the anchors had parted. About then, Mr Croome, the Fourth Officer, came down to ask Captain Adams to join Captains Withers and Taylor to consult on the best means to save the ship. I don't know the result of that conversation between the three captains, but I saw Captain Adams afterwards. He was then very quiet, and began nursing one of the passengers' children.'

For a moment, the poignancy of the tragedy came into the courtroom with its full horror, together with the realisation that what was done to save the *Royal Charter* had been as a result of a discussion between three experienced shipmasters, any one of whom knew more about the subject than Mr Mellor, Mr Pitcher and the Coroner put together. And also that they had been there in fact, with the actual situation under their eyes.

Deciding to make the best of a bad job, Mr Mellor was on his feet again, to demand that expert nautical testimony be sought. He also took the opportunity to have a dig at the owners. This was all the more necessary, he added, because he had heard that the *Royal Charter* had been weakened, after her launching, by being involved in an accident.

Mr Bright got up to explain what had really happened on the Dee, but he was told to sit down—they would not argue this matter, but confine themselves to questions related to the ship's course. With a show of graceful resignation, having made his point, Mr Mellor also agreed to this. The Coroner was sufficiently out of his depth already, without introducing the subject of naval architecture; one can sympathise with his decision to restrict evidence to the only slightly less complicated matters of navigation and seamanship.

Mr Bright then produced the highest expert nautical advice available to him—the Maltese boatswain's mate, Suaicar.

Left to himself, just to talk, Suaicar did very well. He produced the most precise and accurate account yet, confirming authoritatively what the passenger witnesses had said. When he said that the lights shown at 8 pm were for a pilot, as Gapper had stated, not even Mr Mellor could disbelieve him. When he said that the darkness had prevented a line being taken ashore earlier, and backed it up with his own detailed account of how he, too, volunteered to go ashore with a line, it would have taken a brave lawyer to try to trip him up. He rubbed it in. He had been 22 years at sea, he said. Captain Taylor had been up nearly all night, giving orders, and he, Suaicar, had personally helped to carry them out. There was no doubt that the Captain was sober. He described how, three times, an attempt was made to stay the vessel, head coming up to the wind on to the course that would save her, and then being driven back again by the sheer, awful power of the storm. 'Any ship,' he said impressively, 'under such a heavy gale, could not stay in that or any other manner.' Mr Mellor sat back, arms folded, legs crossed, and bided his time.

Guided by questions from Mr Bright, Suaicar told of the various courses steered, and how the wind changed direction. 'I am quite certain that Captain Taylor was perfectly sober,' he concluded.

A juryman asked a question. 'How was it that so many were lost, when one man was able to swim ashore—the man with the line?'

This was a sore point with Suaicar, who regretted that he himself had not made a similarly successful attempt. He replied, shortly, that he had no idea. Then Mr Mellor rose to his feet.

He had momentarily flustered Gapper, made him out to be an unreliable witness, by deliberately asking him about the times at which this or that had happened. Even now, with all evidence to hand, there is no real certainty—the times are approximate only. They could hardly be anything else. But Gapper had been a stout opponent, and had fought back. For Mr Mellor, Suaicar was easy meat. He had him hog-tied and thrown with his first question.

Deceptively quiet, he asked the Maltese how he had known the ship's course when off Holyhead.

'I did not know my course.'

'Oh?'

'I did not see the chart.' Suaicar paused in embarrassment, searching for the exact words in a foreign language. 'I meant to say that—that I did not look upon it to see the course; but how the bay stood.'

Mr Mellor became sharp. 'Have you discussed this matter with Captain Martin and Mr Bright? Is that how you know the course?'

The unhappy Maltese looked helplessly round the court, then blurted out, 'I did hold a conversation about the "Charter" with Captain Martin and Mr Bright.'

'Did they tell you the course?'

'I didn't, to my knowledge, say anything about the course she steered until one o'clock. I can't swear it. I may have.' Suaicar stammered out desperately, 'No one has shown me on the chart what the course of the vessel ought to be, from Holyhead to Point Lynas. No one either pointed out her course from Lynas to Liverpool.'

Mr Mellor let the Maltese stumble on, talking about courses and wind directions. The court rang with NEs and ENEs. But it all sounded very unconvincing now. When Suaicar was done, Mr Mellor slowly produced his trump card—a chart. He showed it to Suaicar, who stared at it as if it were a rattlesnake, and asked the Maltese if he could indicate the point where the ship had missed stays.

Only a navigator, as perhaps Mr Mellor knew, who had drawn track lines and indicated the times on a chart which he had retained, could possibly have answered this question with any pretence to certainty. Even now, we do not know exactly what this position was. Indeed, considering the visibility, for absolute precision, radio aids would have been necessary.

With shaking fingers, Suaicar touched a position on the chart.

From that position, with the wind at NNE, if the ship had not missed stays, could she have cleared Point Lynas?' rapped Mr Mellor.

'Yes, oh, yes,' replied Suaicar, 'she would have cleared Point Lynas.' He stopped and thought, then said quickly, 'No, that is not so, she would not have cleared Point Lynas.'

Mr Mellor made a gesture of exasperation.

'I am not an Englishman, you must excuse me. I do not understand the question, that is why.'

Mr Mellor looked at the wretched Maltese, then pointedly folded up the chart. Suaicar's evidence is utterly useless, the gesture implied. He has been told what to say by his employers, and he cannot even remember that. He has probably never seen a chart in his life before.

Then Suaicar burst out in a rage. After all, he *had* been 22 years at sea. And Mr Mellor had not. 'I have sailed from Liverpool to Holyhead 10 to 15 times,' he shouted, 'and about the same number down. I don't know where the ship missed stays, but it was in 16 fathoms of water, I do know! I only sailed one voyage in the *Royal Charter*. I had nothing to do with steering the ship. I was not on board to pass any opinion to Captain Taylor. But I tell you something. Ships will not stay in strong wind, such as this! There was no place to wear the ship where this was!'

Mr Mellor sat calmly through the outburst, then cut in. 'Is it not a fact that a certain person asked the Captain to cut away the masts, and that he refused?'

'No. I did not hear anyone say that.'

'Is it not a fact that you have already said this, outside this court?'

'I am not aware I said this to anyone.'

Mr Mellor paused, then said quietly, 'Is it not a fact that you yourself have stated that a certain person went three times to the Captain, asking for the masts to be cut down, and that that person was—yourself?'

'No.'

'I will be clearer, sir,' said Mr Mellor ominously. 'Is it not a fact that you yourself told me this—in the presence of Mr Russell and Mr Welsh?'

'You are mistaking the person, sir,' blurted out the flustered Suaicar.

Mr Mellor became suddenly cold and grave. 'Now, sir!' His voice rang through the courtroom. 'Now, sir, did you not say to me, that if the Captain had cut the masts the vessel would have been safe?'

Suaicar was shaking. 'I really don't believe I did say so, and I swear I did not.'

Mr Mellor dropped his voice to a whisper. 'Is it not also a fact that you told me that the Captain was drunk on the night of the wreck?'

The statement, falling into the hushed courtroom, sent out a wave of murmuring and whispered comment. Mr Russell's eyes were gleaming, it might have been with tears or rage. Elsewhere, there were sounds that might have been sobs.

Before they could quite die away, Mr Mellor flung a last question at Suaicar's head. 'Is it not a fact that, on Thursday last, in the presence of Mr Russell and Mr Welsh, you told me that Captain Taylor was drunk on the night of the shipwreck?' And then he sat down.

Chapter 13

THE VERDICT OF THE COURT

Instantly, Mr Bright was on his feet, trying to repair the apparently irrevocable damage done by Mr Mellor's series of bombshells. But in answer to his questioning, Suaicar went off at a tangent, telling a long, rambling story about how the Chief Officer had asked him to swim ashore with a line and how he, Suaicar, had agreed and had tried to do so. He was building himself up again, but it was no help to Mr Bright. At length, however, he did grasp the point of the questions, and said. 'Yes, I did ask the Second Officer, after the second anchor had parted, if anything should be done to the rigging, and the Captain heard me, and called out, "No, my lad, not yet".'

Was this then the basis of the whole story— the veritable molehill from which Mr Mellor had most cunningly constructed a mountain? But Suaicar stumbled off on another track, trying to discredit all reports. A story had appeared in the papers that he had £400 on him when he got ashore. It was a base lie, he shouted. Mr Mellor wasted no further time in cross-examining the boatswain's mate, but had his next witness sworn in at once.

Mr Thomas Welsh took the stand. He was Mr Mellor's cousin. His evidence was to the point. 'I was present with Mr Mellor and Mr Russell, on Thursday last, at Moelfre. I heard the last witness state most distinctly that Captain Taylor was drunk on the night of the wreck. I believe he repeated it more than once. I heard him also say that he had applied to the Captain three times to have the masts cut off. I am positive that the witness was that person.'

Captain Martin interjected. If this alleged conversation took place on the night following the wreck, he argued, not much reliance could be placed on it. The survivors, having barely escaped with their own lives, and having lost many friends in the disaster, would almost certainly be overwrought, and might well also have been drowning their sorrows.

Mr Welsh replied quietly. 'In fact, it was I who asked Suaicar if the Captain was sober or drunk. I do not remember the precise words he made use of. I thought he was sober when he made that remark. I think he knew perfectly well what he was saying. I know Foster, the carpenter, too, and he was present. It was in a private house that this took place, between 7.30 and 8 pm. It was on Thursday, the day after the wreck.'

Again Mr Mellor wasted no time. He had himself sworn in as a witness, and spoke in tones of studied moderation, as of one weighing every point. 'I had relatives, a brother and a cousin, on board the *Royal Charter*, both of whom are lost,' he began, dramatically. 'I came here on Thursday last, to make enquiries as to the wreck, and to see if I could find the bodies. In the course of my enquiries, I met with Mr Russell, and went with him and my cousin to the house where Suaicar and Foster lodged.' He then virtually repeated Mr Welsh's evidence, adding that he himself had put the same questions to Suaicar, and received the same answers; but he had not taken them down in writing. Foster was present. 'I don't remember what Foster said, but he said something.'

The solicitor admitted that he had been 'vexed' at the loss of his relatives. 'I called in the office of Gibbs, Bright & Co, I believe it was the following day, and told a gentleman in there that there was a rumour at Moelfre that the Captain was drunk. He said it was a great lie, and asked who dared to tell such a lie? I told him I would not give the name up then, but that I would do so at the Inquest.'

Captain Martin interjected a question. Who was this mysterious witness?

I asked for information from other persons at Moelfre, concerning the Captain,' replied Mr Mellor, 'and I was told by one of the passengers that he was drunk. That person was Mr James Russell, the gentleman there.' He paused dramatically, while all eyes turned on Russell. Russell, the survivor whom Mr Wagstaffe had seen rambling about the shore after the wreck, 'more like a maniac than anything else', in his grief and rage.

'I asked other passengers,' went on Mr Mellor. 'Mr Gardner was one, but he told me he had never seen the Captain drunk. I was guarded in my enquiries there. I also spoke, I believe, to Mr Gapper, and asked whether the Captain was sober; he replied that he was. I have since ascertained, on pushing the enquiry with Mr Russell, that he had no knowledge of the Captain being drunk.'

There was a gasp in the courtroom.

'He spoke from the information of others. I might have mentioned these things to others.' There was another gasp, then stupefaction, as Mr Mellor added, 'My own impression of it is that the Captain was perfectly sober.'

Mr Mellor's studied air of scrupulous fairness was quite lost on the court. As his case ran steadily downhill, there was a noticeable relaxation of tension. Now, it rested only on the talkative and excitable Maltese, Suaicar, and, somewhat nebulously, on statements attributed to Foster, the carpenter. Foster was the next witness.

151

He told the same story—of unsuccessful attempts to bring the ship round, defeated each time by the terrible power of the wind; of how the next step was to let go the anchors, to stop the drift towards a lee shore; and of how they merely slowed the drift, so furious was the hurricane; how the anchors at last parted under the strain; how then the order was given to cut away the masts; and how she struck on the sand before this could be done. For a little while, the true demon of the piece, the hurricane, blew through the room. But it was now growing dark outside the little courtroom, and as no lights were available, the Inquest was adjourned to the next day, Friday, 4 November.

A mile or so away, divers were working below the surface in the tangled wreck, trying to get at the strongroom. A 4 lb gold bar was brought up, and a cashbox belonging to a passenger, John Hawkins, of Wells, in Somerset. During the night there came horribly ashore a portion of the mutilated body of a baby. It lay in Llanallgo Church by the time the Inquest re-opened on Friday morning.

Foster, the carpenter, explained how, shortly after the ship began to beat on the rocks, she broke up. He explained how 16 men got ashore on the hawser, all of them members of the crew. The sense of tension and horror, of something left still to be explained, again flooded the court. But Foster's narrative dissolved it as quickly. 'There was a female who hesitated to go along the hawser, which caused a delay of half-an-hour.' That was a tit-bit for the press, and pencils scribbled busily. 'After she refused to go, I went down next, and about three other men followed me.' Foster concluded by saying that he had seen the Captain frequently that night, that he was sober, and that, considering the gale, no one could have done more than he did to save life. Answering Mr Bright, he added that the 16 men who went ashore by the hawser did so by order of Mr Stephens, the Chief Officer, to help rig another hawser, but this attempt failed, why, he did not know.

Mr Mellor began to cross-examine. First, he concentrated on matters of course and position. Foster did not know, and did not pretend to know. But he confirmed that Suaicar had indeed offered to take a second line ashore. Mr Bright asked if he had heard Suaicar say that the Captain was drunk, and Foster said that he had not. The Coroner asked him about the conversation in the cottage with Mr Mellor and Mr Welsh. Foster replied that he had no recollection of it. There were hundreds of people continually coming in and out. In any event, he had not heard Suaicar say he had asked the Captain three times to cut down the masts; nor had he made such a statement himself, or heard anyone else make it.

The owners then produced their own witness to a conversation with Suaicar and Foster at the cottage. It had taken place at nine o'clock on

the Thursday night, an hour or so after the talk described by Mr Mellor
and Mr Welsh. The survivors were, of course, continually being questioned, going again and again over the same ground, for the benefit of
relatives and visitors. This witness, however, was a professional—an
English newspaper reporter, Mr J. B. Marsh, of Chester. He had, he said,
taken down in writing the narratives of both Suaicar and Foster, but had
afterwards destroyed his notes. However, he remembered quite well what
he had been told. There was a sudden stir of interest in court. At the conclu-
sion of the interview he had asked Suaicar if he had anything more to
say, or was that the whole story? Suaicar had thought a moment, then
replied, yes, he had heard somebody on the beach saying that the Captain
was drunk. Suaicar had been incensed by this, and said to the reporter,
'I was running about all night carrying messages from the Captain to the
officers, and from the officers to the crew, and I can assure you he was
not drunk. I would like to see the man who said so.'

Mr Mellor got to his feet. But not to cross-examine. He regretted, he
said, that, at this stage of the proceedings, he must leave; he had been
called home on urgent business. To which the Coroner replied that he
also regretted this, as he had hoped that Mr Mellor would have been able
to be present to hear some remarks he was now about to make.

As Mr Mellor left the room, pale, and avoiding the curious eyes fixed
on him, the Coroner turned to the jury. Were they all agreed that the
Captain was sober? They all said that they were. The Coroner then said
that there was no need, in that case, to take evidence of Cormick, a steward,
and Henry Evans, a sailor. He would, however, like a neutral witness,
experienced in nautical affairs—and would send at once for Captain Fell,
of the Underwriters, then at the scene of the wreck, a mile away. He would
also call for Captain Martin, for the owners. While they were waiting for
Captain Fell, the court would like to hear one more witness—Mr James
Russell.

The Scotsman took the stand firmly, even aggressively. He sketched the
sequence with which by now everyone was acquainted: Melbourne—
Queenstown—Holyhead—Point Lynas. He made a point of the delay at
Queenstown; if this had not happened, the ship would have been two or
three hours nearer Liverpool when the hurricane caught her. He told of
how the ship got on the rocks and broke in two; of how he brought his
wife and two daughters up from below—and how they were cut off by
an impassable gap from the hawser which was the only means of escape.
He described his effort to make from fallen rigging a makeshift hawser
of his own; how the attempt failed; and how all of his family, himself
excepted, had died in the sea.

Russell admitted that he had not seen the Captain at all that night.

He had indeed said that the Captain was drunk, but he had also given the questioners—Mr Mellor and others—the names of the people who had told him in the first place. They were the boatswain's mate, Suaicar, the apprentice, Walter Hughes, and a passenger named Bradbury. The two latter, badly injured, were still in Moelfre and could be questioned. He concluded, 'I never saw Captain Taylor, at any time during the voyage, intoxicated.'

As Captain Fell had not yet arrived, Thomas Griffith, a quartermaster, was asked to take the stand. He lived at Amlwch, only five miles from Moelfre, and knew that coast well. In his opinion, if it had been possible to stay the ship, she would have been able to clear Point Lynas and stand out to safety in the Irish Sea. The attempts to do so failed, in his opinion, because 'She was too light, and the wind blew too hard to allow her to go round. I mean by being too light, that she was not low enough in the water. She was stiff enough when she left Melbourne, but she was lightened by the quantity of coals burnt.' He concluded, 'I know of nothing against the Captain.'

Captain William Martin then gave evidence. He explained that he was Marine Superintendent of Gibbs, Bright and that, while the *Royal Charter* was in this country, she was in his charge. The owners had spared nothing in respect of the *Royal Charter*. He had been in her during her trials. They had only thought it necessary to stay her once, she performed so well, answering as soon as the helm was put down. He then went on to explain authoritatively what the *Royal Charter* was doing off Point Lynas.

'The witnesses proved clearly that the ship was three to four miles north of Point Lynas. Here we have Captain Taylor looking for a pilot. He then comes up to the regular pilot ground eastward. There are three pilot stations: the first outside the North-west Lightship; the second is the Ormeshead station, and the third is Point Lynas, or Westernmost station. If a captain fails in getting a pilot at Point Lynas, his next safe course is to steer for the Ormeshead station; and it is on that course that we can trace him five miles to the eastward of Point Lynas. The next thing we hear is that he is encountering a very heavy breeze from NE to N, according to the evidence, he having tried to stay the ship. Failing that, we find him leaving go his anchors in 16 fathoms water. Sixteen fathoms is rather more than four miles from shore; and I have no doubt of his having been driven previously at least five miles to leeward. It was impossible for the Captain to stay that vessel in such a hurricane. It would have been certain destruction to wear her.'

He ceased explaining, and went on earnestly. 'I knew Captain Taylor for 17 years, and I have commanded vessels for this Company for about 16 years. I have always known him to be a temperate man, and he was selected for the command of the *Royal Charter* from being a very smart man, fully competent in everything to command such a vessel.'

James Russell, game to the last, where Mr Mellor had fled, got up to fire one last shot. Was it true, he asked, that the *Royal Charter* had been altered structurally after her launch? It was the shrewdest blow yet. Captain Martin, somewhat inaccurately, replied that she had not. In fact, she had been *strengthened*. But to mention this, in the current atmosphere of suspicion, especially of the strength of iron ships, perhaps seemed inadvisable.

Captain Alfred Fell, who had entered the court a moment or two before, then took the stand. He said that he had been employed by the London Underwriters for 17 years; he had been 20 years at sea, nine of them in command in the East Indies and Australian trades. He referred to the estimated position of the *Royal Charter* at the time she had let go her anchors. 'It was the start of the flood—the wind at NE. I should say it was impossible to stay that vessel. I agree that Captain Taylor did all that could be done under the circumstances to save the ship. I should have done everything Captain Taylor did.'

On that last, decisive note the taking of evidence was concluded, and the Coroner summed up. 'Our object in this enquiry has been to find out whether this disaster has occurred from any mismanagement on the part of the Captain, or was caused by any fault in the construction of the vessel,' he began. The first question to be decided was: was Captain Taylor at fault in bringing the vessel to the spot where she was wrecked? An attempt had been made to prove that the Captain was not sober–'I wish that gentleman was here now'—but the evidence completely cleared the unfortunate Captain's memory. But if the jury disagreed with that, they would say so by their verdict. Was every means used, after the wreck, to save life? Again, that appeared to be the case, but if they thought there was any negligence by Captain Taylor, they would say so.

The courtroom was then cleared for ten minutes, while the jury considered their verdict. It was unanimous. The loss of the *Royal Charter* had been 'pure accident'; the Captain was 'perfectly sober'; and he had done 'all in his power' to save the ship and her passengers.

But before the public could stream out of the little courtroom for the last time, Mr W. H. Smith, the Collector of Customs at Beaumaris, read out a letter which, he said, had reached him only a few moments ago. It had been written in London the previous day and was from Mr J. O'Dowd, solicitor to the Merchant Shipping Department of the Board of Trade, who was journeying to Liverpool the following morning. Both the witnesses and the owners were hereby warned that the Board of Trade proposed to hold an Inquiry into the loss of the *Royal Charter*, and that their attendance would be required.

The story of the wreck was not finished; far from it. The matter of faulty construction had not even been considered. Now, the really big guns were about to thunder.

Chapter 14

DOWN TO THE DEAD IN THE SEA

Whenever the weather allowed, a little salvage fleet lay at anchor above the wreck of the *Royal Charter*. There were one or more steam-tugs, with paddle wheels, lying a little out to sea, and closer in, a vessel which looked like a fishing smack and was called a 'lump' or 'lumper'—in modern parlance, a lighter. She carried heavy lifting apparatus, to which chains were attached. There were a number of boats in the vicinity. Some were out searching for bodies, for it was now the second week of November, but several were anchored directly beside the sunken stern portion of the wreck. An iron ladder hung down into the water from near their bows and amidships was a curious affair with two large wheels attended by two or three men—these were the manually operated pumps for supplying a diver with compressed air. Three new divers had come from Liverpool the previous day, employed to speed up the work, and one of them was about to go down for the first time. He was an object of interest to the spectators on the rocks, few of whom had seen a diver before, but his suit and helmet were indistinguishable from those in use today—'hard-hat' diving equipment has not changed substantially in a hundred years.

There was a slight grating noise as the front glass of the diver's helmet was screwed tight. Then a hand tapped him on the helmet, signalling, 'Go down.' Slowly and clumsily, he began to descend, his heavily booted feet feeling for the resistance that meant they were on a rung of the ladder. The pumps had taken up their thumping, gasping rhythm. There was a thin, wavy line dancing in front of his eyes—the surface of the sea that had engulfed the *Royal Charter*. Then he was under, and had momentarily closed the outlet valve of his helmet, so that the attendant above could check for the bubbles that would mean a leak in the suit. There were none. Now the world around him was green and solid. He felt for the shot line hanging down beside the ladder, grasped it, and transferred his weight to it in curious slow motion, like an elephant trying to do an act on the flying trapeze. The bottom was not far below, but he could still get a nasty squeeze if he fell before he could valve more air into his suit. A few moments later, he was on the bottom, slanting forward like a man bending against a gale, and getting his bearings.

He could see sharply for six feet or so, but it was like being enclosed in a solid green fog. High above his head the surface of the sea was a shimmering silver mirror, alive with changing patterns, cutting off irrevocably all sight of the world of gas and vapour that lay above this realm of water. To one side was a block of shadows that faded off into the gloom—the wreck. What was under his feet, he could not see; and to put his head down close to the bottom would mean that his suit would swiftly inflate to utter rigidity; imprisoned in iron armour, he would float, arms outstretched as if on a cross, feet first towards the surface. His breathing sounded heavy inside the helmet, as he began to move forward, not walking, but leaning forward to pull himself with his hands and push back with his metal-capped boots. Valving a little more air into his suit, he went bobbing towards the wreck like a tethered balloon, his scuffling boots raising a grey cloud from the bottom. No sensible man walks forward upright below the sea, the effort of pushing aside tons of solid water is too great.

Clouds of tiny, silver bubbles rose in bursts from his helmet; as they moved upwards, they continually expanded, grew to the size and shape of mushrooms, of a leaden, metallic colour. Their swelling measured exactly the decreasing pressure in every foot of their rise to the surface. They were the visible sign that this was in truth another world and the clumsy diver, tethered by his line and air hose to the boat above—like a goat chained to a stake—was an alien here, none too well adapted to his new element.

He had been told that this wreck was a bad one. Where the hull, hammered mercilessly on the rocks by the hurricane, had not already collapsed, it was ready to do so at any disturbance. The fighter pilot's world of the free diver was not yet; this man had to haul and thump his way into the cavernous shadows looming ahead under the sea. Already shards of twisted ironwork were reaching out black and ghostly hands towards him, with golden shafts of sunlight from the surface, flickering and twisting like miniature searchlights between them. There were no fish—yet. Weed had not had time to grow, and anyway it was not the season for the growth of weed, for the bottom of the sea has its springs and autumns, too.

He skirted cautiously the monstrous mound of wreckage, utterly distorted, and bearing no resemblance to a ship. His job was to locate the heap under which lay the bullion room, and attach twisted plates and

Alexander McKee making his first dive in a helmet diving suit during December, 1951, at a Royal Engineers' training school in Hamburg. This experience helped him to understand the problems faced by the divers of 1859, wearing identical gear, in their efforts to salvage the gold of the *Royal Charter*. *Photo: Alexander McKee copyright.*

sodden woodwork to the chains, so that the lighter could lift them clear. No one had yet seen the strongroom, and nothing but a few single bars of gold had been recovered; no doubt it had been bent and flattened like an old tin can. On top of it had lain the heavy frames and machinery of the patent steering apparatus, but already the latter had been slung by a veteran diver and lifted clear. The frames remained, and a pile of twisted, gaping iron sheets, like a honeycomb, forming an intricate series of semi-collapsed caverns. It was very dark inside.

Carefully, breathing hard in spite of his cautious movements, the diver scuffled his way into the blackness, groping in front of him with hands blue and numb with cold. One hand was bleeding already from cuts. Held at the back of his mind was fear of the awful weight above him, of iron plates and frames and heavy machinery, ready to fall on him or on the air hose that trailed back to the dim light of the undersea, now far away. He swallowed hard and went on, controlling his breathing with an effort.

The diver was surprised when he saw a face looking up at him. His first thought was to wonder how a human being had got there without a diving helmet. He had almost put his hand on it—not that he would have noticed, his fingers had little feeling left in them. He tried to lever away some of the iron plates and crushed woodwork that were pinning the ghastly thing in place; the head moved a little, that was all. In air, he could easily have done it; down here, it was a tremendous task. He could pull upwards, that was comparatively easy—but to push in any direction even the lightest spar was merely to push himself away from it, like a balloon bumping against a cliff. He had to leave the puffy, lifeless thing where it was, and go in towards that fabulous treasure, shrouded in darkness and death.

The gold was in small mahogany boxes; fragments of them had already come ashore. Nevertheless, the salvage experts confidently expected to recover the bulk of the ingots and specie. They knew by experience that the effect of currents on heavy objects lying on the seabed was negligible. The very smashing of the boxes would ensure that the gold would remain at the point where it had poured out, scattered somewhat by the effects of the breaking sea, but still mostly inside or close around the wreck. The only doubtful point was the number of boxes swept out of the wreck and broken up while the hurricane was still raging, for their contents would have been strewn widely among the rock crevices and among the shingle piled high up the nearby beach by the waves.

*   *   *

The salvage operations appeared to be shrouded in great secrecy, largely because the principles involved were not understood by the spectators, the relatives, or the Rector, Stephen Roose Hughes, all of whom grew increasingly angry at the spectacle of an intensive search for gold while several hundred bodies were still missing, pinned, they believed, beneath the wreck. Now, in this second week of November, they saw many more bodies being washed up, and they pointed to this as the obvious proof that the disturbance of the wreck by the divers was releasing them. Why could not the divers release them all? Of couse, the brutal answer was for someone to lend Stephen Roose Hughes a diving suit and tell him to go down and do it himself. As it was, the authorities whom he badgered threatened legal action, and even arrest, if he attempted any more to inter-fere with the operations of the Receiver of Wreck. The fact was that the furious relatives, and the equally furious Rector, who was in daily contact with their grief, all thought of the wreck of the *Royal Charter* as lying in a field, entirely surrounded by air; the fact that it was lying under water, and that this could possibly make any difference, never occurred to them. Had their premise been true, the dismantling of the wreck could have been accomplished in a matter of days; as it was, although salvage opera-tions continued for years, the greater part of the wreck was never lifted. What was being raised now was at the risk of men's lives.

Something of this Captain Martin may have managed to convey to Stephen Roose Hughes, for the Rector shortly made another, less impossi-ble demand. There was, he said, a place near a rock where, from his exper-ience, many bodies were likely to have been brought up by the current and entangled in the weed; could Captain Martin send down a diver to free them? The latter proposition, that a body could be trapped by weed, arose from the horrible sensation experienced by swimmers when they touched weed which they could not properly see. When the first swimmer put on a face-mask, the myth dissolved. But that time was still far away, and a watchful and expectant crowd gathered on the shore to see the diver go down; there were wild cries when, almost at once, a body rose to the surface, and disappointment when that proved to be all. The diver, on coming up, said that he had seen nothing at all, and looked surprised when the corpse was pointed out to him. Possibly his lines might have disturbed it; certainly it had not been trapped by weed which, as it was winter, must have been largely non-existent anyway. Like winter woods, the seabed in that season looks strangely bare.

In truth, the Rector's Christianity was killing him. As we now know, only too well, horror soon ceases to have much effect; it is felt truly once only—the first time. After that, there is a gradual acceptance. The bell ceases to toll always for us; for if it did, it would be intolerable. It was intolerable for Stephen Roose Hughes, for on him fell the Christian duty of comforting the bereaved who flocked to his church or wrote to him, literally in their hundreds, for news and consolation; his sympathy for the last relative had to be as heartfelt as had been his sympathy for the first. And this goes against the grain of human nature. But he accepted the work gladly, as a task laid on him by God, and although, by the end, he had reached breaking point, he was still able to offer the unfailingly right word. He made himself a kind of living focus for the dead on earth, so that the relatives poured out their hearts to him as they could do to no one else. 'I do not apologise for thus writing to you,' said the mother of Charles Thomas, the 15-year-old steward, 'for oh, my heart is so very sorrowful.' A husband who had lost his wife concluded his letter with, 'Will you tell me what I can do for you, and will you write me a consoling letter to prevent my mind from going astray?' A father who had searched in vain at Moelfre for the body of his son wrote, 'I feel most anxious to hear whether anything fresh has transpired since I left you; will you add another to the many deep obligations I am under by writing to me?'

Letter after letter to be written; and written they were, unfailingly and with feeling, 1,075 of them.

They were not curt notes, nor was there any delay. A Jewish business-man, in particular, went out of his way to thank the Rector for the prompt-ness with which he had dealt with the enquiry and for the length at which he had written. Stephen Roose Hughes had identified the body of his brother from a burial register of 'unknowns' in which he noted carefully every detail that might possibly assist identification later— tattoo marks, which the sailors often wore, as if with that very possibility in mind; receipts for parrots, which many of the dead carried on them; miniatures of women; scraps of letters; locks of hair worn in lockets around the neck; and the physical characteristics of the corpses. In this case, he had the body exhumed and then re-buried with due observance of the rites of the Jews. And like the Christians, the Jew poured out his grief to the Rector, telling him, as so many did, the full details of the sad affair.

But it was time, high time, to call a halt.

The owners were to go bankrupt as a result of the loss of the *Royal Charter*, but they behaved very well, sending the Rector £100 for his own expenses and to remunerate the Moelfre villagers for their rescue work; and they paid for boats to go out in the bay to search for floating bodies. There was no legal obligation for them to do any of this. The boats were often drawn to the bodies by sighting a cloud of circling, crying gulls. Many were found floating around the island at the point of the headland—Ynys Moelfre—and others in Red Wharf Bay. Some were identifiable. A boat manned by John Price and a Coastguard, J. Marshal Davie, picked up one day the semi-clothed body of what was apparently an Irish digger, and on the next found Mr Edwin Fowler, the friend of A. & J. K., who was identified by documents in the sodden clothing, which had also some scraps of poetry written by the dead man and £35 in gold. Washed ashore in Red Wharf Bay, lying almost side by side on the sand, were the bodies of his youngest daughter, five-and-a-half-year-old Ida Fowler, and her young nurse, Emma Calf. It seemed to A. & J. K., who saw them by torchlight in Pentraeth Church, as if the nurse's fidelity to her little charge had lasted until death, otherwise they would not have been found so close together. The most remarkable coincidence that they recorded, however, concerned James Russell who, while down at the wreck with the Misses Moulsdale, of the Rectory, saw a piece of paper washing in the waves and picked it up—it proved to be the deeds of his own modest property in Australia.

These bodies had been freed from the wreck by the salvage operations, declared many people whose relatives had not yet been recovered. But there was another, better reason. The date. When alive, the bodies had been buoyant; when killed or maimed by impact with the rocks, they sank and suffocated, with deflated lungs. The inevitable process of decomposition formed gases which caused them to swell hideously; the swelling increased the size of the body but not its weight; therefore, some two weeks after death they rose again, a horrible, distorted nightmare.

The local reporters were forced closely to examine these bloated bodies, often naked and badly mutilated, some limbless, many of them females and children; and they quite lacked, like their readers, the twentieth century's first-hand experience, and acceptance of, horror. It was with almost savage revulsion that one reporter, finishing his list of identification marks, went on to mock the 'sanguine expectations of some unknown parties at a distance'. He was clearly referring to the current campaign to force the owners to attempt to salvage the bodies instead of the gold. He concluded, brutally, 'It will be almost impossible to identify any bodies that may be washed on shore from this time.' That was printed on 12 November, a clear hint that it was better now that the relatives should not see the bodies, but rather remember them as they had been in life.

It was to no avail. On the following day the County MP, Sir R. W. Bulkeley, Bart, of Beaumaris, wrote a vitriolic letter to the Board of Trade, demanding that they 'compel' the owners to divert the divers to the recovery of the bodies. He had been besieged by angry relatives, who had not confined their complaints to the Rector only. So he was able to write of the 'painful scenes that daily take place in the neighbourhood of the wreck and the callousness of the owners'. 'To the applications of these sorrowing relatives to the agents in charge of the ship, requesting them to use their appliances to weigh up portions of the wreck, with the view of releasing a number of bodies, not the slightest attention is paid; on the contrary, nothing but the most revolting indifference to their feelings is shown. The recovery of the gold appears to be the only object of the owners and underwriters. Whether the Board of Trade or the Admiralty have the power of insisting upon the removal of the wreck, you, sir, are the best judge.'

This letter received wide publicity in the press, far more than the reply by the owners stating what they had done, voluntarily and unpaid, to help in recovering the bodies from the sea and the beaches where they were washed up. The thunder of the local MP may have suggested to a certain solicitor from Oldham, smarting from the failure of his attempt to brand a dead man as a drunkard, a new line of approach. The Board of Trade Inquiry was due to open in Liverpool on 15 November. Mr Mellor would be there, as spokesman for the distressed relatives.

Chapter 15

THE EXPERTS SUM UP

'It has been my painful task to have acted in a similar capacity upon many
occasions during the last four years but never in the course of my experience and, I venture, in the memory of man has an event occurred so dis-
tressing in its character and so lamentable for the extent of its sacrifices
and losses, as the event which we are about to investigate,' said Mr
O'Dowd, opening the Inquiry for the Board of Trade.

His words truly represented the shock caused by the loss of the *Royal
Charter*. And yet, this was not the only 'monster wreck' of the century;
or even of the year. A few months earlier the clipper ship *Pomona*, of 1,800
tons, had been wrecked off the Irish coast as a result of a navigational
error, and 385 people had died. In 1854 the 1,970 ton iron ship *Tayleur*,
bound for Melbourne with 597 passengers and crew, had also been
wrecked on the Irish coast, with the loss of half of them; and was not
seen again until 1959, when members of the Irish Sub-Aqua Club found
her, looking, they said, 'as if somebody had pushed ten haybarns over
the edge of the cliffs'. But both these tragedies had occurred at the start
of a voyage, the *Tayleur* being only 48 hours out from Liverpool. The
drama inherent in the loss of the *Royal Charter* was the fact of her having
sailed 16,000 miles, only to be lost a few hours from her home port. Nor
had her passengers and crew died at sea, out of sight and sound, but
perished miserably within a few yards of the shore and under the direct
gaze of scores of helpless spectators. Nor had there been the accusing fact
that all the survivors were men.

For anything like a parallel it would be necessary to wait nearly one
hundred years, until January, 1953, when the 2,694 ton ferry steamer
Princess Victoria went down in the Irish Sea, with not a single woman or
child saved.

There were two main undercurrents present among the questions and
answers. In effect, the court was trying the dead Captain Taylor for
hazarding his ship; but, as far as the experts were concerned, that was
a minor issue. It was the iron ship, as such, which was on trial. Not just
the *Royal Charter*, which had broken up so quickly on the rocks, but every
iron ship afloat, and those still on the stocks. The experts were not con-

165

cerned with the dead of yesterday, gone beyond recall, but with tomorrow's dead, who might still be saved. They were Captain H. Harris, RN, Nautical Assessor for the Board of Trade; Mr O'Dowd, solicitor for the Board; Mr J. S. Mansfield, Stipendiary Magistrate of Liverpool; and Mr T. B. Aspinall, a barrister appointed by the owners to uphold their interests.

After Mr O'Dowd's opening remarks, he went on to give a concise summary of what had happened to the *Royal Charter*, from the time of her leaving Melbourne to her helpless arrival on the rocks of Moelfre. He intended to call Mr Smith, of Beaumaris Customs, as a witness to the breaking up of the ship; which brought him to the heart of the matter. 'There are two most important considerations suggested by this inquiry,' he said. 'First, this shivering to atoms of an iron vessel seems not only to indicate a deficiency of strength but a positive weakness.' The second point was the conduct of the Captain. Mr O'Dowd was reluctant to throw the slightest imputation on his memory, but nevertheless the court should judge him as strictly as if he was still alive and able to answer for himself before the court. Mr O'Dowd would obtrude no opinions of his own, but confine himself to the calling of witnesses. Let the court judge.

The first witness was David Strongman, one of the quartermasters. He had been on watch and his duties had included sounding the lead; he was able to give them a nautically accurate and detailed account of what had happened. Mr W. H. Morse was next, and, as he was a magistrate himself, his opinion of the Captain's qualities were listened to with care; his evidence was entirely favourable. He was followed by Henry Carew Taylor, who told how Captain Withers had often said that the *Royal Charter* 'would neither wear nor tear, and that her masts were wrongly placed.'

Owen Williams, another quartermaster, gave evidence as to courses steered and what sails were set. Mr Aspinall put to him a series of questions designed to elicit the fact that the women and children were not abandoned. Williams told how, as soon as the hawser was secured, the Chief Officer had sent him aft to call forward the lady passengers—and how the ship divided before he could even reach them. He told how the Third Officer had tried to get a lady passenger to go ashore, and how she had refused. Both officers, he said, could have got ashore and saved their lives, had they wished; but they did not, to the end they appeared anxious only to save the ladies.

Captain Harris asked a few minor technical questions, and then William Foster, the carpenter, testified. He made it clear that the anchors had been properly paid out, with the Captain standing by to see it done correctly. Before the voyage he had helped repair the ship, along with some thirty of forty men; this was usual with such large ships, and the repairs were minor, caulking the decks, and so on. In reply to Mr Aspinall, he stated that he had checked that there were no leaks, after she struck on the sand; she opened only when the hurricane began to beat her on the rocks. 'Nothing could withstand the beating she got there,' he said firmly. 'She was a very strong ship. I would be glad to go out in her again if she had had the luck to get home safe. She was perfectly tight during the voyage.'

Thomas Cormick, steward, said that he was the last living witness to see the passengers in the saloon. They had been sent below by Captain Taylor, to avoid unnecessary casualties when the masts were cut away. They were not put into boats, there was no point in it. He had got into a boat at the last, and it had been simply smashed to pieces. The distance from ship to shore at that point was only ten yards, but it was impossible to swim there. He did not say that survival was a matter of chance only, but made clear that it was.

He was followed by James Russell. Russell, honestly recognising that he had been in error, at once did his best to undo the harm he had originally done to the reputation of Captain Taylor. He had seen him frequently and never known him in an improper state. Answering Captain Harris, he said that it was true that Captain Adams had told him it was going to blow hard; that was at sunset. Mr Aspinall asked him for the time when it had really begun to blow hard. Not before 8 pm, replied Russell. In other words, when the clipper was already north of Anglesey, and the die was cast.

Mr Aspinall then read a letter from John Bradbury, still too seriously ill to be moved. Bradbury was anxious to contradict a report that he had said that the Captain was drunk. He may have done so, in a rambling, semi-conscious state. He could not have done so consciously, as the statement was completely untrue. He had never seen even a single one of the ship's officers anything but completely sober. Bradbury recovered from his terrible injuries, became a pioneer writer of popular guidebooks, and received a bronze medal for saving a man from drowning.

Samuel Edward Gapper, the New Zealand farmer, said simply that he agreed with most of the evidence he had heard. He described how Captains Withers and Adams had conferred with the Captain as to the situation and what was to be done about it. Very little, Captain Adams had told him; they would have to swim before they got ashore. Questioned by Mr Aspinall, Gapper stated that, from some source, word for the ladies to go forward had in fact reached the after saloon, and that they were actually beginning to do so when the ship broke in two. Even then, the officers had not given up the attempt. He had heard John Croome, the young Fourth Officer, tell the ladies he would try to get them ashore in the boats. He had witnessed an attempt being made, and had seen the men washed overboard in doing so. All the officers had behaved, in his opinion, better even that could have been expected in the circumstances.

Joseph Rodgers, the hero of the affair, who was to be officially fêted in Liverpool next day, 16 November, took the stand. The first part of his testimony was damaging to the Captain. As an able seaman, he had taken part in setting the various sails and in trying to take them in again. Some had been set for only ten minutes before being taken in. A picture emerged of the Captain trying various expedients, all of which had failed, and that all was not quite as it should have been aloft. Just how desperate was the situation? people began to ask themselves.

This was soon answered by Rowland Hughes, cox of Moelfre life-boat. He had not seen any signals of distress, nor had anyone else; if they had, the life-boat could not have helped the *Royal Charter*; no life-boat in the world could. He had never seen such a storm. Before 10 pm the wind was east by south, but between 10 and 11 pm it changed round to NE and blew a complete hurricane. It was a hushed court that listened to George Suaicar and then heard Mr O'Dowd say that this concluded the evidence referring to the circumstances of the wreck. They would adjourn for a week, to prepare evidence for the next stage, designed to raise the issue of the strength of the *Royal Charter*. Was she of the usual strength for iron ships? If so, was that strength sufficient?

*   *   *

The very first witness, when the Inquiry was resumed, was Mr Smith, the Receiver of Wreck, the man who, above all others, knew what the rocks had done to the *Royal Charter*. Questioned by Mr Aspinall as to the strength of the vessel, he said, dryly, that she seemed to him to be one of the strongest vessels he had ever seen, for three boiler makers had been working, when the tide was out, on one of her plates which was then exposed. It had taken them three days to loosen it.

Mr Mellor thought he had his cue. Up he jumped. He was a solicitor from Oldham, he said; he had himself lost a brother and a cousin in the wreck. Might he put a question at this point?

Mr Mansfield, the Magistrate, ruled that the question should not be put directly, but through Mr O'Dowd.

Mr Mellor said that the question he wanted to ask was, what had been done for the recovery of the bodies?

The solicitor from Oldham could not have chosen an audience more unsympathetic than this one, nor could he have chosen a worse place or time to ask that question. Every day now, bodies were being washed ashore, miles away from the wreck, some of them hundreds of miles away.

The grave of Joseph Rodgers in Ford Cemetery, Liverpool. *Photo : RCSE Ltd/ Ken Jones*

Pray for the Soul of
JOE RODGERS,
THE HERO OF THE ROYAL CHARTER.
26ᵀᴴ OCTOBER 1859.
RECTED BY THE 'EVENING EXPRESS'

Captain Withers was picked up in Bull Bay, near Amlwch, and was identi-fied by a silver snuff box presented to him by the passengers of the *Glouces-ter*; in his pockets still was £36 in gold. Near him were a dead German, the body weighted down with a belt containing gold coins, gold nuggets, and gold dust, and a woman, badly disfigured, trussed up in the stays and heavy clothing of the time. Another woman was washed ashore as far away as Portaferry, in County Down, Ireland; she was wearing stays and a stocking marked 'S. A. Foster', so it was presumed to be Mrs Foster, of Manchester, the friend of the handsome Mrs Woodruffe, buried weeks ago at Moelfre. At Castletown, in the Isle of Man, another female body came ashore; it was held together only by the clothing, which indicated that the wearer was Miss F. Davis. Recognition was impossible, there being no flesh on the face or hair on the head, the skull showing through; but presumably it was one of the Misses Davis known to Mr Gapper—one of the two girls who were so 'very fond of dancing'. A headless man came ashore at the mouth of the river Conway, in Wales; an unidentified man was picked up at Holyhead. At Moelfre, only James Potts, the unfortunate digger who had broken his thigh and was being given a free passage home; he still had on him some of the money subscribed by the passengers.

All this made nonsense of the idea that most of the missing bodies were still trapped in the wreck, or that, supposing they were, it was a kindness to allow the relatives to look upon the dead faces, where they still had faces.

The court was very brusque with Mr Mellor. Mr O'Dowd said coldly that the recovery of the bodies had nothing to do with the inquiry, which was concerned solely with the loss of the vessel. Mr Smith had already told them that the owners had done everything in reason to recover the bodies. Mr Mellor snapped back.

'What have they done?' he flashed.

Mr Mansfield, the Magistrate, immediately ruled Mr Mellor out of order, and the hearing proceeded without further interruption.

The court was well aware, from the enormous number of letters they had received, that the public was deeply disturbed about the loss of so

The wreck site of the *Royal Charter* at high water, September, 1960—the worst possible place for a ship to be driven ashore, as the masters of the Pilot Boats stated at the Inquiry. *Photo: Alexander McKee*

fine a vessel, a triumph of nineteenth-century engineering; in comparison with her predecessors, almost a floating hotel. There was a vague feeling that it was somehow not right for such a ship to be destroyed. There had to be a reason. Some simple, single reason. But not the real reason. That was too awful to contemplate. The court, however, was going to do just exactly that.

John Sheppard, master of Pilot Boat No 4, and Richard Parry, master of Pilot Boat No 11, next gave evidence. Both were extremely experienced seamen, both had been out that night, both testified to the unprecedented power of the hurricane, which had so nearly destroyed them—both boats had been damaged, one had been reported lost. Both men stated that the place where the *Royal Charter* had struck was the worst possible—any vessel ashore there in any wind was bound to break up. It was all vivid, first-hand evidence, made more effective by the straightforward, matter-of-fact tones of these two master seamen who had ridden out that night of horror—but only just. Both boats had drifted to leeward some seven or eight miles, they admitted. They were obviously very glad to be still alive.

The following witnesses were, in a sense, anti-climax. They were the men who built the *Royal Charter*. Their evidence was very detailed, and they survived unshaken a close questioning by experts. The clipper had clearly been no 'coffin ship', her loss no case of an 'avoidable wreck'. Such cases were not then infrequent, and were to result in 1876, after agitation by Samuel Plimsoll, in the compulsory marking of a 'Plimsoll Line'. Conservative elements were also suggesting that the iron ship was inherently weaker than the wooden ship; and both allegations were being backed by the Royal National Life-boat Institution, which had a vested interest in seaworthiness. But it was clear that the *Royal Charter* had been a good seaboat and better built than the average iron ship. She had not, of course, withstood being beaten up and down on the savage rocks of Moelfre in a 100 mph gale of wind. No ship was built with that object in view, dryly observed her builder, William Patterson, and if she were, it would do her no good. Extra strength meant extra weight. If she had been built of 4-inch iron, like a floating battery, her own weight would have beaten her to pieces.

She was a clipper, with a length seven times her beam; the impact of the rocks had almost divided her bottom into two parts, and then the following seas had broken her, 'as you would a stick across your knee'.

Some idea of what those strains must have been were later provided by HMS *Montagu*, a brand-new battleship which went on the rocks of Lundy in 1906. She was built of steel, not iron, and she had to endure a gale, not a hurricane; but it was impossible to salvage her. The hull, much broader than that of a clipper, was so shattered that it was only held in place by the massive armour belt, according to the then Director of Naval Construction, Sir Philip Watts.

Other witnesses were brought forward to speak for the *Royal Charter*. George Barber, a shipwright surveyor for the Board of Trade, had visited the scene of the wreck with a more than professional interest, for he had lost a nephew in her. He was convinced, he said, that a wooden ship of the same dimensions would have gone to pieces as readily as the *Royal Charter*. William Macdonald, of Liverpool Corporation, stated that he had tested some of the plates salvaged from the wreck, and that they had stood an enormous strain before breaking. Captain Martin said that the anchor cables had been tested to a strain of 72 tons. Captain Francis Boyce, who had been in command on her first voyage, testified to her qualities as a seaboat. (He was not asked about the course steered by Captain Taylor, but said privately that it was intended to gain time and was 'something lacking in leeway'.) Dr Scoresby's book, just published, was quoted. But most effective of all was Mr R. S. Steel, Insurance Broker.

The *Royal Charter*, he said quietly, had been insured at the rate of 70 shillings out and home. That was a low rate. Surveyors' reports were not received before her last voyage; it was not thought necessary, they had such a good opinion of the *Royal Charter*.

Then Captain Harris put directly the question of iron versus wood.

'We make no distinction between an iron and a wooden ship,' replied Mr Steel. The only distinction they did make, he added, was between a sailing ship and a steamship. The rate for the steamship was lower.

As far as the court was concerned, that virtually settled the matter. Insurance brokers had a pecuniary interest in being right. If they were wrong, they lost money. The critics of the *Royal Charter* did not face the penalty of bankruptcy if they proved to be mistaken.

In his summing-up, Mr Mansfield singled out the critics, in their turn, for criticism. If Mr Mellor was still in court, his ears must have been burning. The Post Office, said the Magistrate, had been like the lion's mouth in Venice, from the number of accusations dropped into it. The Board of Trade had replied to them all, suggesting that the people concerned might wish to be heard at the Inquiry. But not a single one had come forward to make his accusation in person. Where the names of other people had been quoted, as authorities for some statement, these people, when contacted, had denied making any such accusation. Consequently, he deduced that the imputations were malignant and groundless. He would not even mention them in his report to the Board. As far as Captain Taylor's conduct was concerned, he was a gallant and brave seaman, and those who had attacked his character had done so from vile and unworthy motives. The conduct of the captain and officers, and, indeed, of many of the passengers, too, had been such as to make one proud of being their countrymen; perhaps a nobler spectacle was never witnessed, except in the memorable case of the loss of the *Birkenhead*.

Mr Mansfield and Captain Harris made their report to the Board of Trade on 28 November. They exonerated the ship—in strength of hull, in strength of anchor cables, and in the quality of her sails she was at least the equal of the average vessel of her class. However, some want of preparation aloft to meet stormy weather was noted. Stating that they were judging by the event, they said that the decision to cut away the masts should have been taken earlier, before the anchor cables parted. But they perfectly appreciated the arguments in favour of the course actually pursued—the *Prince* had found herself in a similar position off Balaklava in 1854, and the cutting away of the masts had fouled the screw and was the direct cause of that disaster. The Captain of the *Prince* had been blamed because he *did* cut away the masts, therefore it was hard to blame Captain Taylor because he did not, although, in their opinion, it might have eased the strain on the cables and so prevented them from breaking. They appreciated that, if the screw was stopped while the masts were cut away, in order to prevent its being fouled when they fell, that would have increased the strain on the cables and they might have broken in any case. They had to take into account also the 'unexampled fury' of the gale, which entirely neutralised the powerful action of the screw propeller, so that the ship was 'no longer under command—a circumstance which Captain Taylor could not have anticipated.' They concluded that the ship was not lost by default of the master; and that 'the officers and crew to the last were indifferent to the preservation of their own lives and solely intent on their duty.'

*   *   *

The news took some time to reach Australia and, meanwhile, some eager beaver of a newsman, like the theatre critic who reviews a play without actually bothering to see it, announced the safe arrival in Liverpool of the *Royal Charter*. Presumably, the news which actually reached him was of her safe arrival off Queenstown, and he concluded that nothing much could happen to her on the last lap of her long journey. As a result, many letters of congratulation on their safe arrival home were written to the long dead passengers by their Australian relatives and friends. But the booming guns of the next mail ship announced disaster. Mr Fenwick never received the news of the loss of his wife and children, for he had died at Melbourne only a week after they had died at Moelfre. There was speculation at the diggings, where the *Amherst and Back Creek Advertiser* stated that, 'several miners, who had large sums of money, embarked by the *Royal Charter* with the intention of settling in England. Considering the number of "pile" claims obtained at Scandinavian Lead, we may conjecture that a large number of miners from this lead have perished, with the fruits of their hard-earned toil, in the angry waves which engulfed the *Royal Charter*.'

In England the storm subsided. There were only a few gusts still to come. The parting of the anchor cables of the *Royal Charter*—and the failure of one cable of the *Great Eastern*—caused stricter standards to be laid down and enforced. The argument of iron versus wood went on, but was soon overtaken by steel. The era of the hybrid ship, using both sail and steam, had not much longer to run. In a comparatively few years the power, efficiency, and reliability of steam had increased so much that the sail also was on its way out, a loss only to the artist or to the romantic.

The gold was almost all recovered, one way or another. But its actual ownership was not easy to define, and the underwriters by no means came off as badly as they had feared. They had insured the consigned bullion for £322,440, the rest of the cargo for £5,000, and the ship itself for £120,000. They were now the owners of the wreck, but their losses had been considerable and salvage costs were heavy. On some days, however, the divers brought up a good haul. On 7 December, for instance, they recovered 12 boxes, 12 bags, and gold bars and dust, to the estimated value of £100,000; and on 21 December they brought to the surface 24 bars of gold, 5 broken pieces of bars, 601 sovereigns, and some other coins, making a total of more than £20,000. There was not much doubt as to the original ownership of the boxes and the bars, but the bags of gold, and the loose coins, may well have been the personal property of passengers, deposited for safe keeping in the strongroom. There was no way whatever of deciding. By Christmas, 1859, barely two months after the disaster, reports of the total amount of salvaged gold varied between £275,000 and £370,000; and a month later all reports were unanimous in stating that of the consigned bullion, all but £30,000 had been recovered. And a month after that, the underwriters sold the wreck to Gibbs, Bright for £1,000. The sum found on the bodies, or on the shore, and handed in officially to the Receiver of Wreck, totalled only £1,200. Unless found on an identified body, it was forfeited to the Crown. It is clear, in retrospect, that much of the salvaged gold was not bullion at all, but had been originally the property of the passengers and crew. The total amount of the treasure cannot have been much less than half a million pounds.

Gibbs, Bright carried out salvage work for a further two years, interested not only in gold, but in the brass, iron and wood as well, and then in their turn sold the remains to a group of Anglesey people, who carried out operations on the site until 1873. When they lifted the sternpost, more than 500 golden sovereigns were found among the twisted ironwork. There are probably a few gold coins or broken bars on the seabed still, but it is unlikely that they could be found by anything except chance.

The last *Royal Charter* death occurred more than two years after the tragedy. Worn out by the physical and emotional demands made on him by the sorrowing friends and relatives of the dead, Stephen Roose Hughes became seriously ill a few months later. He appeared to recover, but died in March, 1862, while sitting quietly by his fireside after tea. He died in poverty, for not only had he given his heart to the bereaved, but the whole of his little fortune.

*   *   *

I came over the hill at Moelfre and went down towards the wreck of the *Royal Charter*, one hundred years and some months after it had happened. It was near high water, as it had been for Charles Dickens, and the scene was exactly as he had described it—absolutely no sign on the quiet sea, blue in the sun, that anything very terrible had ever happened there; only now, there was a small white memorial stone, from that distance only a speck on the hill above Port Helaeth. I crossed the field where Mr Wagstaffe had seen the abandoned body of the man who had died while being carried up to the village, and dropped down onto those sinister rocks where the tide sucked quietly. Then I dumped my kit on them and prepared my underwater camera for action. I had one great advantage over Dickens, who might have made exactly the same journey as I had, from Portsmouth. Mine was the century of the common diver, so to speak; the five pounds worth of simple equipment I had carried over the hill at once opened up to me the whole of the seabed in the area. The wreck lay in only 18 feet of water. 'Bags of good vis. in Anglesey,' I had been told. But there wasn't, because masses of plankton had just begun to drift into the area; I could see it clearly through my mask, like slowly drifting rain, as I lay on the surface and took a deep breath for my first dive into that abominable peasoup.

Bad though the visibility was, some three or four feet, and although I never saw anything positively identifiable as the wreck in that first 30 minutes, it was quite sufficient for my purpose. I had come, because I wanted to see the place for myself; to understand exactly why the *Royal Charter* had broken up so quickly, and why most of the dead had been stunned rather than drowned. As I went headfirst down into that dim green world that had destroyed the *Royal Charter*, I had the answer. There was no need for a detailed examination, with breathing apparatus. It was

175

(*Opposite*) The author after making his first dive with an aqualung in August, 1960. The aqualung cylinder is really an ex-RAF oxygen bottle, its harness is made from women's belts, the weightbelt is an ex-army belt converted and, for protection from the cold, the 'suit' consists of three old, worn-out jerseys. *Photo: Alexander McKee copyright*

The headland where the *Hindlea* was wrecked in October, 1959. Taken at low water, September, 1985. No sign of the ship is visible now. *Photo: Alexander McKee*

Coxswain Richard Evans after winning his second gold medal for the rescue of crew from the Greek steamer *Nafsiporos*, during December, 1966, in winds gusting to 120 mph. *Photo: Don Smith (Radio Times copyright)*

all horribly plain and obvious. There were rock ledges only a few feet down; beyond them, there was sometimes a slope, sometimes a drop into deep water, fringed with weed. Whenever I went straight down into that deep water, invariably I became aware of a solid rock face rising up somewhere towards the surface in the murk, in front, or to the side, or behind. I had to be very careful not to go down too fast, because of the danger of collision. It was quite the worst ship-trap I had ever seen.

If I have perhaps seemed a little hard, here and there, on the authors of wild accusations, it is because, before I had ever gone into the evidence in detail, I had made this short underwater reconnaissance.

And also because of the wreck in the bay, the first thing I saw as I breasted the headland from Moelfre—a small steamer, smashed up against the headland, only her upperworks showing, obviously a modern wreck, and lying about half a mile from the *Royal Charter*. It was the 650-ton *Hindlea*, wrecked in a hurricane on 27 October, 1959—by remarkable coincidence, exactly one hundred years and one day after the *Royal Charter* disaster.

An hour or so later, having fallen on the rocks and broken my leg, I was talking to Mr Richard Evans, cox of Moelfre life-boat. Nobody knew her story better than he did, because he had taken off the crew; and because he had done so, no one was better qualified to assess what had happened to the *Royal Charter*—he had made the rescue in a hurricane, with winds gusting to 104 mph, and had been awarded the Gold Medal of the RNLI for it, a decoration as rare as the Victoria Cross. The *Hindlea* had been a coaster, a modern steel ship, with steel anchor cables, and engines far more powerful and efficient than those of the iron clipper. They had availed her not at all. True, the steel cables had not parted; but nothing could withstand the force of that sea and that wind, and her anchors had dragged. And there she lay, shattered on the rocks.

The only difference, after a century of industrial invention, was this. That where Rowland Hughes, cox of Moelfre life-boat in 1859, had failed to launch his oared boat, Dick Evans, with his motor-powered vessel, had not only managed to do so, but had carried out the rescue. There had been, admittedly, only eight men to be saved, but even that was a miracle. 'There but for the Grace of God I would be' is what he feels when he passes the wreck today. 'What possible chance was there of any anchor chains holding a ship in a 104 mph hurricane? 'Wind and sea of such velocity has to be seen to be believed, especially when on a lee shore with breaking seas, such as was the case with these two vessels—the *Hindlea* and the *Royal Charter*.'

Man has tamed and shaped the land; but he has not yet tamed the sea. And probably he never will.

Chapter 16

GOLD FEVER

The news broke on 9 July, 1985. 'THE SUNKEN MILLIONS: DIVERS FIND FABULOUS GOLD HAUL', read one headline. 'HURRICANE THAT BLEW A FORTUNE TO THE DEEP', ran another, retelling the story of the *Royal Charter*. The source material was probably taken from the original edition of this book. Published in 1961, for two dozen years it had been the 'bible' on the wreck story used by treasure-seeking divers and general public alike. One of the many who had got hold of a copy and was now following with increasing excitement the news of sunken gold and conflict between rival diving teams over the wreck site, was John H. Bradbury.

This was not the John Bradbury of the *Royal Charter* who, before he died in 1904, had been the last living survivor of the disaster, but his great-grandson. John H. Bradbury's mother, Mrs D. M. Bradbury, was one of more than two dozen people who had written to me after publication of *The Golden Wreck*.. Like many other relatives, she possessed information and relics, one of which was a candlestick inscribed, 'Presented to John Bradbury by William Martin & John Fell, Captains in charge of the wreck, Decr 9th 1859'.

Among the newspaper cuttings she sent to me was one from the Manchester *City News* of 8 November, 1919. To commemorate the sixtieth anniversary, a reporter had been sent to Moelfre:

During a recent visit to the scene of this great disaster I was fortunate enough to meet several of the inhabitants of the village who well remember the wreck and the events that accompanied it. One of these—Captain Owen—in whose house I was accommodated, gave me many graphic details. He was early at the wreck, and the first thing he saw was a man, whose clothing had been torn from him by the violence of the waves, being carried away to a cabin on the shore by four men. He proved to be a Manchester passenger—the late Mr John Bradbury. This young man had an extraordinary escape . . .

Suffering from a broken leg and other injuries, nevertheless John Bradbury

179

had emerged from the breakers with his life, but the fortune he was bringing home with him was lost in the sea. Mrs D. M. Bradbury recalled of
her husband's grandfather:

> He always said he was coming back from Australia with thousands
> of gold nuggets, and would have been a very wealthy man—but
> everything went down in the wreck and as far as I know nothing
> has ever been recovered.

Her son, the present John H. Bradbury, is a direct descendant of the
shipwrecked John Bradbury. Apart from this connection with the *Royal
Charter*, he had become intrigued by his ancestor because there were so
many questions still unanswered about him—when did he go to Australia,
and why? Above all, why was he coming back to England in 1859?

Therefore, when his wife saw a news item on television about the new
gold hunt on the *Royal Charter*, and the whole story 'blew up', as he expressed it, in a blaze of publicity, John decided to drive down to Moelfre from
his home in the north of England.

> My feelings when seeing the site of the wreck were almost totally
> unemotional, as I am not a sentimentalist. I thought the site was bleak
> and barren and uninteresting, and would hardly describe the ledge
> of masonry as fearful—just bad luck the wind blew up. Neither was
> the diving operation in any way like a Wembley Cup-final. The work
> seemed to be demanding infinite patience and to an onlooker far from
> laced with excitement. The local community were friendly and help-
> ful when approached but clearly viewed the latest operation as yet
> another inevitably fruitless dig. The salvage team clearly had a degree
> of dedication and purpose and were totally polite and courteous whilst
> at the same time discreet and diplomatic.

Although none of the divers would talk about the gold, Bradbury was
struck by their enthusiasm. 'There's a glint in their eye,' he told me.

The project supervisor, Bernie McDonald, spoke of their finds. There
was crockery, a pair of elegant spectacles, coins and medallions, and one
morning when Bradbury was there, a diver brought up the base of a
candlestick identical in every respect to the one given by the wreck
supervisors in 1859 to his great-grandfather. Such candlestick holders were
probably part of the ship's furniture, he thought.

While he was in Anglesey, John H. Bradbury visited the Receiver of
Wreck, a Customs Officer who holds salvaged goods for a year and a day
after recovery, pending proof of ownership. If proved, the items of 'wreck'
then revert to the owner—with a suitable award to the salvor.

The local folk were phlegmatic and sceptical about yet another 'red-herring' operation, but many holiday-makers from the mainland, and of course the news-hungry pressmen, were intrigued by the mystery of the lost 'treasure', plus the reported conflict over the 'gold bullion' by two rival groups of divers. The whole story was new to most of these people and, according to Bradbury, many of them were asking for copies of my book which, although it had gone through one hardback and three paperback editions, was unobtainable.

For a week I remained ignorant of the fact that the *Royal Charter* had suddenly become 'news'. I was so hard-pressed by another project that I had no time to watch television or do more than skim the newspapers. My first intimation was a telephone call from John H. Bradbury on the evening of 15 July, 1985. I had researched the book in 1959, written it in 1960, and had it published in 1961, so the call came literally from out of the blue. However, I managed to remember having had an interesting correspondence with Mrs Bradbury who, I now learned, had died in 1975. Her son told me that 'all hell had broken loose' over the new salvage attempt on the *Royal Charter*. I thanked him, made a note of it, and went back to my urgent project.

But it was not to be. A few days later I received a letter from Peter Day, dated 17 July:

> Further to a very brief meeting yesterday, with Margaret Rule, I would very much appreciate meeting you to discuss matters concerning the 'Royal Charter'. If one day more is to be written about the ship and her fate you MUST be the one to do so and perhaps now is the time for you to be made aware of work, finds and events over the last years.

I quickly whipped through my files and, sure enough, there were two cuttings from the *Sunday Express* of 2 April and 4 June, 1972, regarding a large-scale excavation being carried out by John Leyland Smart (50) and Peter Day (27). These were not the divers currently working the wreck who, calling themselves Bestspeed Limited, were directed by Joseph McCormack and Bernie McDonald. On the contrary, they were a local group who had been interested in the *Royal Charter* for a very long time. On 20 July I rang Mr Day, who told me briefly what had happened that year, 1985, stating that there was to be a court hearing on 30 July, at which both groups of divers would appear. Like John H. Bradbury, Peter Day had a direct connection with the *Royal Charter* (through a Welsh relative, a great uncle, Robert Williams, a foreman shipwright on her construction).

Then I received a third communication, dated 5 August, from a University historian. He referred to 'an increasingly emotional, not to say violent, issue . . . Differences are being pursued by both legal and illegal means.'

I had already seen in *The Daily Telegraph* of 30 July a news item reporting a night raid from the sea on the shore encampment of Bestspeed Limited: a dinghy and two inflatables sunk, an engine smashed, aqualung cylinders removed. That was what was reported. How accurate it was, I could not judge.

I was tempted to go to Anglesey right away without waiting to convince my publisher that a revised and updated version of *The Golden Wreck* was called for, and without waiting for that long-expected break in the bad weather which had ruined most of the summer of 1985 and made it the worst season for diving off the South Coast that I could recall. But I held off, and then got one of those minor illnesses dubbed a 'virus infection'; and while I recovered the wind howled off the sea and raged against my windows, as it had done for months. Underwater visibility was measured not in feet but in inches.

As I recovered, so did the weather. When Ilse and I drove off for Anglesey on 10 September for a five-day visit, we found that we had chosen four days of perfect weather, one day indifferent—and that one spent on the road home. This was important to my purpose, which was to dive both the *Royal Charter* and the *Hindlea* (or what was left of them), take underwater photographs if possible, to re-photograph both wreck sites from the surface in colour, and photograph various related places, such as Llanallgo Church and Point Lynas lighthouse, which the accident of breaking my leg on the afternoon of my first full day in Moelfre in 1960, had prevented. And also of course to interview all concerned—both rival salvage groups and also the local historians, marine scientists, underwater archaeologists, and local authority and museum representatives, with the object of reporting their varying views as accurately and vividly as possible. Subject only to my own imperfections and the law of libel.

A preliminary hearing before the honourable Mr Justice Sheen had been held in the Admiralty Court, Liverpool, on 30 July. The plaintiffs were Bestspeed Limited and the defendant was John Smart. Joseph McCormack, a director of Bestspeed, had sworn an affidavit on 18 June, in which he stated that the *Royal Charter* had left Melbourne, Australia on 26 August, 1859, carrying 68,397 ozs of gold (£273,000-worth at the then existing prices) and £48,000 in sovereigns; that she had been wrecked on Trwyn

Salvage work on the *Royal Charter* in the 1970s. A mixed crew on the pontoon, sorting finds. Jack Smart, in overalls, is in the centre. *Photo: RCSE Ltd/Ken Jones*

A squashed pewter dish and other artefacts from the wreck, including stoppers and a chess pawn. *Photo: RCSE Ltd/Ken Jones*

Porth-y-Mor near Traeth Lligwy; that not all of the treasure had been recovered, and that Bestspeed had been trying to salve it for about six weeks. Their operation was based on a farmhouse with a permanent forward camp on the cliffs overlooking the wreck, which had always been manned by two people living in small tents, but for the past month they had had a marquee there as well. Their team consisted of about ten divers. They were shifting boulders, sand and gravel by means of an air-lift powered by a compressor on shore. They had recovered some small items from the engine room and expected to reach the cargo in the next few days.

Having stated the size of his operation (which might help him to establish a claim as 'salvor in possession'), McCormack then described the rival team and what its equipment consisted of.

> At about high water on 17th June 1985 the Defendant (John Smart) who lives close by the wreck at Traeth Bychan, Moelfre, Anglesey, arrived on site with a 40′ × 40′ barge containing a Portacabin (plus lifting derrick, airlift and compressors) and assorted articles of diving equipment plus a fishing craft and 2 inflatables and the Plaintiffs fear that it is his intention to take over the site and attempt to salve the cargo from the wreck. About 9 to 10 personnel have been observed. It is believed that the Defendant undertook an attempted salvage operation about three years ago which proved to be unsuccessful and was abandoned and that he has not returned to the site since that time.

Basically, the difference between the two expeditions was that McCormack's was shore-based with only light boats and nowhere for them to shelter if a northerly gale blew up (although, if there was time, they could be run up on the nearby sand beach of Traeth Lligwy). Smart's larger and more numerous craft, which had been purchased and prepared specifically for the *Royal Charter* project, did have shelter—a tiny, almost land-locked harbour beside his house at Traeth Bychan.

McCormack then went on to stress what everyone almost always forgets, when 'treasure' is sought or recovered—the cost of the search and the recovery.

> The Plaintiffs have invested a large amount of time, effort and money in this operation over the last six weeks and have almost completed the difficult work of exposing the wreck. Their expenditure to date is in the order of £15–20,000 and the operational costs amount to £2,000 weekly. The Plaintiffs are concerned that the Defendant intends to dispossess them of the wreck and intends to reap the benefit

of their work and investment for himself. They are further concerned for the safety of those concerned in the operation, both on their own behalf and on behalf of the Defendant in that explosives are being used on site and whilst they can ensure their own personnel are in a position of safety when the charges are detonated they have no control over the whereabouts or safety of the Defendant or any men he employs.

McCormack's deposition of 18 June was followed on 26 July by another one, also made on behalf of Bestspeed Limited, by Bernie McDonald, whose title was Archaeologist and Project Supervisor. He swore to having visited the *Royal Charter* site 'in excess of sixty times over the four years prior to the Plaintiff's initial operation', including the conducting of an archaeology class for members of the Liverpool Sub-Aqua Club at Easter, 1985. McDonald stated:

> At no time has any Representative of Seaton Marine or of the Defendants (John Smart) made known to me their interest in the 'ROYAL CHARTER' other than when the Defendant first arrived at the wreck site on 16th June 1985. I did suspect that the Defendant and Seaton Marine were interested in the wreck prior to their arrival at the wreck site, only as a result of local speculation and hearsay.

McDonald added that his wife, Susan McDonald, had telephoned John Ledger of Seaton Marine Services to tell them all that Bestspeed were the 'salvors in possession' of that wreck. This, the marine equivalent of the old saying, that 'possession is nine-tenths of the law', is best established by having marker buoys up top (which is also an invitation to piracy) and leaving a lot of equipment around on the bottom, just to prove that you have been working there. Joe McCormack was certainly well acquainted with this problem, for he had taken part in one of Sid Wignall's expeditions to locate and excavate the Spanish Armada wreck, the *Santa Maria de la Rosa*, off the Blaskets in Southern Ireland. Just what happened in that case is described at length in *Full Fathom Five* by Colin Martin (Chatto & Windus, 1975).

In addition, McDonald was an expert in the use of explosives underwater, holding a certificate from the Merseyside Police.

> I have made use of explosives in the salvage of the vessel (the *Royal Charter*) to date . . . I have had some considerable experience in the use of explosives on marine archaeological finds and in fact when working on the wreck of the Royal Yacht 'MARY' (belonging to King Charles II and sunk 1675) I made extensive use of my knowledge of explosives in recovering many artefacts under the supervision of

Dr P. M. Davis and Members of the Merseyside County Museum. The use of explosives in recovering archaeological artefacts is accepted in the circles of marine archaeology as a valid method of recovery. I am quite confident that the limited use of explosives by me on the wreck of the 'ROYAL CHARTER' in no way damaged the artefacts to any greater extent than they would be by the normal method of chipping away concretions with a chisel and hammer.

With this affidavit, McDonald submitted a copy of a list of artefacts recovered from the *Royal Charter* which he had delivered to the Receiver of Wreck at Holyhead on 24 July. They included six gold sovereigns dated 1842, 1844, 1850, 1851, 1852, 1859; two gold nuggets (belonging, perhaps, to some unfortunate miner); four gold rings; a silver crown and a silver florin—the private possessions of individuals.

The result of the preliminary hearing was a kind of temporary compromise. During the lunch recess, Mr Smart's counsel drew up by hand a document which became an agreement by both parties and became a court order. Bestspeed were allowed to continue their salvage operation without hindrance, but Mr Smart was to receive lists from them of all they recovered, each day, and was permitted to employ two agents to watch on his behalf what was salvaged and to inspect any storerooms. If the final decision went in Mr Smart's favour, then the artefacts recovered and listed by Bestspeed would have to be given to him. But a full-blown court case was likely to be very costly. The position would be reviewed on 1 October, 1985, although the High Court action might not be until mid-1987.

This was the situation when Ilse and I drove from Hampshire to North Wales on 10 September. We had done this sort of thing before, with some of my war books, which were always written from the viewpoints of both sides. The people concerned had been shooting at each other some years before, but this did not prevent us from being friendly with them all.

Chapter 17

THE WRECKS REVEALED

Hayling Island, where I live, overlooking the English Channel, is some 300 miles as the motor car drives from the Isle of Anglesey, which juts out into the Irish Sea. Hayling is part of the land which the South Saxons took from the ancestors of the Welsh after they landed at Selsey Bill in AD 477. Place names indicate that they embarked from near Emden, then part of the Frisian empire in what is now West Germany. The first 200 miles of our journey were all Saxon. The first surprise, which alerted us to the reality of Welsh history, was the appearance of a castle or two—on the English side of the border. Not that we do not have fortifications on the Channel shores, but they are all coastal defences—Romans guarding against Saxon raids, Saxons guarding against Danish Viking raids, English guarding against invasion by Frenchmen, Spaniards, more French, and finally Germans. The idea of a contested frontier on land is not part of the English consciousness, but it must be of the Welsh. Anyway, here it was—out on the flat plain before the road rose up to the mountain wilderness of Wales.

On the way we had passed the occasional road sign depicting a running stag, as a warning to fast drivers of fast animals crossing, when on the curve of the road as it rose to a mountain landscape was a much larger sign showing a red dragon, also apparently about to cross the road. One had a mental picture that made Wales a most exciting place! When we arrived after a nine-hour journey, there had been no startling developments in the hunt for the 'many millions' in gold supposedly lying just over the headland. The newspaper headline 'MAN DIES IN DIVE ON WRECK' referred to a 22-year-old diver who had been killed 48 hours before on another Anglesey shipwreck, the *Meath*.

Next morning we drove out to the picturesquely named Tynygongl, a few miles inland from Moelfre. We were looking for a house called Pen y Bryn, which lay on a hillcrest approached by many narrow side roads, with here and there the grey, naked rock protruding from the earth. This was the home of Peter Day and his wife Pat, who was the daughter of John Smart ('Jack' to his friends). Peter weighs about 18 stone and not much of it is fat; he sells fire-fighting equipment and works from home,

187

with the telephone ringing all the time. He explained that it was his father-in-law who had started the Royal Charter Salvage Expedition back in the early 1970s.

They had begun active work on the wreck in 1972, following background research. During 1971–72 Peter wrote to all the relevant authorities—the Receiver of Wreck; Lloyds; Gibbs, Bright; and so on; and contacted possible supporters—including British Ropes and Dunlop; and to the Press, and to schools. I was familiar with this process from the *Mary Rose* project ten years earlier—1962 instead of 1971—and I also had received welcome support from British Ropes. Like us, they had had to learn by trial and error how to dig most efficiently underwater.

They had set up their equipment and been rewarded by a Day One Disaster. The basic digging tool was a big airlift which discharged the excavated soil and shingle onto an ex-Army pontoon. In spite of the shallowness of the water, their airlift had worked so efficiently, and brought up so much spoil, that it nearly sank the pontoon. The answer to that problem proved to be a second ex-Army pontoon so that their makeshift raft became in effect a twin-hull catamaran with better buoyancy and stability.

The lower parts of the *Royal Charter* still existed, but deeply buried under sand and gravel. Their primary objective was to find out which way round the wreck lay; had she indeed broken in two—or even into three parts—as some of the witnesses quoted in my book had stated? But in the first stage they were also interested in the artefacts they began to uncover, however prosaic. Peter's list of 1972, which he sent to the Receiver of Wreck, recorded such items as a Schweppes bottle, a champagne bottle (full), wine bottles (full and empty), a leather book spine, silver spoons, some gold sovereigns, a brass porthole, a gold tie-pin and, most intriguing, a gold eternity ring engraved *From W Newlove to M Davis 4th Feb 1856*.

Once, when they had dug down 12 feet into the seabed, Peter must have hallucinated, perhaps from cold and tiredness, for he seemed to see above him a row of corpses, their dead faces looking down on him.

In 1973, many of the smaller artefacts were still the pathetic remains of passengers and crew—wooden pieces from a game of draughts, a child's leather shoe, gold and copper coins (one sovereign was marked '1859—SYDNEY MINT AUSTRALIA'), but increasingly the finds represented machinery—a broken fire box door, four clinkering irons, six iron furnace bars, 13 brass boiler tubes, a piece of steam pipe with coupling and brass elbow.

The effect of the digging, however, was to make it much easier for casual underwater divers to visit the site in their absence to recover artefacts for themselves. One such diver was observed by an academic to surface with

Finds from the 1970s salvage work on the *Royal Charter*: wine bottles, sloe gin jars, cod bottles—all collectors' items. *Photo: RCSE Ltd/Ken Jones*

Typical small finds from the wreck: pottery, copper coins, spoons, a pencil and a ladle. *Photo: RCSE Ltd/Ken Jones*

Pathetic remains of boots and shoes from the first dig site. *Photo : RCSE Ltd/Ken Jones*

Machinery from the *Royal Charter*. *Photo : RCSE Ltd/Ken Jones*

a gold watch which, when he got it ashore, he promptly smashed to pieces on a rock in order to separate the gold from the (to him) worthless interior.

There were changes in the team over the years, but certain key people stood out, such as John Russum, the first engineer of the project, who gave up his job in Leeds to work on the *Royal Charter*; and Martin Bave, from Wolverhampton, who was the most methodical and developed an uncanny ability to spot things on the seabed, being the first to find gold items—a tie-pin and the ring. Both these men eventually bought houses nearby.

At last, they got down to the lower plates of the engine room. Now, the idea was not to recover artefacts, but to determine and draw the outline of what remained of the hull—portside, midships, starboard side and their levels; plus the levels below the ship. Their ultimate aim was to be able to put an 'X' on the seabed and say: 'That's where the bullion is!'

I was shown some of their drawings and plans, plus many photographs of the finds made over the years, and it was clear that Peter believed there had been more gold in the wreck than had been publicly reported. To find this had been their ultimate objective, the intrinsic value of many of the artefacts being nil; or, at the most, worthy only of display in a local

Members of the Royal Charter Salvage Expedition. Left to right: Peter Day, Dave Albiston, John Russum. *Photo: RCSE Ltd/Ken Jones*

museum where, as relics of the *Royal Charter*, they would prove fascinating, bringing contact with those who died in Anglesey's most terrible disaster. Jack Smart's team, the Royal Charter Salvage Expedition, had made no claim for the artefacts they had recovered from 1972 onwards.

In 1983 a diver from another sub-aqua club had found six gold sovereigns, which were declared to a Receiver of Wreck. Early in 1985, said Peter, they were completing work ready for a final onslaught on the bullion. Their previous floating base—the two ex-Army pontoons—had been smashed in a storm during the winter of 1979–1980, but now they had fitted up a barge which was to deploy a formidable list of excavation equipment, including four six-inch airlifts, two four-inch airlifts, plus a prop wash device. With that sort of power available, he reckoned, they would know within two weeks, one way or the other, if the gold was there or not.

In April they went on site for a trial working, but came off site about 18 May for work to be done on the barges:

We were ready to take the barge on site about 12 or 15 June, when one chamber of the barge was found to be flooding. When the tide went out it was looked at and it was found that someone had burnt a hole in the bottom with oxyacetylene equipment. We had no oxyacet on the barge, so a portable set must have been used, and it was clearly sabotage. The police were brought in and verified the facts. But we patched that up and Brian Meason went on site on 12 or 15 June. At that time there was a rubber dinghy and some divers on site—which was quite common. Never in our time on the wreck did we ever dissuade anyone from diving on the site unless they were a nuisance. We knew some of these particular divers, who were not on the wreck itself but were working in the rock gullies. Two days later they arrived with a solicitor and served us an injunction to stop us diving. Their story was, they had arrived in early May and that we had abandoned the site; they were using explosives and if we dived we might get hurt. Lord Boston (who owns the land) met them, and he was told: 'We're just here for a few days, then we're off to a site in Scotland.'

Once, eleven men went to my father-in-law's house, with a threat to attack me. The police were called, but it seems a mistake had been made about a green boat seen on the site which somebody reported was ours, whereas in fact our boat was not in the water that day but was on land three miles away with a dry hull.

Having spent the morning talking to Peter Day, we went down to Traeth Bychan, which is a sandy bay just south of Moelfre, to meet his father-in-

The Expedition at work over the wreck at low water. *Photo: RCSE Ltd/Ken Jones*

law, 'Jack' Smart, whose house is built on rocky ground with the sand beach on one side and the tiny, almost land-locked harbour on another. A very convenient site for working the *Royal Charter*; indeed his drawing-room was dominated by a huge lithograph of the ship. In the boat park was a damaged yacht which they had salvaged after it had been sunk in a gale a week or so earlier.

Jack Smart was a small, quiet man of about my own age, who expressed no animosity about the rival team working on the *Royal Charter*. The site of his home was a diver's dream, with bad-weather harbour, boat park and launching beach quite literally on the doorstep, and a wonderful view out over Liverpool Bay to the Great Orme and Puffin Island.

On television diving is very easy, because all you have to do to go underwater is press a button and sit in a chair—and this gives the public a false impression. In a real diver's life, boats and access to the water—and the moving of a lot of heavy gear—are the fundamentals; the diving comes later. This was exactly the point which was now worrying me. Like Jack Smart, I was past that glorious stage of life when, in one's youthful forties, one can get by through brute force and ignorance. My knees no longer worked very well—the joints were rusted up—and my left leg had never recovered from the breakage in 1960 and the two operations which had followed. The foot stuck out at an unnatural angle and there was no feeling or resilience in it—it was just like having a metal leg (which in fact it partly was, in the form of a plate). I really did not feel like finding a fisherman, who might know nothing of divers and diving, and then arguing about how best to get into the water, and more important still, how to get back up out of it. I recalled an appallingly ridiculous incident down in Devon, years back, on an outing with Southsea Branch of the British Sub-Aqua Club, when we concluded that the old Devonian seadogs whose services we had hired were really old Devon tram conductors most of the week. Never again! I quietly hoped that one of the two rival salvage groups—or both—would offer professional facilities.

I had written to Joe McCormack (with a slight hint in the postscript) but it had been returned by the Post Office undelivered. Now Peter Day suggested the use of his boat, which I had seen parked outside his home;

The author after breaking a leg on the cliffs above the wreck site in September, 1960.
Photo : Ilse McKee

fast, flat, low, roomy, it had seemed to me ideal for the use of an elderly gentleman in sad need of repair and a couple of new knees. I thanked him, but it was late in the day. By the time we had gone back for that boat and my kit, and I had suited up and got a bottle on, most of the light would have gone. On the other hand, the light now was terrific—soft, golden, late afternoon glow and an almost flat, calm sea (after many months of howling winds and chill, driving rain). Should I go and to hell with it? Tomorrow might bring another gale. Yes, I ought to go now. On the other hand, I might be putting these people to a lot of trouble for nothing. McCormack might prevent me diving. However, at least I might be able to speak to him or some of his team. Yes! So I decided to do it the quick, spartan way. Don't bother with the time-wasting aspect of suiting up and kitting up; just wear swim trunks and mask, fins and snorkel for a quick look, if the 'salvors in possession' would let me go down just holding my breath.

Back we drove to Tynygongl; Peter hitched the boat on its trailer to his car, and I got into my car. At the beach, my kit went into the boat, a tractor drew the boat across the sand and into the water, we got in, the engine roared, the bows reared up and we planed off round the headland at a fair speed in knots. Jack Smart's son John was driving and Roger Crowhurst, who had joined us, would be back-up diver if necessary. Unavoidably, I should be arriving at the Bestspeed camp in an opposition boat crewed by some of the 'enemy'.

This time it was near to low water on 1 September, 1985, whereas on my last visit, on 8 September, 1960, the tide had been high, covering many of the rock ledges and all the gullies which were now exposed, blackly weed-covered against the declining sun. The weather was identical—blue sea, blue sky with white cumulus clouds, and a golden calm over all. The exposed ledges looked menacing; of course, I had never seen them before, nor had I seen the wreck site from the sea. There was one other difference: the salvage raft and attendant inflatable boat floating above the wreck site, literally a stone's throw offshore.

As I raised a camera to take the Bestspeed raft against the background of the rocks which had destroyed the *Royal Charter* and pounded most of her passengers to death—I was momentarily conscious of this as we closed in, for it seemed a sinister spot in this light—there were shouts and wavings of arms from the divers on board. Apparently they did not like being photographed.

Some raw language was being used but in an accent so thick (although clearly not Welsh) that I was unable to interpret the subtleties of it, so I joked back: 'Don't you want your pictures in my next book!' Then someone else, in understandable tones, called out reproachfully, 'We didn't expect that of you.' To which I shouted, that I did not intend to take sides, and that I wanted to talk to McCormack. So they sent off for him and I landed on the rocks as a preliminary to climbing the cliff.

It is no exaggeration to say that I was terrified. The last time I had been here I had broken my leg. Having carried out a snorkel dive over these rocks and the *Royal Charter* area just offshore of them, I had then gone for a walk towards the wreck of the *Hindlea*, plainly visible above water, crushed against a headland. On my way back, walking a rock ledge, there was a jump down of four feet to reach the place where I had left my kit, and at one point a grassy knoll made the jump a matter of two feet only. I chose that. I had a camera swinging round my neck, the knoll was rounded, and perhaps I landed awkwardly. My left leg snapped under me—I distinctly heard it go—and then I was sprawling face downwards on a grassy slope. Later, this was to help me describe what John Bradbury must have felt, when he broke a leg during the *Royal Charter* shipwreck. Nor was that all, for eventually it brought me Richard Evans, cox of the Moelfre life-boat and rescuer of the *Hindlea*'s crew. But to begin with, I lay there for an hour trying to attract attention by shouting out at deliberately spaced intervals; and turning onto my back, because I was afraid that if I passed out when lying face down in the grass, as I was originally, I might choke; and I very nearly did pass out during the effort of turning over and struggling round.

Eventually two caravanners, a Mr and Mrs Baker, heard me calling and at first thought I was hoaxing, I looked so comfortable. While Mrs Baker returned to their caravan to make me a thermos-flaskful of tea, Mr Baker went for the nearest telephone, which was in the cottage of Captain Owen; and he rang Dick Evans, who knew all the traditional local stories regarding the *Royal Charter* wreck and could judge exactly how little blame attached to her captain, for the same conditions had destroyed the *Hindlea*. We talked together for another hour—one cannot exactly call it an interview, but I learned a lot—and then, about 4 pm, Dr Parry Jones arrived, strapped the leg and gave me an injection. I had broken the leg about 2 pm and it was about 4.45 pm when a stretcher party reached us. Despite the injection, and the dopey feeling, the break hurt like hell whenever I was moved which, unavoidably, was often, for I must have been taken up the same path as the survivors of the *Royal Charter*—up the cliffs and

The Bestspeed salvage barge moored over the wreck of the *Royal Charter* at low water, September, 1985: (*Above*) seen from a boat a few yards away, and (*below*) from the cliffs overlooking the site. Substantial portions of the wreck lie below where the hoses curl in the sea, only about 20 feet down. *Photos: Alexander McKee*

over stone walls and fences to the ambulance, which could get no further than the caravan camp.

The local paper printed a much more likely story than the real one, stating that I had 'slithered about 20 feet down the cliff-face', adding that in Bangor Hospital I was said to be 'comfortable'. I can now translate exactly this old medical standby: for 'comfortable' read 'in bloody agony'. But the distance jumped was two feet and I can still recall, after a lapse of 25 years, that my first, overwhelming impression was of surprise. And then, a realisation of sudden helplessness.

So, as I clambered over the rocks in 1985, I was more than usually cautious, fighting that memory; and these rocks were treacherous, seaweed often concealing deep holes and crannies between them. This was the mincing machine on which the hurricane of 1859 had pulverised men, women and children by the hundreds, as they were swayed between ship and shore.

On the cliff top now Bestspeed's air compressor was roaring away, supplying digging power to the airlifts offshore by means of a hose laid across the rocks and over the water. Aqualung cylinders were being carried up and down the cliff face, the 'empties' going back to another compressor which filled them with breathable air. A marquee acted as an advanced headquarters, and near it were two damaged metal boats which, like those used by Jack Smart and his friends, had supported the digging and sieving equipment between them. One story was, that the damage had been caused by saboteurs, but it seems they were simply driven ashore in a storm. Then Joe McCormack appeared, walking down to the cliffs from his main base at the farm.

Although not as large as Peter Day, he was a squarely-built man with a direct manner. 'What can I do for you?' he asked.

I said that I was updating *The Golden Wreck* and would like his side of the story. Plainly, he did not find that very impressive. I added that what I would most like would be to dive the *Royal Charter* and photograph the remains. He explained that Bestspeed were contemplating a book, and I would understand that he could not let me take a camera down. But I got his permission to snorkel dive on his operation, while his divers were working, although without a camera and, of course no breathing apparatus.

As I did not want to risk another leg-break at another critical time, I avoided the rocks on my return, made my way to a small stony beach just south of the wreck site and waded out to the boat from there. Had the *Royal Charter* been driven ashore here, most of the people would have survived; and had she been driven into the sandy bay of Traeth Lligwy to the north, all would have survived. But it could have been worse; had the ship struck on the tiny island of Ynys Moelfre, at the tip of the headland, no rescuers could have crossed to help those few who reached the rocks alive. Now I was going to have a really informative look at the place where she had struck, for the digging must have revealed a lot.

We moored to the Bestspeed raft, telling them that the 'boss' had said okay; I rolled over the side in swimming trucks and basic equipment only—the gunwale of the boat was only about 18 inches above the water—and swam about 50 yards to where their airlifts were working. The visibility was very good, some 10–12 feet, perhaps more. The relief, now that I was buoyed up by the water above the rocks and not scrambling over them, was immense. I took half-a-dozen rapid breaths, held a last deep one, and went down.

I arrived at the side of a ten-foot deep crater, with stone blocks poised at the top and a diver working a six-inch airlift. From the surface of the sea to the bottom was about 20 feet. In a succession of dives I covered most of the working area. A long length of plating, presumably part of

The Bestspeed team at the wreck site in the summer of 1985. Centre (in cap and holding a salvaged pistol) is Joe McCormack. Bernie McDonald is in the front row at the right. *Photo: Liverpool Daily Post & Echo*

the port side of the *Royal Charter*, had been exposed and then undercut for part of its length in case there was anything underneath. I put out my hand to first touch it and then hold on against the slight current while I looked around. There were masses of pink starfish all over the site, some adults, some tiny babies. Then a shoal of small fish, only a few inches long, moved in ahead of me, and I much regretted that I had no camera. There were scattered pieces of rusted and concreted machinery and a metal tube that might have been a mast, except that the diameter was rather too small.

There were two Bestspeed divers working and normally I went down either behind them or to one side of them, so as not to interfere. The digging was of course stirring up clouds of sand, reducing visibility, and just once I misjudged in the midst of a vast cloud of muck and, bursting free into clear water, came face-mask to face-mask at a range of two or three feet with a diver intent on digging. He seemed much startled, as well he might be, at the spectacle of an unknown and nearly naked man arriving on his work patch without benefit of breathing apparatus. I gave the universal 'all's well', to show I was friendly, and flippered back up to the surface.

The *Royal Charter* had indeed, as Dick Evans had said, struck first on sand. Indeed, she was still there—at least, the lower parts of her hull were—largely buried under it and now being uncovered again. No wonder Captain Taylor had hoped that she would survive until the morning, when daylight would reveal the scene and let him decide how to get his passengers ashore. The rising tide and the close proximity of the rocks—only a few feet away from where the remains of the hull now lay—had instead doomed almost all of them.

I had gone in at 5 o'clock in the afternoon and I came out at 20 minutes past, having seen a good deal of the wreck site, but I was now a little chilled, so I got back into the boat and thanked the Bestspeed divers for letting me see the wreck. Jack Smart had been watching from the hilltop and, timing my dives, had been much amused by the contrast between the young aqualung divers necessarily clad in expensive dry-suits and the cheap, skin-only diver going down among them.

> Your dives were in 20 feet of water at that state of the tide, plus an estimated 10 feet for the excavation, 30 feet approximately in all (or 9·2 metres), giving an estimated average bottom time of 15 seconds, an impressive performance without protective clothing in our waters.

On the way back to Traeth Bychan I noticed that there was definitely no trace of the *Hindlea* any longer. In 1960, she had been wrapped round a headland, split into two halves. However, next morning I was to see her again, in weather even calmer and more beautiful than before.

Roger Crowhurst said there were just a few bits of her up in a cove, that he would go first and scout around for something larger. I wanted pictures to show what happened to steel ships (let alone iron ones!) when a hurricane got hold of them off a rocky coast. Also, as in 1960, I wanted to test new underwater photographic equipment in good and easy conditions. For my first *Royal Charter* dive I had bought a cheap 35mm camera, put it inside a dive-mask and then clamped half a football-bladder to the mask. That was more-or-less the state of things 25 years ago. What I had now was an automatic-exposure camera coupled to an automatic-exposure flash unit, an outfit designed to eliminate human error (which I have in plenty).

Alas for human planning, although the visibility was good, there was a host of white particles in the water, so that no object further away than 18 inches was clearly visible. I had fitted a wide-angle lens, but even so this was pushing things. I went down the anchor to the edge of the rocks, swam out over the sand at 35 feet, and came back to the rock where, near our anchor, there was a section of hull plating with frames attached. I was not happy with my exposures there, so roamed off and found an incredible rock pinnacle, over six feet high, every inch of it occupied by huge white or bright yellow anemones.

I then surfaced, swam back to the boat, changed the new Nikonos V flash camera for my old and trusted Nikonos III, went down the anchor line and shot it all again with natural light. I surfaced, went back to the boat, and waited for the anchor to be hauled up. It jammed, so I went down again and cleared it. By now, Roger had found larger parts of hull structure near the headland, so the boat towed me over there and I went down for the fourth time. There was more plating here, immovably jammed into crevices in the rock, so that the scattered remains of the ship were in effect welded to the underwater landscape which, as before, was liberally sprinkled with pink starfish of all sizes, some of them, arms and all, spanning no more than the diameter of an old farthing. A big green pollack, about two feet long, came swerving in at me, but my film was finished and my air almost exhausted.

In the afternoon it began to rain, making appropriately sombre our visit to the little cemetery and chapel at Llanallgo, with the *Royal Charter* memorial under the dark trees. The chapel is tiny and the scene here when the bodies, many of them battered and torn, had been laid out for grief-stricken relatives to identify, staining the stones with sand and saltwater, must have been sickening.

Denise Black, Anglesey's principal museums officer, was able to see me briefly later that day, just before a Borough Council meeting at Llangefni which had the *Royal Charter* on its agenda. She said that this ship was merely

Diving the scattered remains of the *Hindlea* in September, 1985. *Photo: Alexander McKee*

The monument in Llanallgo churchyard, where many of the *Royal Charter* dead are buried. 1985. *Photo: Alexander McKee*

the 'tip of the iceberg' as far as Anglesey wrecks were concerned. The Council acknowledged the historical potential of all the wreck sites, not merely the best-known, but were worried about the cost of conserving artefacts if they decided to become involved. The guns from Charles II's yacht *Mary*, (recovered in 1971 during an underwater free-for-all, as I now knew) had still got bronze disease. Then there was the legal tangle—who actually owned the gold, the hull, the artefacts and so on? Above all, the Council were not anxious to take sides in a conflict between rival salvage teams. And there was the potential of all the many thousands of wrecks around Anglesey—those that had been found already and those that will be found in the future.

At the meeting of the resources and recreation committee that evening, two items related to the *Royal Charter* came up. Firstly, should the Council consider making premises near to Moelfre available for a Royal Charter Museum? The majority voted against. Secondly, what participation should the Council have in the *Royal Charter* project? The majority voted against any participation.

Part of my life is spent filing press cuttings about items of special interest. I had scissored, kept and could find the reports of renewed diving on the *Royal Charter* in 1972 by Jack Smart and Peter Day; and I had also brought with me to Anglesey a small crop of cuttings covering the discovery of the wrecked Royal Yacht *Mary* in 1971 and the dispute, which went on into 1972, by what were referred to as rival claimants, one group from Merseyside, the other from Anglesey. By 1972 the matter was being debated in Parliament, and a plea was made by a Dr David Owen, Labour MP for Sutton, Plymouth, for the Government to help preserve the wreck. 'No one wished to stifle local initiative or Welsh national feeling, but a yacht of such rarity and antiquity was a national heritage,' he was reported as saying. Winding up the debate for the Labour opposition, the MP for Woolwich, Mr Hamling, who was a trustee of the National Maritime Museum, reinforced appeals for early legislation on historic wrecks. There was need to protect wrecks from 'pirates' who would seek to strip and destroy them, he said.

Angela Croome, secretary of the Council for Nautical Archaeology, described how, within days of the discovery, no less than five diving groups were on site 'manoeuvring with a vigor worthy of the Cornish wreckers of the 18th century'. She reported that a shot was fired, a cannon raised by one group hijacked by another, and so 'ugly' did the situation become that a Royal Navy minesweeper was called in.

And, of course, there was the inevitable 'expert Naval diver' to claim the wreck as 'historically the most important find in home waters'. As the discoverer, legal protector and excavator of the *Mary Rose* from 1966, I took such boasts with as much salt as one might get into the *Titanic* (about 48,000 tons).

In Peter Day, I was talking to one of the members of the local Anglesey group which had found the *Mary* by accident in 1971, just before he made his first aqualung dive. The *Mary* had been a small Dutch-built yacht of 100 tons lost with all 35 of her crew and passengers in 1675. In comparison, the *Mary Rose* was a 700-ton battleship (the first British 'great ship' to carry complete batteries of heavy siege guns and therefore a 'key' vessel to fill missing gaps in the histories), sunk in battle in 1545 with reported losses varying from 400 to 700 men. My discovery of her was deliberate, part of a careful and costly search effort begun in 1965. In the absence then of any law to protect historic wrecks (there was only the commercial Merchant Shipping Act of 1894) I had pioneered a new concept in protecting underwater history by obtaining a lease to the actual seabed around her from the owner—the Crown. The Crown was also the owner of the hull, fittings, armament, ammunition and stores of the *Mary Rose*, because she had been a Royal ship belonging personally to King Henry VIII. This much clarified the legal position. At the same time it ensured that, even if I wanted to, I could not profit from the *Mary Rose* project; and indeed was bound to count as a loss all the time and money I put into it; but this was true of all the other enthusiasts who joined me in the early days (although not of all those who got on when the project took off and necessarily became a bandwagon).

The *Mary* was a Royal ship, too, although not, to my mind, so directly and personally as the *Mary Rose*, and of some historic interest. The *Royal Charter*'s gold clearly came under the Merchant Shipping Act and was open to commercial salvage; even the passengers' possessions were of little importance nationally. A nineteenth-century gold watch, ruined by sea-water, is little more than a curio compared to the tiny sundials with inset compass—the Tudor equivalent—worn by some officers of the *Mary Rose* more than four centuries ago.

However, when Jack Smart's team of divers found the *Mary* in 1971, they did not know what ship it was, who it belonged to, or when it had sunk. It was an entirely accidental discovery made by a diver who had in previous seasons, with members of a Stockport sub-aqua club, looked for this very wreck, but in the wrong place.

On the day of their discovery Jack Smart and his team had been engaged in a different project. This was to recover a cannon from another site where guns had long ago been used as a fog-warning to ships; when replaced by newer methods the cannon had been simply thrown into the sea. Using tidal lift, they had raised a cannon and were on the way back home when they decided to stop at the Skerries, a group of rocks called in Welsh Ynysoedd y Moelrhoniaid, lying off the north-west coast of Anglesey not far from Holyhead. Terry, one of their divers, wanted to get into the water, so Peter Day rowed him over to the rocks in a boat, and can remember him coming back from his dive, shouting: 'There's bloody lead blocks like daisies all over the seabed!'

Lead blocks implied ship ballast and there were also bronze cannon down there, one with the easy-to-read date of 1661. It was obviously a valuable site, whatever the origin of the ship.

On the weekend when Jack Smart and Peter Day planned to return to the Skerries site and raise one of the cannon, they were told by the Coastguard that some other divers had got a bronze cannon with a Dutch inscription on it (the *Mary* had been a gift from the Dutch to Charles II). When they approached the Skerries they could see about 40 boats there, full of divers. By Monday morning, however, they had all gone home bar the determined four-man crew of one diving boat. The owner of this boat, Malcolm Beelinson, was well known to Jack and, after discussion, the two groups joined forces. Working together, they lifted one cannon that day; on Tuesday a second cannon; and on Wednesday two more.

'Then things started going wrong,' recalled Peter Day. On the way back, they had gearbox trouble. Two men set off in an inflatable for spares while Jack and Peter continued the journey home astern. As they limped into dock in the early hours, the two who had set off for spares were just finishing their cup of tea! Next morning the two cannon raised on Wednesday were unloaded. The only vehicle Jack Smart had available was full of coffins (his business then was as a Liverpool coffin-maker). So the coffins had to be unloaded first, then the heavy cannons hoisted in, and the coffins replaced on top of them. It was macabre.

That done, it was back to the boat and repair the gearbox. After testing the engine and gearbox at sea, the boat was anchored and Peter Day was put into the water for his initiation 'open sea' dive. At the end of it, as he climbed back up the ladder into the boat, he heard voices on deck.

'Mr Jack Smart?'

'Yes, that's me.'

'We're Customs Officers.'

It seemed that persons unknown had reported to a Receiver of Wreck that a cannon had been stolen. Peter Day commented:

We had no knowledge of any stolen cannon but eventually realised that the enquiry concerned those recovered from the *Mary*. As it happened, our other four colleagues had already been into the Receiver of Wreck's office in Holyhead to mention the four cannon recovered. There is no doubt that those cannon raised by Jack's team were the first items to be recovered from the *Mary* site, and declared to the Receiver, and Jack's team were the first to be given a receipt.

On the Friday, we went back to the wreck and were anchoring when quite a large vessel arrived with 20 to 30 people on it. They physically drove us off the site, shouting that they'd got a seabed lease and we had to keep off. They were all from Liverpool and picked up two cannon which had our ropes on them. Four of our team anchored on the site, and there was a shout from the other vessel: 'We have put a charge down and if you lot go in we will set it off.'

Our colleagues took this to be an empty threat. One of the team went down and they, fully aware of his entering the water, set off the high explosive charge. Our colleague floated to the surface unconscious; ears, eyes, nose and mouth bleeding. Later, when he had recovered consciousness and his senses, we contacted Holyhead Police Station. We were told that as the incident had happened off-shore it was outside Police jurisdiction. Explosives were the norm with these people who were granted a licence to explore the site.

205

Our last full day in Anglesey, Friday, 13 September, was a rush. Joe McCormack rang up at breakfast time. If I came to his camp in the afternoon, I could see the artefacts.

The morning was already booked for a visit to Dr Cecil Jones at the Marine Science Station, Menai Bridge, part of the University College of North Wales. Dr Jones was a member of the Department of Extra-Mural Studies whose function is to relate the work of the College to the local community. Thus he works not only with distinguished internal colleagues (some of who I was to meet) but with local divers, historians and people with an interest in promoting the study of the sea:

> The view that most of us hold on the *Royal Charter* is that although she is an important piece of local history she is not a historic wreck in the sense that she represented some unknown or badly-documented type of ship. Our main interest is in filling the gaps in the history of seafaring at times like the Dark Ages and the Mediaeval period. The ships used then (like the Ford Model A's of the day) are still a mystery and examples like the Pwll Fanog Ship (date approximately AD 1400) can help fill the gap. The shipwreck sites that interest us most are those which contain information about ship technology which is available from no other source. (We know a lot about steam clippers of the 1850s!)
>
> On the other hand, every shipwreck site holds information of value to the biologist and ecologist. The marine concretions on the wreck formation are of considerable interest as they represent a record of the faunal pattern of the site and tell us something of the forces acting on it. Thus even vessels from the First World War period are valuable scientific sites which tell us something about what happens to man-made structures when they find their way to the sea-bed.

This had long been my own view, formulated more than 25 years before, when it was a case of do-it-yourself marine science—or do without. Today Bangor is one of the two university centres of oceanographic skills in Britain (the other is Southampton), and it is likely that the Menai Straits may become a marine nature reserve (or park) where controlled scientific experiments on lobster rearing in the wild can take place—'lobster ranching' on a systematic basis. This time, the book I was asked to sign was called *Farming the Sea*, published in 1967. As part of my practical research, I had in 1966 helped set up an experimental lobster farm off Hayling Island, and was broadly optimistic at the prospects for farming crustacea. 'Now it's all come true,' said Dr Jones, 'and I'll show you, if you can stand the humidity and the smell.'

First we saw the fish tanks where turbot were bred to eatable size. These

Part of the Marine Science Station, Menai Bridge, showing the island that houses the conservation facilities for dealing with timber and other items from historic wrecks. *Photo: courtesy of University College of North Wales*

fish were used to being fed by humans, so when Ilse put her hand into the surface water, a large turbot with a healthy appetite rose up off the bottom like an undulating flying saucer and tried to bite her fingers off!

Next came the lobster-breeding laboratory. Female lobsters may lay 10,000 eggs, but in the wild only about three per cent will survive to maturity. In the first stage, they float as part of the plankton; in the next stage they are tiny, miniature lobsters. But if you put 20,000 tiny lobsters into one tank overnight, then in the morning there would be only a few left, I was told. Hunger and cannibalism would have done for the rest. Here, they had hit on a simple solution—a centrifuge which prevented the tiny creatures from killing each other until they had grown large enough to be caught and put into small, almost matchbox-sized tanks. They were soon ready to go into the sea off Anglesey on some rocky coast at a size where their chances of survival were infinitely greater than at the plankton stage, and with nature now taking care of the costs instead of the College budget. The breeding programme is the result of research by the Ministry of Agriculture and Fisheries at their Conway Research Station, the Bangor project being supported by the Lancashire and North-West Joint Fisheries Committee, with Bangor providing the venue and its staff assisting.

We were shown the breeding stock, the male and female lobsters which are kept permanently in a large tank, and an example of a lobster reared to adult size in the laboratory. This one was very aggressive, explained Dr Jones, probably because it had never met any creature likely to attack it.

How everything had changed, since I wrote my book!—as Dr Jones remarked. In 1966, there was no certainty that oil would be found in the North Sea, for instance. I had thought it would be, because I favoured the experts who believed in its creation by organic means rather than a rival group who speculated on a chemical creation. If the first group were right, then oil must be associated with the gas which had just been discovered there. Strangely, in those days, as Dr Jones recalled, a marine scientist who actually went into the sea to observe his subject at first hand was regarded as some dangerously adventurous exhibitionist and looked down on. Nowadays it was the other way round: there must be something incomplete about a marine biologist who did not dive. And this brought us to the wrecks.

From diving the Menai Straits, with its viciously fast currents and different underwater environments—some of them exactly right for the rapid growth of sponges—Dr Jones knew that a 70-foot long ship, carrying 200 tons of cargo, could disappear, particularly if the cargo was stone or some other natural-appearing material. The diver could not tell the wreck from other rocks covered with sponges, usually *Halicondria panacea*, the breadcrumb sponge. I had had the same trouble during 1960–1964, scraping *Halicondria* off rocks on 'Church Rocks' in Hayling Bay, in order to decide whether what I had found was building material or natural rock in its natural state. One of the ships they had found in the Menai Straits, buried and camouflaged by sponges, was 50 feet long, of mediaeval date, and had been carrying a cargo of slates. Dr Jones also showed me some of the recoveries from a smaller vessel found in Llyn Peris, Snowdonia. The Pwll Fanog slate-carrying wreck proved to be of Viking type; although

The research vessel *Prince Madog* at the Marine Science Station, Menai Bridge, in September, 1985. *Photo: Alexander McKee*

The Menai Straits, a short-cut between the Isle of Anglesey and the mainland of North Wales, has claimed many ships. September, 1985. *Photo: Alexander McKee*

the Vikings raided rather than settled in Anglesey, clearly they influenced local boatbuilding methods.

These vessels were of historical importance and the College were thinking of running a course in underwater archaeology on the theme of the interpretation of shipwrecks by marine scientists. I agreed with this, for I had long been an opponent of the simple view that the archaeologist should be king of all he surveys—I thought there should be a prominent place for the historian, the ship expert, and the marine scientist, also.

Dr Jones pointed out that west of Anglesey the reefs stretch out in shallow water for seven miles from shore, and must have collected many ships over the centuries. Most would be broken up but could still prove valuable for studying the 'scrambling processes'. And, if dated, those ships would preserve the record of marine biology in the area back to the day they sank. The real record went back many millions of years, but even a Roman wreck might preserve almost 2,000 years of biological history offshore. Marine concretions could tell us much about the health of the underwater environment at the time of the ship's sinking and thereafter.

Generally, Dr Jones felt that the *Royal Charter* affair could do nothing but good for Anglesey. It gave employment and provided publicity for the wreck potential of the area, provided of course that a clear distinction was made between marine archaeology and salvage diving by treasure-hunters. I felt the same way. The *Royal Charter* was a modern wreck and should be dealt with in accordance with the ordinary salvage laws as laid down in the Merchant Shipping Act, and designed to deal with maritime accidents such as the loss of the *Hindlea*. If there was gold there still, good luck to the first man to find it. He would need all the luck he could get, because of the complexity of the legal problems posed by the genuine treasure carried by many of the passengers.

Rather late, for we had had a fascinating discussion, we drove back to Moelfre, parked the car and walked round the headland by the cliff path to the Bestspeed camp overlooking the wreck, then up to the farm where Joe McCormack was. We had had only a brief talk that morning over the phone. He had been direct and very blunt.

He had read *The Golden Wreck*. It was 'a bit flowery'. All right for the general public, but . . . On some days in summer there had been two or three hundred people at a time on the cliffs, looking down on the salvage operation. They all knew of *The Golden Wreck* and wanted to buy a copy, but they were unobtainable. Bestspeed were doing their own book and a film and they would mention my book as the 'bible'. Personally, he was not worried about being credited in other books—he was only worried about the gold. 'If I find that, the credit doesn't matter.' This was so refreshing, I laughed. Because most of my circle put more into the sea than we take out, we tend to be perhaps over-sensitive to the question of 'credit', since it is all we are likely to get, if we are lucky.

When Ilse and I reached the farm, Joe McCormack was scrupulously polite, showing us first the artefacts laid out for us in his caravan, and then a great many more, mostly in conservation tanks, in an out-building of the farm. As he pointed out, the treatment of these objects represented a lot of work for a very busy diving team.

I noticed particularly the gold pencil, the gold watch, the golden spoon, the silver candlesticks with the ship owner's crest—and the shoes. These brought home the reality of the tragedy—all these poor people (many of them temporarily rich), travelling in civilised surroundings in what was only a fragile iron hull. Comfortable cabins, elaborately laid tables. And then the hurricane, and the rocks, the water roaring in; terror and truth.

McCormack handed us two gold sovereigns to look at. Perfect, both of them. Gold is one of the very few materials which does not deteriorate or undergo chemical change when immersed in seawater. Almost everything else required conservation—a long, expensive and, as I now knew, uncertain process. There were also two gold nuggets, the first I had ever seen—twists of gold, really—being brought home by some miner from the Australian goldfields. It could have been John Bradbury's great-grandfather, but how could one ever know?

There were also many silver spoons and forks, some already cleaned and shining, but, McCormack pointed out, no knives had been found. Why was that? There was what we were told was the Captain's telescope, part of a sextant, a brass porthole, a deck light. There was part of a book, the remains of a picture in a frame and two pistols together in a holding tank. Two stiffening rods which we were told came from smashed bullion boxes were shown us. There were some ingots in a corner—the top one was certainly brass. Mr McCormack said he was happy to hand all this over to the Receiver of Wreck.

He stressed that it was not the case that all Bestspeed was interested in was the gold. His team was concerned in a carefully mounted operation to salvage all matters of historical and archaeological interest. They were of course interested in the gold, but only as a means of financing this and future operations.

Then, perhaps referring to the book *Full Fathom Five*, which I had noticed in his caravan, he said philosophically: 'You win some, you lose some.'

*   *   *

We might just make Point Lynas lighthouse before evening came on and the light failed. I wanted to see the place because it was often referred

211

Point Lynas lighthouse, September, 1985. *Photo: Alexander McKee*

to by the witnesses of 1859, to grasp where the pilot ground was and its exact relationship to the rocks where the *Royal Charter* finally arrived. The golden light was starting to go as we left the car and walked the last few hundred yards up the path, not because of the lateness of the hour but of a violent and rapid change in the weather, just as it had on that fateful October evening long ago.

The house holding the light was inside a high-walled building not unlike a square Norman castle. Although it was after visiting hours we were allowed to go up and talk to the Pilot on duty. Almost at the foot of the headland on which the building stood there was a large area of violently disturbed water, known as an overfall. The Pilot told us that in a storm the spray from the rocks that caused it would hit the windows. It could be frightening, which we could well believe. The pilot ground, he told us, was either south-east or north-west of Point Lynas light, according to which place was best sheltered from the wind. To the South, the *Royal*

Charter site was not quite visible, being blanked off by a headland, but two ships lay waiting at anchor a few miles out. The sunlight was cut off as though by a blind. The forecast, we were told, was for 'Severe gale, Force 9'—and it was coming already.

Walking back down the hill, we faced a sky of high, torn cloud flung into tendrils by the force of the winds at altitude—the outriders of the storm. But this one was only 'severe', not the hurricane-force winds which drove the '*Royal Charter* Gale'.

In my mind's eye I could see the doomed ship passing Point Lynas out in the Irish Sea to the west and, because there was no wireless and no forecasting, her captain in ignorance of what was approaching him and of how radically and brutally the wind would veer against him and pin his clipper to that rocky coast like some monstrous butterfly. And I recalled the words of Coxswain Evans:

> You know very well that people do write and talk about those things after a tragedy such as the *Royal Charter* and the *Hindlea*, what should have been done, what wasn't done, why this, and how the other, but!! I leave this to your imagination. Wind and sea of such velocity has to be seen to be believed, especially when on a lee shore and with breaking seas.
>
> This part is very exposed to NW and northerly winds and with the wind of great force from the north we have tremendous seas. As you will notice on a map, north wind and sea at Moelfre comes straight through the gap between Northern Ireland and Scotland from the Atlantic Ocean, which means that the sea has several hundred miles to form into tremendous waves.

But for the gold, who would have remembered the victims of the *Royal Charter* Gale? Probably no one, except perhaps the great-grandsons and granddaughters of the 'twenty-eight men' who dared to go down onto the rocks that night.

Is there still bullion remaining in the wreck? Peter Day is reasonably sure that a sizeable fortune lies there still. I found his explanation believable, based as it was on thirteen years' research and a mountain of documents and correspondence. Also, my estimate of where the bulk of the gold might be, if there were substantial amounts remaining, seemed to match Peter's ideas. Joe McCormack did not take me into his confidence at all, but he, too, clearly believed that a search was well worth the effort and the cost.

During October, 1985, there were fresh developments of a startling nature, which I did not witness as I was diving some 2,000 miles away off Cyprus, carrying on an investigation of Mycenaean harbours probably dating to around 1300–1200 BC, the time of the Argonauts and the Trojan War—rather a contrast to an auxiliary steam clipper of the mid-nineteenth century!

Both the local and the national press carried sensational stories of events at Moelfre which, as they are now to be the subject of a Court case, cannot be publicly discussed.

Coxswain Evans at the wheel of the modern life-boat, the *Watkin Williams*, which he used in the *Nafsiporos* rescue. *Photo : courtesy RNLI*

(*Opposite*) The new life-boat house, from which Coxswain Evans successfully launched to rescue the crew of the *Hindlea* in conditions as bad as those experienced during the '*Royal Charter* Gale'. Seen from the diving boat coming back from the *Royal Charter* and the *Hindlea*, September, 1985. *Photo : Alexander McKee*

The *Royal Charter* monument on the cliffs, with the salvage craft working on the wreck at low water, September, 1985. *Photo: Alexander McKee*

LIST OF SURVIVORS

Passengers (18 *out of some* 376)

Christopher Anderson of Bradford	(*)
Carl Bartel, musician, of Prussia	(*)
Thomas Bowden, goldminer, of Torquay, Devon	(*)
John Bradbury, travelling to Manchester	(*)
James Dean, goldminer, of Wigan, Lancashire	(*)
William James Ferris, storekeeper at Ballarat	(*)
Samuel Edward Gapper, farmer, of New Zealand	(*)
Samuel Grenfell, goldminer, of St Ives, Cornwall	(*)
Thomas Gundry, returning with fiancée	(*)
Neston Hagen	
John Judge, an Irishman of 'herculean size and strength'	(*)
John Loone	
James M'Cappin, cabinetmaker and upholsterer, of St Kilda, nr Melbourne	(*)
Colin McPhiel	

Ernest Mantion ⎫
M. Marcion ⎬ possibly the same
W. Meaton ⎪ person
L. E. Mention ⎭

W. Henry Morse, magistrate, of New South Wales	(*)
James Russell, of Linlithgow, Scotland	(*)
Henry Carew Taylor, travelling with nurse and child	(*)

Riggers, working their passage (5 *out of* 11)

William Barton, of Liverpool	(*)
Thomas Cunningham, of Liverpool	
Patrick Devine, of Liverpool	
George Pritchard	
James White, of Liverpool	(*)

217

Crew (18 out of more than 100—no officers saved)

Thomas Cormick, second steward	(*)
William Draper, seaman	
Thomas Ellis, storekeeper	
Henry Evans, seaman, of Caernarvon, North Wales	
William Foster, carpenter	(*)
Thomas Griffith, quartermaster, of Amlwch, Anglesey	(*)
Walter Hughes, apprentice (seriously injured)	(*)
William McArthur, seaman	
George McGivren, seaman	
John O'Brien, seaman	(*)
John Richards	
Joseph Rodgers (Joie Rodriguez), seaman, of Liverpool (Maltese)	(*)
John Stannard, steward	
David Strongman, quartermaster	(*)
George Suaicar (or Suicicar), boatswain's mate, of Liverpool (Maltese)	(*)
Thomas Timms, seaman	
Owen Williams, quartermaster, of Caernarvon, North Wales	(*)
Edward Wilson, seaman	(*)

*Gave some account of the disaster afterwards, either in a letter, or in newspaper interviews, or in evidence at the Inquest and at the Inquiry. The spelling of the names is that used by contemporary newspapers.

Some survivors did not stay to talk to the press and be counted, but made for home by the earliest connection; and therefore the above lists may be incomplete.

LIST OF WITNESSES

of the Gale

Rowland Hughes, Cox, Moelfre Life-boat (evidence)
John Sheppard, Master, Pilot Boat No 4 (evidence)
Richard Parry, Master, Pilot Boat No 11 (evidence)
Captain Mends, Captain, HMS *Hastings* (log entries)
_____, Keeper, Point Lynas Light (log entries)
Correspondent, *The Times*, on board *Great Eastern*, Holyhead
Correspondents, *Caernarvon & Denbigh Herald*, at Llandudno and at Rhyl
Correspondents, *Liverpool Courier*, at Liverpool and in the Mersey

of the Wreck

Rev Stephen Roose Hughes, Rector, Llaneugrad and Llanallgo (as reported by Charles Dickens)
The 'Twenty-eight Men,' of Moelfre and nearby (as reported by their spokesmen)

of the Shore Scene, soon after

Councillor Wagstaffe, of Liverpool (letter to the press)
J. A. Gregory, solicitor, of Liverpool (letter to the press)
Correspondent, *Manchester Guardian*
Correspondent, *North Wales Chronicle*
Correspondent, *Liverpool Courier*
Correspondent, *Northern Daily Times*

of Miscellaneous Scenes

Rev W. Scoresby, passenger in the *Royal Charter* on her maiden voyage (*Journal of a Voyage to Australia and Round the World for Magnetical Research*).
William Gilmour, Surgeon Superintendent of the *Royal Charter* for two years (long letter to the press, giving pen pictures of officers and crew).
Charles Dickens, novelist, visited Moelfre 30 December, 1859 (*The Uncommercial Traveller*).

A. and J. K. (Kennedy?), Irish family, who were to meet the Fowlers at Liverpool, but instead went at once to Moelfre, where they wrote their book (*The Wreck of the 'Royal Charter' Steam Clipper*).

W. F. Peacock, author, visited Moelfre, June 1860 (*A Ramble to the Wreck of the 'Royal Charter'*).

Thomas L. Pelling, deputed to receive the salvaged gold (letter to the press).

John William Mellor, solicitor, Oldham, visited Moelfre day after the wreck (evidence).

J. B. Marsh, reporter, Chester, visited Moelfre day after the wreck (evidence).

Correspondent, *Liverpool Courier*, visited Bangor, Moelfre, Llanallgo Church, a few days after the wreck.

Mrs Roose Hughes, wife of the Rector (letter quoted in pamphlet *The Hughes Fund*, edit. Hugh Nanney, 1862).

R. M. L. in *Sea Breezes*, June 1951, article *Rodgers of the 'Royal Charter'* (personal recollections of Rodgers).

Frederick Foster, midshipman (letter written on board the *Royal Charter*, 24 October, 1859).

Joseph Robinson, passenger (letter written on board the *Royal Charter*, 24 October, 1859).

Charles Thomas, sailor (letter written to his mother 15 days before the *Royal Charter* left Melbourne for the last time).

The principal local newspapers which reported the wreck were: *Northern Daily Times, Liverpool Mercury, Liverpool Courier, North Wales Chronicle, Caernarvon & Denbigh Herald*, and *Yr Herald Cymraeg* (*The Welsh Herald*).

The argument of wooden versus iron ships, together with some historical detail, is to be found in *The Life-boat*, journal of the RNLI, 2 January, 1860.

The repercussions of the wreck on Anglesey are fully dealt with in an article by R. R. Williams, *Anglesey and the Loss of the 'Royal Charter,'* published in the *Transactions 1959* of the Anglesey Antiquarian Society and Field Club.

Some details of the Gold Rush will be found in *Liverpool Shipping: A Short History*, by Dr George Chandler (Phoenix, 1960).

The author is indebted to the Superintendent of the British Museum Reading Room, the Deputy Superintendent of the British Museum Newspaper Library, the Secretary of the Public Record Office, the Assistant Keeper of the National Maritime Museum Library, and the Central Library, Portsmouth, for research facilities afforded.

During 1961–1972 further information was provided by readers, including:

Alan Orme, chief sub-editor *Telegraph & Argus*, Bradford, who provided an interview with Christopher Anderson and information about William Bean from the pages of the 3 November, 1859 issue of *The Bradford Observer*.

Mrs S. Wikeley, Birkenhead, whose mother-in-law was to have come home in the *Royal Charter*.

E. Foy, Liverpool, relative of William Foster.

David Brough, Accrington, relative of Thomas Brough.

Mrs T. Schofield, Ormskirk, relative of John? Brough.

Clarence Ellis, Holyhead, chairman, County Library Committee.

Miss M. Withers, Wrexham, relative of Captain Withers.

Sylvia M. C. Thomson, Dunedin, New Zealand, relative of Andrew Cowie.

Alfred Archer Coates, Scarborough, relative of Captain Francis Boyce.

Mr and Mrs F. Gordon Roe, London, relatives of Captain Francis Boyce.

Roy Anderson, North Shields, regarding the *Tayleur*.

Mrs J. B. Kerr, Victoria, Australia, regarding the *Tayleur*.

Joseph Ritchie, Knebworth, Herts, relative of Anne Taylor, sister of Captain Thomas Taylor.

Michael Turner, Bolton, relative of Captain Thomas Taylor.

Mrs N. Sotheby Pitcher, Rye, Sussex, relative of the Pitcher family, ship-builders, Northfleet.

R. Glyn Hughes, Old Marston, Oxford, who lost relatives in the *Royal Charter*.

Michael Feeny, Collooney, Co. Sligo, regarding the Misses Moulsdale.

Mrs D. M. Bradbury, Newquay, Cornwall, relative of John Bradbury.

M. D. St G. Kirke, Stratford-on-Avon, relative of Anne Kirke, wife of the Rev C. V. Hodge.

Norman Clark, Ontario, Canada, relative of James Tate.

Mrs Sheila Dixon, Sale, Cheshire, regarding the grave of Joseph Rodgers in Ford Cemetery, Liverpool.

A great niece of Thomas Gundry, whose letter was readable, but not her signature.

For more recent events, covering the period 1971–1985, but particularly during my visit to Anglesey in September, 1985, I am especially indebted to:

John H. Bradbury, Houghton Le Spring, Tyne & Wear, descendant of John Bradbury of the *Royal Charter*.

Denise Black, BA, FMA, Principal Museums Officer for Anglesey, Llangefni.
Peter G. K. Day, Tynygongl, of the Royal Charter Salvage Expedition.
John Illsley, Department of History, University College of North Wales, Bangor.
Dr Cecil Jones, Marine Science Station, Menai Bridge, and Welsh Institute of Maritime Archaeology and History, University College of North Wales.
Joseph McCormack, Bootle, Merseyside, of Bestspeed Ltd.
John Leyland Smart, Traeth Bychan, of the Royal Charter Salvage Expedition.

And finally, my thanks to Coxswain Richard Evans of Moelfre for his aid to me on the cliffs after my accident, and subsequent correspondence 1960–1961 regarding both the *Royal Charter* and the *Hindlea*. His life story has now been told by Ian Skidmore in *Lifeboat VC* (David & Charles, 1979).

THE 'TWENTY-EIGHT'

Thomas Roberts	John Lewis
Owen Roberts	Joseph Williams
Owen Roberts, junior	Thomas Owen
David Williams	William Williams
Mesech Williams	Richard Mathew
Robert Lewis	Israel Mathew
Thomas Hughes	William Pritchard
John Hughes	Owen Hughes
William Owen	Richard Evans
Richard Hughes	David Owen
Evan Williams	John Lewis, junior
John Parry	William Owen
John Owens	Lewis Francis
Thomas Parry	John Francis

MICHAEL LEAPMAN

THE LAST DAYS OF THE BEEB

Gossipy, scandalous and packed with inside information THE LAST DAYS OF THE BEEB is a shocking and sensational account of a public corporation whose internal feuds—climaxing in the enforced departure of the Director-General—are never long off the front pages. The whole truth is now revealed about one of our most familiar but secret institutions.

'Well-written and all too readable'
Aubrey Singer, ex-Managing Director of BBC Television in *The Listener*

'Plenty of juicy flesh to put on the bones of the scandal we already know . . . It also offers a serious and generally disturbing accounting of the rows over programmes'
Patrick Stoddard, *The Sunday Times*

CORONET BOOKS

MORE NON-FICTION AVAILABLE FROM
HODDER AND STOUGHTON PAPERBACKS

☐	41107 4	MICHAEL LEAPMAN Last Days of the Beeb	£3.95
☐	24169 1	R. V. JONES Most Secret War	£3.95
☐	41197 X	NIGEL WEST GCHQ	£3.95
☐	33781 8	A Matter of Trust	£2.95
☐	40573 2	NICHOLAS BETHELL The Last Secret	£2.95

All these books are available at your local bookshop or newsagent, or can be ordered direct from the publisher. Just tick the titles you want and fill in the form below.

Prices and availability subject to change without notice.

HODDER AND STOUGHTON PAPERBACKS,
P.O. Box 11, Falmouth, Cornwall.

Please send cheque or postal order, and allow the following for postage and packing:

U.K.—55p for one book, plus 22p for the second book, and 14p for each additional book ordered up to a £1.75 maximum.

B.F.P.O. and EIRE—55p for the first book, plus 22p for the second book, and 14p per copy for the next 7 books, 8p per book thereafter.

OTHER OVERSEAS CUSTOMERS—£1.00 for the first book, plus 25p per copy for each additional book.

NAME . . . .

ADDRESS . . . .

. . . .